Law and Object

Law and Objectivity

KENT GREENAWALT

New York   Oxford

OXFORD UNIVERSITY PRESS

Oxford University Press

Oxford   New York   Toronto
Delhi   Bombay   Calcutta   Madras   Karachi
Petaling Jaya   Singapore   Hong Kong   Tokyo
Nairobi   Dar es Salaam   Cape Town
Melbourne   Auckland

and associated companies in
Berlin   Ibadan

First published in 1992 by Oxford University Press, Inc.
200 Madison Avenue, New York, NY 10016

First issued as an Oxford University Press paperback, 1995.

Oxford is a registered trademark of Oxford University Press, Inc.

Library of Congress Cataloging-in-Publication Data
Greenawalt, Kent, 1936–
Law and objectivity / Kent Greenawalt.
p.   cm.   Includes index.
ISBN 0-19-506741-X; 0-19-509833-1 (pbk)
1. Law—Interpretation and construction.
2. Objectivity.   I. Title.
K296.G74   1992
340—dc20   91-17633

1 3 5 7 9 8 6 4 2

Printed in the United States of America
on acid-free paper

To Andrei,

Our youngest son, loved with wonder and joy

PREFACE

This study about law and various senses in which it might be considered objective arose from an invitation to deliver the Julius Rosenthal Lectures at Northwestern University School of Law for the academic year 1988-89. I had been concerned with the capacity of legal norms to provide definite answers to legal questions, the fit of law with moral norms, the way legal reasoning relates to other forms of reasoning, and the degree to which that reasoning reveals or obscures the true bases of legal decisions. I also had a longstanding interest in whether standards of criminal law and constitutional law should be rigid or contextualized, should take acts as they reasonably appear, and should address people's mental states, as well as external events. All these major inquiries of modern jurisprudence may be cast in terms of the objectivity of law. Perhaps underestimating just how controversial a word "objective" has become, I decided upon that broad rubric for these lectures.

I began my study with the conviction that people often mix up quite discrete questions about the objectivity of law and that discussion of most of the questions suffers from severe oversimplification. I hoped that clarification of the questions, and their complexities and differences, would help contribute to understanding of relations among the questions. Given sharply radical critiques of "traditional legal thought," such an endeavor seemed timely. I also counted in favor of the topic my insufficient familiarity with the work of critical legal scholars, feminist legal scholars, and scholars writing about how legal interpretation resembles other interpretive efforts, a consequence of my scholarly work having been focused elsewhere in recent years. I knew that coming to grips with the broad subject of objectivity and law would require some amending of this deficiency.

Uncomfortable as I am with such categorizations, I suppose that much of my own prior work falls broadly in the category of "traditional legal thought" and "liberal jurisprudence." Part of my reason for working on this topic has been to develop more fully many of my own jurisprudential views. Although my work has proceeded against a setting of the views of others, especially those who are radically critical of traditional conceptions of law, my aim has been to state positions in which I believe and to explain and justify them. My purpose is not to defend some preexisting version of "traditional legal thought," nor to mount a point-by-point response to challenges made by critics.

I knew from the beginning that I wanted the lectures to be accessible not only to legal scholars and others with a special interest in jurisprudence, but to law teachers, law students, lawyers, and nonlawyers who care about law but have not concentrated on legal philosophy. This ambition led to development of some points that those acquainted with the most recent literature may now take for granted; it also meant suppression of many qualifications and intricacies of analysis. I have retained the ambition of accessibility in the transition from lectures to book. I have kept the personal lecture style, and I have generally tried to maintain clarity of language and methods of explanation that are easily comprehensible to readers with little background in legal philosophy. I have resisted the temptation to attempt a full academic treatment, with extensive references, for each of my topics, something that would be impossible in a single book. What I say here about many things is closer to my first word than my last one, and I hope to return to many of the subjects in more depth on other occasions. However, the lectures themselves have been considerably expanded. I now make much more effort to respond to opposing positions and to deal with subtleties I then disregarded.

Many people have contributed to this work. It benefited from discussion at Northwestern following the lectures and from trenchant criticisms at faculty seminars at the University of California in Los Angeles and New York University law schools and at a legal theory colloquium at N.Y.U. presided over by Ronald Dworkin and Thomas Nagel. Larry Crocker, Elaine Pagels, and Michael Perry, who reviewed the entire manuscript at some stage, and Norman Dorsen, Harold Edgar, Lewis Kornhauser, Charles Larmore, and Peter Strauss, who looked at sections of the manuscript, provided very useful comments. As my research assistant during the semester when I was delivering the lectures, Jamie Titus suggested important points and sharpened my analysis and language on many issues. Eric Orts prepared the bibliography and gave me extensive and thoughtful suggestions for improvement. Kenneth Ward made a careful review of the manuscript; he also helped with citations and with guiding the work through the last stages before publication. I have used the manuscript as material in variously titled seminars at Columbia and N.Y.U. during the past three years; the testing of my ideas against the perceptive, often skeptical, views of participating students has been of great value. Research for the summers of 1988-91 was generously supported by the Samuel Rubin Program for the Advancement of Liberty and Equality Through the Law, the Mildred and George Drapkin Faculty Research Fund, and general gifts to Columbia Law School.

Besides thinking and writing, most of my effort has involved reading materials new to me. As a consequence, the citations I provide are primarily to sources I have read recently. Work that has been part of my intellectual baggage for a long time—I think especially of H. L. A. Hart's *The Concept of Law*—tend to be slighted. I hope authors who have had a pervasive influence on my thinking will forgive the stretches in this book where I do not cite support for long familiar ideas.

Sally Wrigley, with some contribution by Madelaine Amare at the early stages, has typed successions of drafts quickly and expertly, occasionally correcting my infelicities of language. Her steady assistance has much lightened the burden of continuing revisions. Finally, the patient encouragement of Cynthia Read and the editorial work of Catherine Clements and Ellen Fuchs at Oxford University Press have helped greatly. With this, as with each of my previous books published by Oxford University Press, every stage of the process has been handled in the way an author most hopes for: respect for his ambitions for the book, with valuable proposals on how best to realize those.

Because this book emerged from the Rosenthal Lectures, I should like to include the comments I made in March of 1989 in beginning the lectures, indicating part of what they meant to me.

> Anyone would feel honored to lecture in this distinguished series of your great school, but there are also more personal and deeper meanings for me. I visited Northwestern in the spring of 1983. I had learned from the writings of Dean Bennett, Tony D'Amato, Mayer Freed, Ian McNeil, Michael Perry, Martin Redish, and Victor Rosenblum, so I cherished the opportunity for dialogue with them; I discovered many others on the faculty, and numbers of students, whose perspectives enriched mine. Alone in Chicago, commuting back to my family on weekends, I also found a friendly, congenial, and supportive community. Being amongst your faculty, students, and staff made an arduous semester a genuinely pleasurable one. So I came to consider Northwestern Law School a kind of second home.
>
> More painful associations are present too. My friend and colleague William Cary, who became America's leading scholar on Corporations law, began his career here; he died of cancer while I was visiting in 1983. Years earlier Bob Childres, a superb teacher on your faculty and one of my closest friends, had also died of cancer.
>
> When I was invited to deliver these lectures, I recalled the happiness of Paul and Iris Brest's visit in 1983. I eagerly anticipated sharing these days with my own wife Sanja. Last spring, I suffered some seizures. Her loving

care helped me to regain physical strength and cope with strong medication, to overcome self-doubts, and to begin initial work on the lectures. The prospect of spending these days together seemed even more significant. On the last day of August, an apparently routine operation showed that Sanja had cancer; she died in early November. Friends on your faculty were generous in their sympathy. The decision whether to do the lectures was left entirely to me, and the schedule of these days here was sensitively adjusted to my feelings. For me, preparing and delivering these remarks will always be linked to last autumn's events and my overwhelming sense of loss. They will also be linked to the concern shown by members of your faculty, the kind of concern to which one clings when carrying on is difficult.

The sensitivity and concern of members of the faculty continued during my three-day visit at Northwestern, and that time provided emotional support as well as intellectual challenge.

During the last two and a half years, family and friends have aided me beyond measure. Often in unexpected ways, those who have cared for me and for Sanja have made the burden of these days a little less heavy and have contributed to my finding renewed meaning in what I do. The greatest help has come from my three sons, Andrei, Sasha, and Robert. Their love for each other and for me, largely the gift of Sanja's love for us all, has been a powerful assurance. My understanding that their lives give meaning to my own has remained strong in even the worst moments.

New York   K. G.
June 1991

CONTENTS

Law and Objectivity

1

Introduction

How Law Might Be Objective

Is law objective? This question generates argument and confusion. Radically different conceptions of law, of social life, and of human understanding produce the argument. Exaggerations contribute to the confusion, but a major cause is ambiguity. There are many questions about the objectivity of law, and some are closely related to others. Unless two people happen to begin with the same problem in mind, initial clarification and analysis is needed for useful discussion. Perhaps "objective" has become so unclarifying and controversial a label, we would do better to find another vocabulary, or diligently limit ourselves to the other labels that already exist. Indeed, this study suggests other appropriate phrases to distill competing positions. But whatever would be most desirable conceptually, many questions about law have often been put in the language of objectivity.

This book examines a number of senses in which the law might be objective or something opposed to being objective—such as subjective, indeterminate, or arbitrary. The book is divided into three major parts. The first part undertakes a preliminary inquiry about law's determinacy, the extent to which existing legal rules and principles provide definite answers to legal questions. For this part, the standard of a determinate answer is, roughly, what virtually all lawyers and other intelligent persons familiar with the legal system would believe, after careful study, the law provides. To say that the law provides an answer is to say that the answer should guide someone trying to act in accordance with the law. (That answer, and the legal system that yields it, may or may not be believed to be just.) The discussion in Part I draws significant conclusions, but is a highly incomplete account of legal standards and practices,

3

in some measure because it reserves most analysis of legal reasoning for the last part of the book.

That part of the book mainly considers the relationship between "legal" standards and various sources of evaluation that I loosely call "broader" standards. Is law objective, or can it be objective, because it is anchored in sound political morality, economic efficiency, cultural morality, or some other criterion? With respect to these three criteria I have mentioned, I inquire how far law does conform with them, how far it should conform with them, and how far they are appropriately used in resolving legal cases. For legal cases with no easy answer, the possibility of "the law" providing an answer is closely tied to the law's relationship with these broader standards. Part of that relationship is the manner in which legal reasoning is linked to reasoning used to develop and apply these standards. In the course of Part III, I consider whether any distinctions exist between legal and broader standards and between legal and other reasoning, and if so, how such distinctions should be drawn.

The middle part of the book considers a range of questions about whether law treats people in an "objective" way. Among the possible ways that law might be objective are in (1) addressing external acts, not thoughts and emotions; (2) taking acts as they reasonably appear, rather than examining intents, motives, and understandings; (3) viewing acts in light of what "reasonable people" would be expected to do, not in light of what the particular individual might do; and (4) establishing criteria of liability and designing remedies and punishments with regard to general classes of people and circumstances, rather than individuals and particular situations. Further questions may be raised about the "objectivity" of categorizations that appear "neutral" in some respect but operate to the disadvantage of important groups. In Part II, I spend some time considering feminist claims that apparently neutral rules operate to the disadvantage of women and that the whole enterprise of abstract categorization reflects a harsh and unbending masculine perspective that is harmful for human beings. Part II is important in its own right, but its facing of troublesome problems of legal choice also lays the foundation for the appraisal of questions of interpretation in Part III.

The Lawyer's Perspective: Law School and Legal Work

The book tries to illuminate the law both for ordinary law students and lawyers and for theoreticians. A brief sketch of my beginning acquaintance with law may help readers who are not theoreticians to put the book in context and relate it to their own concerns.

When I came to law school, I had rather firm assumptions about the law. I thought that law was a set of legal rules that applied straightforwardly to events in life, that the lawyer's task was to know a lot about these rules and use them in trying cases and giving advice. I am not quite sure just how I developed this view.[1] Perhaps it was from listening to radio dramas—my parents did not purchase a TV during my formative years—in which the law of criminal guilt was clear and the only issue was "Who done it?" Perhaps I had a deep psychological need for certainty. In any event, I assumed that if the facts were discovered, the application of law was almost always simple, that reasoning within the law was essentially objective, that the law deals with people in an impersonal or objective way, and that a healthy fit usually exists between the law and correct moral principles and community standards.

In recent decades, the coverage of legal issues in the news media and in entertainment is more sophisticated than what I remember. Perhaps few students today begin law school as naive as I was then, particularly since the spread of critical theory among professors who teach college courses in humanities and social sciences may yield students who are much more skeptical about "truth" in any domain than were the members of my "silent" generation of the late 1950's. But I suspect the vision of law as a set of definite, impersonal, rules with fixed applications to particular cases has not lost its hold on the mind of the general public; probably there are still some students who begin law school with a picture of law that is not so different. They suffer, as I did, a rude awakening.

In law school, students are exposed to case after case in which the right result is debatable, in which every reason for a decision one way is met by a contrary reason. It becomes easy to think that the law is largely indeterminate, even to think that legal reasons are just manipulative techniques that lawyers and judges use to support results reached on unstated grounds. If cynicism sets in, any claim that law is objective may look like a cruel, patronizing delusion, one lawyers perpetuate to conceal what really happens.

Having had only slight involvement in the private practice of law, I cannot speak with confidence about how perceptions of law evolve as one immerses oneself in the business of being a lawyer. But I believe the intuitive perspective of most lawyers resembles that of law teachers who concentrate on particular subject matters rather than the shifting fashions of legal theory. I think they would say something like this:

For many circumstances the application of relevant legal standards is clear; for other circumstances the law is uncertain. The percentage of doubtful cases depends on the general area of law—the law of wills is more certain than constitutional law—and also on the subdivision within the general area. There is often rough agreement on the force of legal arguments. Some arguments have substantial force; others seem to have little or no genuine force but serve to obscure the true bases of decision. Law generally, and desirably, treats people in an objective or impersonal manner, but with some frequency particular, or subjective, characteristics count. Certain broader sources often underlie the law and are a basis for decision in hard cases, but neither law nor legal interpretation can be reduced to a subcategory of a single outside source or to a combination of them.

I contend that this somewhat crude appraisal is essentially accurate, but even its proponents are hard put to give a precise account of its underlying assumptions. This book tries to develop these underlying assumptions and to defend the developed view against more simplistic and extreme alternatives.

My treatment of various topics usually begins with concrete examples and moves to more general conclusions. I hope this strategy of presentation will clarify what is involved and avoid some of the confusion that can be engendered by grand abstractions. This strategy fits my aim to speak comprehensibly to nontheoretitians; but it also reflects my own sense that in legal and political philosophy close attention to illustrations can teach us more than unfocused debate about large generalizations.

Traditional Legal Theory and Modern Skepticism

How various positions in modern legal theory bear on these inquiries is complex. A fuller account must await more detailed discussion, but some introductory remarks can help set the stage for what follows.

Traditional versions of natural law and positivism each consider law to be objective in important senses. The natural law perspective that dominated thinking about law for much of the history of western civilization has taken for granted that the main source of law's objectivity lies in its derivation from a moral law that conforms with divine law. According to a less familiar, secular version of natural law, the objectively valid moral standards from which law derives rest on some connection with natural processes or stand by themselves.

The simple positivist conception that law derives from a political sovereign grew in the late eighteenth century with the emergence of powerful nation-states. Those who maintain that conception hold that the objectivity of law is a consequence of the enactment of rules by a political authority. The rules give directions that are objectively ascertainable by others, and the answers to legal questions are determinable whether or not those answers conform with moral principles.[2] Because natural lawyers had long assumed that positive legal enactments could settle matters of indifference (e.g., what currency to adopt) and provide more precision than does natural law for the practical administration of principles derivable from natural law (e.g., the scale of sentences for theft), the notion of positive rules providing answers was hardly novel. But the comparative emphasis on the actual rules rather than on underlying moral principles increased dramatically with legal positivism.

A third way in which legal standards might be considered objective is if they follow in some structured way from cultural patterns or a basic social reality. According to Friedrich von Savigny, for example, positive law is rooted in the spirit of the people, the *volksgeist*; according to Marx, modes and relations of production substantially determine legal superstructure. Though both these conceptions suppose that law will differ significantly according to a particular culture or stage of history, law is seen as deriving in some fashion from underlying social roots. The more familiar view in modern America that economic efficiency is the ultimate source of all or much law is similar if it supposes that law in certain societies inevitably moves toward results that an effectively working market would yield.

Regardless of the grounding law has been thought to have, law has been widely understood as dealing with external behavior and involving abstract categorization. It focuses on objective circumstances and treats people in an impersonal or objective way. In liberal political philosophy, these features are considered aspects of "the rule of law," a political virtue that enhances individual choice and prevents arbitrariness.

Modern challenges to claims that law is, or should be, objective have drawn from an amalgam of perspectives: candid recognition about how legal institutions work; belief that values are relative or matters of preference; attention to the subjectivity of interpreting language and rules; awareness that any culture is composed of complex, partly conflicting strands that make deriving any single set of legal institutions impossible; and skepticism that abstract categorization is desirable in human relations. Legal realism, hermeneutics, feminist legal thought, and critical legal studies[3] are movements whose adherents often reject various assertions of law's objectivity.

Among the most unsettling of the skeptical notions for ordinary thought about the law are the ideas that language and rules are much less determinate than lawyers have generally supposed and that abstract categorization is undesirable. The first of these ideas is a major concern of Part I, which focuses on the possibility of normative categorization. The second idea emerges as an important theme in Part II.

I

Legal Rules and Determinate Answers to Legal Questions

2

The Import of Normative Language and Rules— Nonlegal Illustrations

This first part of the book addresses the skeptical possibility that answers to legal questions are rarely if ever determinate. Drawing from legal realists, some modern writers have emphasized the indeterminacy of legal norms.[1] Often a central aspect of their critique has been an assertion that the language and content of legal rules are open to a wide spectrum of interpretations. If that thesis is sound, perhaps objective legal answers cannot be derived from authoritative rules. If the application of any single rule is indeterminate, questions that invoke broad sets of rules and principles are not likely to be determinate either. If the language and content of law are indeterminate, those who decide legal cases may not be essentially different from legislators and from executives exercising discretion. They may make political judgments that carry the day only because of their political authority. In that event, much legal decision differs little from unguided political decision.

Part I has two major aims. The first is to show that any extreme thesis that "the law" is always or usually indeterminate is untenable. Is rebutting that thesis challenging a straw man? Does anyone *really* think the law *usually fails* to provide answers to legal questions, in a sense of "fails" that has some practical significance? I am not sure. I do know the position has received vigorous defense in discussions with able students and scholars I respect.[2] Detached passages in some articles suggest the position, even if the authors' actual acceptance of it may be in doubt. The subject generates enough misunderstanding to make it worth establishing that the law does often and indisputably have determinate answers to legal questions.

My second aim has more general importance. It is to explain *how* one can conceive the existence of determinate answers without relying on highly controversial assumptions about truth or value.[3] Many of those who believe in determinate answers are not sure how to defend their beliefs. I try to explicate the ways that the law yields many undoubtedly correct answers.

A preliminary question I need to face is whether the determinacy of law is important. No doubt, it matters what factors judges should take into account and whether their authority to resolve significant practical issues is warranted. But if those problems are resolved, perhaps we shouldn't worry too much about whether "the law" provides answers or where "the law" ends and other things begin. So goes the objection. There is much that is sound in it. When one addresses the complicated issues of interpretation with which Part III deals, saying where law ends is difficult and deciding whether "the law" provides answers does not always seem to be of great moment.

Nonetheless, a good deal is at stake in the problem about a determinate law. The "naive" vision of a legal system holds that the law does yield many answers, that finding an answer does not depend on a particular individual's moral or political values or perspectives about interpretation. Certainly this vision is caught by the traditional idea of a "rule of law, not men." The right answer does not depend on something idiosyncratic about the person who is deciding, or on controversial moral and political claims that are the stuff of debate in the legislative process. Whether this vision of a rule of law, not individuals, is just an illusion does matter. Suppose legal decisions are essentially indistinguishable from decisions based on ordinary moral and political arguments, at best the product of a highly deliberative process for considering such arguments. Then the idea that there is something special, more solid, about the law should be dispelled, or seen through clear eyes as a false myth that is useful for the elite or for a supine and ignorant populace. For some writers, revelation of the character of judicial decision exposes the power of the judiciary as illegitimate.[4]

The "rule of law" idea connects to my basic standard for a determinate answer in this part of the book. The main criterion for judging the existence of a determinate answer is whether virtually any lawyer or other intelligent person familiar with the legal system would conclude, after careful study, that the law provides that answer. This standard well reflects the notion that the answer is there, not dependent on an individual's particular opinion. Let me emphasize that this is a rough criterion for seeing whether the law really does provide an answer in some simple, indisputable, sense. I am not asserting that somehow near unanimity *automatically* constitutes a determinate answer. My focus is not on the factual question whether the answer is highly likely to be given by lawyers and judges who are consulted, but on the normative question whether the law requires a particular answer. People *might* agree on an answer that was incorrect or not required. But almost universal agreement that an answer is required is strong evidence of such an answer, given the nature of law. To cover the possibility of misjudgment, I add as a further criterion of a determinate answer that no powerful argument consonant with the broad premises of the legal system exists for a contrary answer. Whether there are determinate answers in the law meeting these joint criteria matters for our understanding of a legal system.

I postpone discussion of legal norms themselves until the following chapter. Here I offer variations on two nonlegal illustrations that raise normative questions in social contexts and help suggest a number of important theoretical points about determinate answers. I move from individual imperatives, to collective imperatives, to rules addressed to many people and circumstances. I do not suppose that conclusions based on nonlegal illustrations can be easily transposed to the law, and I want to be clear that I am not claiming such a transposition. However, nonlegal illustrations have a double value. They force us to see whether skepticism about the determinacy of law is based on skepticism about language and rules in general or rests instead on something peculiar about the law. The simpler examples also compel attention to any features of legal systems that might justify greater skepticism than is warranted for the examples.

Directives and Rules in Business Settings

The Determinacy of Simple Imperatives

THE BASIC THESIS

When Sam enters the office of his boss, Beth, she says, "Good morning, Sam, please shut the door." Beth has used imperative language; her words are directed toward Sam's performing an action. The word "please" might indicate a request that Sam is free not to perform. However, coming from a boss to a subordinate in typical settings, a "request" like this amounts to a directive, one that the subordinate is required to perform. If nothing in Beth's tone of voice[5] or in Sam's past relations with Beth suggests other than a straightforward significance to Beth's words,[6] Sam has a clear idea of what he needs to do to comply. He is supposed to walk to the door of Beth's office and shut it immediately. Sam's understanding does not depend on any prior relationship between Beth and Sam; he will know what to do even if it is the first day on the job for him or Beth. This example shows the obvious, that imperative language can be substantially determinate in context.

How is this possible? First, Beth and Sam share a linguistic competence in English. Both understand the significance that is now assigned by English speakers to the words "shut" and "door" and to the syntax and tone of voice in which imperative utterances are usually formulated. But more is needed than an understanding of English. Beth has said "the" door and she has not specified when she wants it closed. Suppose that Sam's own office door and the door to a cabinet within Beth's reach are both open. How does Sam know Beth means the door to her office? He knows this because people often want their office doors closed when important matters are to be discussed, and most people do not ask others to close cabinet doors within their own easy reach. (Matters could be otherwise; if all office doors in the firm were rigidly set in open positions, Sam might look for a door he was capable of closing.) Sam knows further that in contexts like this, a request to close the door means right away. What is more, Beth is confident that Sam has this knowledge, and consequently, she feels no need to specify which door is to be closed and when. In some sense, Sam must construe Beth's words and Beth in turn intuitively relies on Sam's almost certain construction when she formulates her words.[7] But the effectiveness of Beth's communication does not depend on anything idiosyncratic about her or Sam; indeed, it is what they share with people generally that makes it so easy for Sam and others to recognize what Sam needs to do to comply. If Sam walks over to the door and shuts it, he has complied with Beth's directive. If, in full command of his faculties, he sits down in a chair and doesn't budge for five minutes, he has failed to comply.[8] If he walks behind Beth's desk and shuts her cabinet door, he is either crazy or playing some joke, but he has also failed to comply.[9]

Our example indicates how the significance of an imperative commonly depends on both shared linguistic competence and shared assumptions about the social universe people inhabit, how some forms of action in response to an imperative can determinately, or objectively, be said to comply with the imperative, and how other forms of action can determinately, or objectively, be said to fail to comply.

INSTANCES WHEN COMPLIANCE IS DOUBTFUL

On some occasions, whether Sam has complied or not may be arguable. Barring exceptional circumstances, these occasions are not too frequent with simple directives to shut doors, but they can arise. When they do arise, Beth's directive may not be determinate as to whether Sam has fully complied. Suppose that Sam walks over to a table, pours himself a glass of water, drinks it, and then shuts the door. Did Beth mean Sam should shut the door before doing anything else? The temporary delay may or may not lead Beth to think that Sam has failed to comply fully, and Sam may or may not perceive himself as slightly insubordinate. Suppose that Sam shuts the door enough so that no one can see inside and most noise is blocked, but the door does not "click" shut. Has he successfully shut the door? For most of my family life, that would count as shutting a door in our apartment; but we now have a dog who can push open doors that have not clicked shut. If I ask one of my sons to shut the door to my room partly because I want to keep the dog out, my request has not been fulfilled completely unless the door clicks shut. With virtually any request or directive, doubt can exist whether certain responsive behavior constitutes compliance or noncompliance, or constitutes only partial compliance rather than full compliance.

EXCEPTIONAL CIRCUMSTANCES

Unusual circumstances may call for Sam to act in a manner different from that which obviously would comply with Beth's directive in ordinary circumstances. Suppose that as Sam puts his hand on the door, he sees Beth collapse or notices the company president approaching Beth's door. In either event, Sam should not close the door.

Just how to state this conclusion is perplexing. We might say that although Sam has not complied with the literal significance of Beth's directive, the directive effectively lapsed[10] because its force did not cover the unexpected circumstance.[11] We might say, alternatively, that the actual *meaning* of the directive incorporates assumptions about underlying conditions for obedience, including conditions up to the time of compliance. On this view, the directive itself excludes the circumstances in which Sam finds himself. Focusing on the directive's meaning, we might distinguish full meaning from literal meaning; or we might take the view that the idea of literal meaning is itself misguided, that there is nothing other than meaning *in context*, and that the meaning of Beth's directive in context does not reach these circumstances.

These nuances in the philosophy of language are not crucial for my purposes, but it is worth pausing over them for a moment, if only to indicate why I subsequently use the language I do to treat them. In *some sense*, Beth's directive does not require Sam to close the door if the president is approaching or Beth collapses. Sam has *not failed to comply* with a directive that really applies to him at the moment he acts. We should not say, however, that Sam *has complied* with the directive to shut the door.[12] The action he should now perform is not *called for* by the directive, and that action would be the same if Beth had never given the directive. So Sam's appropriate action is neither compliance nor non-compliance with any directive to shut the door that applies to him at that moment.

One basic question is whether the present absence of an effective imperative to close the door is somehow part of the "meaning" of Beth's directive. The idea that it is part of the meaning is most persuasive if the situation has arisen previously. Suppose on some prior occasion Sam has closed the door in the president's face and Beth has responded, "Sam, you should never do that. I didn't want you to close the door if he was approaching." When Beth asks Sam to close the door on subsequent occasions, she and Sam may understand what she says as meaning "Shut the door, unless the president is approaching." On this view, the meaning of Beth's directive does not require Sam to close the door if the president is approaching; therefore, his failure to close it cannot be a failure to comply.

If the meaning includes all the implicit understandings Beth and Sam may share, must a distinction be drawn between full meaning and literal meaning? It is difficult to think of the *literal* meaning as including understandings as to which an outsider listening to the conversation might have no inkling. One might scrap the idea of *literal meaning* altogether in favor of *meaning in context*. However, I am inclined to think that the idea of literal meaning makes sense and that a literal meaning includes some basic assumptions about the conditions in which an utterance is made,[13] but does not include all the understandings shared by speaker and listener.

A different way to conceptualize the nonapplication of Beth's directive is to say that the directive lapses, or lacks force for the situation. On this view, the unexpected intervening event renders the directive inapplicable. This approach is most persuasive if the event is one neither Beth nor Sam has foreseen. Suppose it has never occurred to them that between the time Beth says, "Please shut the door," and Sam shuts it, Beth may collapse, a devastating earthquake may occur, or Sam may discover a fire in the building. It is a strain to pack all these exceptions into "unless clauses" that are part of the *meaning* of Beth's directive. It is also a strain (though a lesser one) to say that part of the *meaning* of the directive is that the listener should exercise discretion not to do what is directed if unforeseen extraordinary events occur. It makes more sense to say that the directive simply lacks relevance or force because of what has happened.

Let me summarize my best understanding of this somewhat tangled conceptual topic. When exceptions to an imperative are part of an antecedent understanding between speaker and listener that limits conditions of application, the exceptions are part of the meaning of the imperative. On occasion they will be part of its literal meaning, but often they will be part of a meaning that extends beyond literal meaning.[14] When exceptions arise because of circumstances that were not previously conceived, the exceptions are not part of the meaning of the imperative. Rather, the force of the imperative lapses because of intervening events.[15] (I have not yet addressed situations in which the understandings of speaker and listener diverge; that subject is covered below, and its general treatment there applies to this topic as well.)

I now return from this brief tangential attempt to characterize the conclusion that Sam does not need to shut the door. Ultimately what matters is not the characterization but the conclusion: Sam's failure to shut the door if Beth collapses or the president approaches is appropriate, and carrying out the simple terms of Beth's directive would be inappropriate. In declining to shut the door, Sam has not "failed to comply" in the sense of not complying with an imperative that is presently requiring him to shut the door. If he actually shuts the door in these circumstances he will be castigated for extreme stupidity.

Does the problem of unusual intervening circumstances undercut the previous conclusion that when imperatives are spoken, some actions objectively represent failures to comply? If some circumstances render the simple content of an imperative inapplicable, how can we say with confidence that in any other circumstances Sam objectively is required to shut the door?

We can examine this question in light of a suggestion Frederick Schauer once made that unless the language of rules is taken in a highly literal sense, their "ruleness" is undermined.[16] He urged that when rules are interpreted broadly in terms of their purposes they fail to function as rules, but rather become reminders or "rules of thumb" about the advantages of behaving in a certain way. At least as far as an individual imperative is concerned, my example shows that this dichotomy is a false one.

Sam supposes that Beth wants the door closed to prevent interruption or overhearing and, more generally, to serve the firm's welfare. An ensuing conversation between Beth and Sam will not be possible if Beth collapses or the president wants to see Beth. Other obvious purposes, Beth's health or retaining the good will of the president, may be disserved if Sam shuts the door. If purpose is put at the abstract level of the company's welfare, shutting the door will disserve the very purpose that led Beth to ask Sam to shut the door. Beth does not want or expect Sam to shut the door if she collapses or the president is about to walk in. (If she had wanted that, she might have said something like, "Shut the door, and do so no matter what is happening to me or who is right outside the door."[17]) Sam and others in similar situations are expected to act with some sensitivity to the reasons for the directives, not carrying them out when unexpected events raise exceptionally strong countervailing reasons.

It hardly follows that the directive has no force but to remind Sam of the advantages of shutting the door. Under ordinary circumstances, Sam's duty as a subordinate is clear. Sam may appropriately raise a question before he acts, "Do you really want the door shut, considering how hot the room will get?" But if Sam says nothing or Beth repeats her original directive in response to his inquiry, Sam has lost whatever power and responsibility he might otherwise have had to decide whether the advantages of circulating air, openness to fellow employees, and so on, outweigh the reasons for shutting the door. That decision has definitely become Beth's, not his. Further, even if Sam thinks Beth's own interests would be marginally better served by leaving the door open, such considerations do not provide a basis for his not closing the door, as long as they are within Beth's apprehension when she issued the directive. The directive constrains Sam's behavior to a very considerable degree and, as far as his responsibility as a subordinate is concerned,[18] virtually dictates his course of action except in genuinely exceptional circumstances. The reader's experience will attest that in an extremely high percentage of situations in which someone is directed or requested to shut the door, no genuinely exceptional circumstance intervenes. Thus, interpretation in light of purpose need not turn an imperative into a rule of thumb. Many, many standard circumstances will remain in which a determinate, objective answer will exist to whether behavior complies with an imperative like Beth's, "Please shut the door."

EXCEPTIONAL CIRCUMSTANCES AND INSTANCES
WHEN COMPLIANCE IS DOUBTFUL

If exceptional circumstances may call upon Sam not to carry out the terms of Beth's directive, he is left some latitude in identifying which unanticipated circumstances are exceptional enough to prevent him from carrying out the directive. Not all circumstances will be clearly either ordinary ones in which the directive applies and continues in effect or exceptional ones in which the force of the directive lapses.

Somewhat unusual circumstances may arise when the application of the directive and the manner in which Sam should respond to it are unclear. Suppose when Sam gets to the door, he notices another subordinate, Sandra, approaching Beth's door with an evident wish to talk to her. Especially if he is relatively new on the job, Sam may not be sure whether Beth wants him to shut the door, indicating to Sandra that she should wait, or keep the door open until Beth can hear briefly what has brought Sandra to her office. Sam may lack the time to inquire of Beth what she wants him to do before Sandra reaches the door, and in any event, he may suppose that Beth would be embarrassed to say that she wants the door shut to keep Sandra out even if that is her wish. In short, Sam, and a reasonable person in his situation, may be unsure what effect Sandra's approach has on the directive, and he may have reason to act one way or another without seeking a clarification. If Sam closes the door and Beth questions him, he might say, "I did what you asked and I assumed that covered this circumstance." If Sam does not close the door and Beth questions him, he might say, "I thought you probably wouldn't have wanted me to exclude Sandra," or "I didn't think your request really covered this situation." In this circumstance, there might be no objective answer to whether Sam should shut the door; the effect of Beth's directive may be indeterminate. The significance of the directive in these circumstances may depend partly on how much Sam knows about Beth's management style and general wishes. If the force of the directive *is* indeterminate, Sam's own personal sense of appropriateness will influence his reaction. This *range of indeterminacy of application* by no means detracts from the conclusion that in many circumstances Sam must shut the door if he is not to disobey the directive and that in other circumstances his failure to shut the door will definitely be appropriate.

WHOSE PERSPECTIVE CONTROLS

Circumstances in which the application of the directive seems to be in doubt raise questions about the manner through which the meaning and effect of the directive are to be ascertained. In this initial part of the book, I am taking as determinate only those answers on which vitually everyone agrees. In these situations, speaker's and listener's perspectives will rarely diverge, but it is analytically clarifying to focus briefly on possible divergence.

To examine the appropriate criteria for determining meaning and effect, we need to consider wants versus more complicated feelings and the speaker's expectations versus the listener's perceptions. As a rough beginning, we might suppose that Sam's standard of action is what Beth wants and that the range and effect of her directive are determined by what she wants. But that would certainly be an oversimplification. Imagine that Beth prefers open doors but has been told by her own boss that she must ask subordinates to close doors, or that she dislikes Sam and would be delighted to have a clear instance of insubordination so that she could fire him. Beth might actually *hope* that Sam will not comply, but she has nonetheless directed him to shut the door. Insofar as Beth's subjective state is relevant, it must be her sense of what Sam would understand her to be directing.

An approach to meaning and effect that focuses on the speaker must take into account the speaker's expectations of the listener. But is the speaker's perspective finally conclusive of the directive's significance, or does the listener's perspective have more relevance than that?[19] Suppose Beth has actually misspoken and wants her window, not her door, shut. The listener's perspective would seem to control. We would not say Beth has *instructed* Sam to shut the window if she has said, "Please shut the door,"[20] even if she is consciously thinking "window" all the time.[21] Perhaps the significance of the directive should be taken to be what Sam reasonably would take it to be.[22]

If the directive's significance is unclear in context, as when Sandra approaches Beth's door, which perspective, if either, should be taken as finally determinative if the speaker's and listener's perspectives diverge? This question itself is probably misconceived. One needs to be more precise and ask determinative for what purpose? If Sam is deciding what to do and asks a fellow employee for advice, the fellow employee will probably be guided by his best guess of Beth's understanding of her directive's coverage. That guess, of course, may depend partly on more general ideas about how people in firms should relate to each other.

Some people may think that if bosses have not spoken very clearly, subordinates should act as they think best. I am assuming that for matters of this sort most people understand the objective to be to conform to the boss's sense of what she has directed. Thus, the friend would advise in terms of speaker's intent. However, suppose the issue is not what Sam should do but whether what he has done warrants criticism. If he acts as a reasonable listener in his situation would, he does not deserve criticism. For that purpose, the reasonable listener's perspective should be determinative. Insofar as a listener's perspective controls in doubtful instances, that perspective might focus completely on the listener's reasonable perceptions of the speaker's expectations, including the speaker's likely resolution of doubtful instances the speaker has not considered, *or* the listener's perspective might leave the listener some "discretion" to decide which doubtful instances fall outside the range of application of the directive.

Only when we know the purpose of the inquiry are we in a position to evaluate what perspective controls the significance of an imperative. That depends largely on social practices and expectations. Social practices not only help fill in the content of communications beyond the literal meaning of individual words, they also help determine the perspective from which meaning should be assessed.

This truncated discussion of perspectives has powerful implications for the scope of imperatives, and legal norms in particular. Without exploring those implications here, I shall make three important points.

First, *if* the "determinate" applications of an imperative extend beyond applications that virtually all reasonable people would agree to and include applications that are "correct" by some more refined standard, then the range of determinate applications will depend on the test of significance for the imperative. Insofar as an imperative's significance rests on the actual speaker's perspective, for example, the determinacy of applications will turn on what is in, or somehow would be in, the speaker's mind. If no perspective takes evident priority, we may have to say that a particular imperative is determinate from one perspective but not from another, and then debate which perspective or perspectives should count.[23]

Second, in some contexts it is critical to know how much the language in which the speaker has framed an imperative limits the listener. To use a phrase employed by legal scholars, is the language canonical? The answer to that question is often intertwined with the perspective one is to take toward the significance of an imperative.

The third point is that all these complexities do not threaten the major conclusions I have drawn thus far. Usually speakers' and listeners' perspectives coalesce across a wide range. Most circumstances call for compliance; some render "compliance" evidently inappropriate; some would leave people uncertain or in disagreement about whether compliance is called for.[24] In this part of the book, I am counting as determinate only applications upon which virtually all informed people agree. These would be applications that virtually all listeners would recognize as covered by the speaker's words and purposes.

Responsibilities as a Subordinate and What Is Good Overall

A distinction exists between Sam's responsibilities as a subordinate and his overall responsibilities; but his responsibilities as a subordinate, and therefore the force of a superior's imperative, usually have substantial normative force for what he should do taking everything into account. My discussion of these two points concentrates on the clear case of ordinary circumstances in which Beth's directive plainly requires Sam to shut the door.

For a variety of reasons, Sam might not believe Beth's directive is conclusive about what he should do as a human being. Suppose the company is planning to dump toxic wastes that will endanger the community's water supply. Sam has warned a few friends, but they do not believe him. A community leader is lurking in the hallway, and if Sam leaves the door open a crack, she may hear Beth's development of the company's plans and be able to forestall their implementation. Sam is aware that if Beth knew these circumstances, it would only intensify her wish to have the door closed.[25] If Sam leaves the door open, he breaches traditional notions of employee responsibility, but his broader responsibility as a member of the community may call for that action.

This illustration raises a more general question about Sam's view of the authority of Beth's imperatives. He may accept widely shared understandings about employee responsibility, but believe exceptional circumstances like these call for violation. Or he may be a social radical who thinks that the policymaking of private companies should be open to public view and that subordinates should have as much to say as bosses about whether office doors should be open. Sam may think that "requests" by superiors should be only requests, not directives, and that junior employees should feel free not to fulfill requests if they have opposing judgments or preferences.

Why should Sam, or an outsider who views Sam's situation, suppose that Beth's directive carries authority? One answer may be that hierarchy is necessary or beneficial, that power to decide most matters is correctly located in superiors, that primacy in decision contributes to an efficient economy, and so on. From such a perspective, one reason Beth's directive carries authority is that it should. But is there a response that does not tackle this question? Can one just refer to prevailing assumptions of business people and members of society, saying that people recognize the authority of superiors and that one's duties *as an employee* are circumscribed by this cultural understanding? Doing what employees are generally supposed to do is part of what it means to play the "game" of being an employee.

Sam might answer, "I did not choose to play this 'game.' I have to work to make money, and these destructive assumptions about subordinates' duties warrant resistance." Sam's response raises a practical and conceptual problem. The practical question is what Sam, and others, actually should do when subject to directives. Saying that Sam has a duty as an employee, in the conventionally understood sense of employee duty, is not to answer the question of what he should do overall. Violation of employee duties might, on occasion, do more good than harm or it might represent and foster proper relations among human beings. Moreover, violation might help alter the understanding of appropriate duties. Some years ago, running personal errands for bosses, predominantly male, may have been assumed to be part of the job of secretaries, almost all female.[26] Some secretaries' refusal to perform personal errands testified to the intensity of their feelings that the practice demeaned the secretaries; the refusal may have helped shift the performance of personal errands from an accepted conventional duty to something outside the range of secretarial duties.[27]

In favor of Sam's performing employee responsibilities, one might urge that conventional understandings define expectations, and that the parties have effectively agreed to these understandings. Subordinates' duties are sometimes the subject of explicit agreement. More commonly an employer assumes that someone who takes a job implicitly undertakes to perform duties that accompany the job, or at least those duties perceived by the prospective employee when he accepts employment. By accepting the job, Sam may have implicitly promised to act as employees are generally expected to act. If promises and similar undertakings have moral force, those conventional understandings that were not explicitly foresworn by Sam when he took the job bear on what he has agreed to do and, therefore, on what he should, overall, do.[28] It does matter, of course, whether Sam chose his job in conditions of freedom or could be said to have been coerced to accept particular conventional notions of duty because no employment opportunities without them were available. But if Sam has taken his job with adequate freedom, Beth's directive exerts *some* normative force for what he should do overall. Not only will it ordinarily be prudent for Sam to do what Beth says, serious moral reasons exist for doing so.

The conceptual question is a bit harder to untangle than the practical one. I have so far assumed that we properly talk of conventional duties that are attached to positions even if the conventional duties may not coincide with what positional duties *should be* or with what it is right to do overall on particular occasions. That is, I have assumed that we can say, "Sam violated his duty as an employee," without offering a judgment either that what he did was, overall, wrong or that his duty was one employees should have in a good society. A radical might challenge this conceptual assumption. Pointing out that our concepts affect our actions, he might claim that talking about duties and responsibilities of employees as something different from the duties and responsibilities of human beings gives the actions expected of employees a higher status than they should have. The radical might say that we should reserve the language of duty and responsibility for actions that, overall, one can commend to performance. If the radical based his claim on present conceptual practice, an investigation of actual practice would be needed to see if people do talk about their duties and responsibilities as employees even when they are unsure whether these should be performed. Perhaps, present ordinary usage is too confused to give clear guidance, but I do not believe it supports the radical's challenge.

The radical might concede that his proposal deviates from present usage, saying, "Any conceptual practice of isolating employee responsibilities is itself destructive because it generates uncritical acceptance of undesirable directives. All those who recognize that destructiveness should *now* use concepts in the way they would be used in a good society. Therefore, we should refuse to speak of employee duties except as a subcategory of actions that people should, overall, perform." (This account closely parallels a possible natural law argument that one should not speak of legal duties when complying with human law requires the violation of moral duties.) One powerful answer to this proposal is that a conceptual practice of distinguishing employee duties and responsibilities from duties and responsibilities, overall, is actually preferable to the alternative and would remain so in a good society. That practice allows us to talk most clearly about what are generally conceived to be employee duties and whether they are warranted. A second answer is that even if conceptual practices might be different in a good society, evaluating substantive challenges to the existing social order is made too difficult when the use of concepts departs drastically from common understandings.[29]

As I indicate in more detail in Chapter 5, one's view of who has authority will sometimes bear on the apparent scope of a directive and on the range of applications that appear determinate; but ordinarily a challenge to the *authority* of Beth's imperative is separable from the question whether its *scope* and *force* determine for many circumstances what Sam should do *if* he aims to comply. Sam may understand perfectly well what act Beth demands, and he may understand perfectly well that no condition has arisen that would cause her directive to lapse; yet he may think he should not perform the act.

Collective Imperatives

It may seem that thus far I have made relatively little progress toward a conclusion that rules can have determinate applications, but that assessment would be wrong. The succeeding steps can be filled in fairly quickly.

I begin with a collective imperative. Suppose that upon Sam's entrance to Beth's office, she asks two of her coequals in the firm, who are in her office, whether they would prefer the door open or closed, and each says "closed." Beth then says to Sam, "We'd like the door closed, please." This sentence, which amounts to a directive to Sam to close the door,[30] represents a "collective intent." If Beth's individual request in her office adequately expresses an individual intent, people can also adequately express a collective intent in some situations.

A collective intent can be based on acquiescence rather than a positive affirmation by some members of the group. Suppose that Beth's initial remarks at the meeting take a slightly different course. She says, "Unless someone disagrees, I'll take it that we want the door closed." When neither colleague responds, she says to Sam, "We'd like the door closed, please." Her comment to Sam again indicates a kind of collective intent. The silence of the two colleagues does not show that either really *wants* the door shut or even wants Beth to tell Sam to shut the door. Each may have had a slight preference for an open door but, thinking that the other preferred a closed door, wished not to waste time, or each may have wished to avoid starting the meeting by disagreeing with Beth. When Beth alone told Sam to close the door, we know she wanted to issue the directive, if not necessarily to produce the directed result of a closed door. When an intent is collective, and perhaps more frequently when it is based on silent acquiescence, one may not be confident that each of the participants *wants* either the result or the issuance of the directive. Thus, *contribution* to a collective intent supporting a directive can be consistent with someone's having (1) an initial preference for an outcome contrary to that which her contribution supports, (2) a hope that the directive will not be issued, and (3) a hope that if it is issued, it will be disregarded. Of course, that scenario is atypical. Those who support directives usually want them to be issued and followed.

What are the conditions for a collective intent in these circumstances? It is not enough that Beth's associates know that their joint silence may be taken as supporting a directive to have the door shut. Suppose Beth had said, "I shall take your views today about whether to shut the door as finally dispositive on whether to shut the door for all future meetings among us three." Her colleagues are likely to feel that this use of their present inclinations for future action would be unwarranted. When on a subsequent occasion, Beth says, "We'd like to have the door shut, please," her directive may not reflect the acquiescence of the two others, yet they may not bother to argue about it. What is sufficient to make Beth's directive an appropriate indication of a collective intent is that her two associates both understand how their silence is to be taken *and* agree that it should be taken in this way. When Beth then directs Sam to shut the door, she has their genuine acquiescence. Beth's associates will feel that if Sam does not comply with the directive, he has acted contrary to their authority as well as Beth's.

What constitutes a collective intent depends partly on what actions are taken by people as underlying a collective intent. When it is unclear whether peoples' actions contribute to a collective intent, the presence of such an intent will be debatable. What amounts to a collective intent is importantly conventional, but that does not mean that the *content* of a collective intent can amount to anything those who are later construing it agree upon. They must stick fairly closely to reasonable understandings of what those whose actions underlay the formation of a collective intent thought they were doing, or at least they must stick fairly closely when the reason for divining collective intent is essentially to give effect in some sense to the wills of those involved in creating it.[31]

The Determinacy of Rules

The shift from directives to individuals for particular situations to rules that are addressed to many people and cover many situations does not alter my conclusions about the determinacy of many applications of imperatives. If single and collective imperatives can determine appropriate responses, so too can rules issued in advance.

Suppose that Sam receives the following notice issued by the company management: "The keeping of doors open has been shown to waste a great deal of energy used to heat or cool offices. Except when someone is entering or leaving, all officers of the company should keep their doors closed." This rule differs from collective imperatives in not being given on the spot when particular behavior is desired. Also, Sam may be less confident what mental states and whose mental states the rule represents. It may even be unclear whether Sam should be guided by judgments about any company official's actual mental state. Perhaps he should take the rule as if a single person issued it.[32] In any event, Sam knows the company officials have authority; he further knows that they communicate in this way. At least if the rule has been issued recently, he knows he should keep his door closed in the ordinary circumstances the rule plainly contemplates. When Sam is in his office working on his own or meeting with someone else, his office door should be shut. As with Beth's individual instruction, instances of doubt may exist. May Sam open his door if the air conditioning is not working? May he do so if a client of the firm says, "I'd feel more comfortable if the door were open?" Getting immediate clarification in respect to borderline cases is not possible as it often is with individual directives; so Sam and others like him will need to use their own judgments more frequently.

When directives take the form of rules generally applicable to people and situations, time elapses between their issuance and the performance of acts under them; this affects how reliably they may be construed. But time is a matter of degree. Seconds elapse between Beth's directive and Sam's shutting of the door; her words two seconds ago may no longer represent her wishes now. If Sam receives the general directive to keep doors shut, he can be almost certain that this applies two days later or two weeks later. As long as office structures and heating and cooling remain the same, the behavior the rule covers remains clear.

As time goes on, it may be more difficult to say how much force the rule has, to what extent it remains firm policy. Some rules seem to lapse in force as time passes by. Others do not. When I started as a student at Columbia Law School in 1960, signs prohibited parking on the western side of Riverside Drive on Monday, Wednesday, and Friday, from 11:00 A.M. to 2:00 P.M. The signs, or ones like them, remain. Traffic conditions and street cleaning practices remain similar. What the signs are taken to require has not altered thirty years later. Three decades have not affected the ability of virtually all drivers to comprehend what the signs require. Obviously, the force of rules can survive shifts in persons occupying the positions under which they were originally issued. If the understanding in Sam's firm is that firm rules survive changes in the presidency, the requirement that office doors be shut will remain in effect the day after the resignation of the president who approved the requirement.

Although the passage of time need not undercut the possibility of determinate applications, one must recognize two major difficulties with rules and their effects, the significance of which can increase over time. First, people sometimes issue rules, and even simple directives, that are formulated in more extreme terms than they actually hope to achieve. Maybe what company officials are truly aiming for is to have doors shut most of the time; maybe Sam's leaving his door open for five minutes while he gets a cup of coffee is not the type of behavior the officials seek to curtail. Sam might guess this from past experience and act accordingly. Has he failed to comply?

Does everything depend on nuanced apprehensions within the company? As far as how Sam *should* act as an employee, perhaps everything does depend on a subtle appreciation of the aims of the managing officials. If a parent says, "You must study all afternoon," and both parent and child know from past occasions that a few half hour breaks to watch television are all right, then taking a few breaks is not contrary to what the parent has urged. But when Sam leaves his door open in accord with the managers' aims, has he *justifiably failed* to comply *or* has he *not failed at all*? Certainly he has not complied with the rule's literal meaning, which requires that doors be closed except when people are entering or leaving offices. If Sam had just joined the company, he would probably assume that he should close the door. One cannot pack into the *literal meaning* of the rule everything that Sam is aware of as a seasoned employee. In deciding if Sam has failed to comply, it might matter what the company officials would say if Sam's behavior were noted. They might say either, "That's not really a violation," or, "That is a violation but not one that concerns us." In the latter event, they might intentionally have used language in their rule that was a bit broader than the behavior that bothered them so as to simplify identification of violations.[33] Only more knowledge about precise understandings within the firm would allow us to label Sam's behavior as consistent with the real norm the rule represents or as an acceptable deviation from the rule.

The second major difficulty with rules is that some never quite get off the ground. Here is my recollection of a faculty discussion and vote some years ago and what followed. Serious concern had been expressed that what individual faculty members had said in faculty meetings about prospective appointees occasionally had gotten back to the candidates. All agreed that this was a serious breach of faculty confidentiality, but some faculty members also were concerned about reporting of evaluations to candidates and to members of other faculties that did not identify the names of individual Columbia faculty making the evaluations. Despite mention by some faculty members that an absolute bar on reporting such evaluations in vague terms would be difficult to square with our making requests during our own appointments process that other faculties share their evaluations with us, we adopted an absolute bar on giving such information, and that resolution was moderated only by considerable comment that the matter should be reevaluated after more careful review. If a member of the appointments committee said to a dean of another school, "Well, many people here thought X had very interesting ideas but was not rigorous in developing them," the member would have violated the stated faculty policy.

The matter never came back to the faculty. As far as I could tell, the resolution had little restraining effect on reporting of general attitudes, and when I inquired some months later of a key member of the faculty, he said that he did not recollect any resolution nearly as sweeping as the one I remembered. Believing that the resolution was foolishly overbroad to begin with, and having other things on my mind, I did not check the minutes to determine if my recollection was accurate. This subject was definitely within the faculty's authority at our law school, and our faculty members are fairly conscientious about trying to comply with rules and policies voted by the faculty; but somehow on this occasion, as I recall it, what was required was too far at odds with ordinary and previously accepted practices to alter them much. Very quickly after the vote, the newly stated faculty policy ceased to be an operating constraint in the life of the school.

The passage of time accentuates these difficulties about rules and their effect. The understanding of what words are meant to prescribe may shift over time. Even if the high officials of Sam's firm originally wanted doors shut for short breaks, a more relaxed attitude may evolve, without any change in the governing rule. The rule remains in effect, but the sense of its content shifts slowly. And what is to be said of rules that have ceased to restrain those subject to them, are forgotten by those who voted on them, and are never brought to the attention of those joining the firm? If my recollection is correct about what happened years ago, is the rule against generalized reporting still "in force" for our faculty? It was properly adopted and has never been formally altered, but it is a dead letter in the life of the school.

We need to conceive of an evolution of meaning and effect that includes the understanding of those now responsible for administering and complying with rules. That significance may change in a way not indicated by literal language is sharply illustrated by an amusing example involving the strike zone[34] in American baseball. Through the season of 1987, the rule book provided that a pitch over the plate and between the batter's armpits and knees was a strike.[35] According to a baseball official, umpires over the years had shrunk the strike zone and (perhaps with some exaggeration) in "recent seasons, pitchers hadn't been able to get strikes on pitches above the waist."[36] In the summer of 1987 a conscientious major league umpire could properly call a pitch just below the armpits a ball, even though the supposedly authoritative rule book literally specified otherwise.[37]

Uncertainties about changes in meaning and effect, themselves the results of social changes of various kinds, make it harder to say as time passes when rules yield determinate answers to questions about what people should do. However, as to what were originally conceived as standard circumstances, general rules are still frequently understood, and applied if there is a stage of application, in essentially the same way as they were when first issued. For these circumstances we can comfortably say that determinate answers have not altered much over time.

Rules as Parts of Systems of Rules
Governing Competitive Games

I now turn to an example of a rule that controls activities in a game. This setting reinforces major theoretical points already made and shows how the import of a rule may be plain even if the words of its formulation are unclear as applied to a specific situation. I empathize with feminist disquiet over unnecessary uses of sports analogies in talk about law, but organized sports are among the few activities in our society that are governed by highly specific and detailed rules. My confidence is greater in analyzing them than possible alternatives because of their place in my own experience.

Informal basketball games are often played "half court" with one basket. In some games, when a member of the defensive team rebounds a missed shot, that team must "take the ball back" before a shot by it will count. The rule covering how far back one must go is often phrased "as far as the foul line."

An intense school yard game involves players, all of whom have played many times before. In prior instances all baskets made

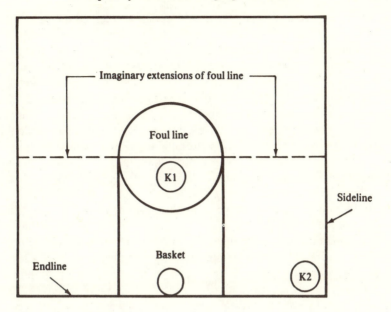

Key

K1 = Kate's first shot

K2 = Kate's second shot

Figure 2.1 Half of a basketball court

without going back to the foul line have been disallowed. On two occasions a teammate of Kate's rebounds a shot by the other team and passes the ball to Kate. The first time Kate is half a step in from the foul line; the second time Kate is in the corner. On each occasion her shot at the basket goes in, and an opponent says, "No basket." Both times Kate responds, "My shot counts."

Are Kate's claims objectively wrong? I think they are. The first instance is easiest. Shots taken in front of the foul line always have been disallowed. All players have understood the rule to require that one really go back *to* the foul line, not just *close* to it. Kate might argue that she went back far enough to serve the purpose of the rule, but games would be plagued if highly contextual decisions had to be made about how far is far enough. In any event, all the players have accepted an interpretation of the rule that is literal in this respect.

When she shoots from the corner, Kate might claim her actions conformed with the literal meaning of the words in which the rule is usually phrased. The corner is *further* from the basket than the foul line, so she has taken the ball back "as far as the foul line." The language "as far as the foul line" *might* be so interpreted, but the decisive answer to Kate's argument is that all the players have understood the rule differently, to require that one cross an imaginary line extended from the foul line to the sidelines and parallel to the endline. Thus, back "as far as the foul line" is to be understood in this way. A somewhat different way of stating the same conclusion is that the phrase "as far as the foul line" is not to be taken as a definitive formulation of the content of the rule. The rules of half-court basketball may be largely arbitrary, but they are what participants accept as the rules. Kate's "interpretation" is contrary to "the rules," as they must be understood in any plausible account of what rules are for informal competitive games. By contesting a clear, shared understanding among all relevant participants (including herself up to the time she proposes a change), Kate tries to play in a way that is "not according to the rules."

Kate might respond that rules, even the rules for informal games, need a capacity to grow. One method of growth is disagreement over, and resolution of, borderline instances. But Kate cannot rely on that argument. Kate urges a *sharp change* in the existing rule. Our culture shares a basic understanding that sharp changes in rules of informal competitive games are not made after the fact when urged by a team that would benefit. They are agreed upon before the game, or to cover plays that have not yet taken place. Even when the possibility of an instant retroactive change in the rules is considered, Kate's assertions that her shots should count as baskets are objectively wrong. The rules yield a determinate—negative—answer to her claims.

Now comes the question of authority. Why should the import of the rules constrain Kate? Is she free to play by different rules or to act upon different methods of changing rules? Suppose she has bet on the game and that her team wins if her shot from the corner counts but loses otherwise: is she morally free to refuse to pay the bet?[38]

The answer here is easy. Kate has played before. She knew the rules and roughly the manner in which they might be changed. By agreeing to play in the game, she implicitly agreed to accept the rules that governed it. Bound by her implicit agreement, she should pay the bet.

My basic conclusions hold if we introduce a referee named Ralph:

> Ralph has often played with members of both teams. The players have agreed Ralph's decision will be final on all questions, and Kate's claims to have her shots count are directed to Ralph.

If Ralph counts either shot, his decision will be objectively wrong under the relevant rules. Ralph implicitly has agreed to referee according to the rules, including both the import of existing rules and the manner in which changes may be made. Ralph lacks authority under the rules to count her shots, and his implied promise binds him to reject Kate's claims.[39]

A legal system and its norms are, of course, much less simple than office practices and half-court basketball games, but these examples have allowed me to illustrate significant theoretical principles. The import of individual imperatives and rules may be determinate as applied to standard instances. That determinacy may exist even when the linguistic formulation alone could be read differently. Understandings shared by many people within specific contexts often provide the basis for comprehending the import of rules; they constrain the methods by which rules may be changed; they usually give rules normative force, providing a reason for compliance. These conclusions refute any universal thesis of radical rule indeterminacy. My major remaining tasks in Part I are to show how these conclusions apply to the law, and to deal with some of the complexities of a legal system.

3

Determinate Applications
of Legal Rules

People have long believed that given existing legal institutions and standards, many legal problems have definite, objective answers, the answers provided by the law as it exists. For this belief to be sound, law need not be firmly rooted in morality, economics, or culture, but legal standards must yield answers. The most ambitious claim of determinacy is that the law provides an answer to every legal question, but that claim has few modern defenders, and I am not one of them. In this part of the book, I am defending a modest claim about determinacy: that many legal questions have determinate answers that (1) would be arrived at by virtually all those with an understanding of the legal system, and (2) are unopposed by powerful arguments, consonant with the premises of the system, for contrary results. One might think, especially in light of the last chapter, that this claim has all the bite and profundity of a truism, but passages in some skeptical writings appear to cast doubt on it. Joseph Singer has written, for example, "legal reasoning is indeterminate and contradictory. By its own criteria, legal reasoning cannot resolve questions in an 'objective' manner . . . ."[1] David Kairys has said that "legal reasoning does not provide concrete, real answers to particular legal or social problems. Legal reasoning is not a method or process that leads reasonable, competent, and fair-minded people to particular results in particular cases."[2]

Few, if any, writers have asserted the most extreme thesis about indeterminacy—that no legal questions have determinate answers—in a clear or careful way, and almost no one may actually believe *that thesis*, but it is useful to establish why that thesis is absurd. When that is done, one can address more clearly whether particular legal questions have determinate answers (and in what sense), the frequency of indeterminism in the legal system, and the implications of that indeterminacy for the legitimacy of courts and other legal authorities.

I begin this chapter by emphasizing that the law often has determinate answers to particular legal questions. Most often the answer to whether liability of a certain kind arises from an action is no. I next discuss briefly the frequency of determinate answers relative to indeterminacy. I then address the possibility of determinate answers in the context of a simple statutory formulation, analyzing arguments that even an apparently plain application of the statute may not be determinate. I consider specific arguments bearing on the legal problem and also three general contentions that might conceivably be thought to undermine a claim of determinate answers. These contentions are (1) that unreliable fact-finding makes determinate answers impossible; (2) that legal rules guide rather than determine action; and (3) that deep uncertainties about the role of courts render all results indeterminate. I show why a sensible thesis about the determinacy of law is not threatened by these contentions. I then address the problem of how shared understandings for the law are to be ascertained, a much more complicated matter than the analogous procedure for an informal game. This subject introduces some problems about the determinacy of law that arise because of the different levels of authority within a legal system. Finally, I briefly indicate the distinction between what the law requires and what it is best, overall, to do. I urge that, at least for officials acting in an official capacity, legal requirements carry normative force that is broader and more compelling than simple legal duty.

The Frequency of Easy Questions and Determinate Answers

What Is a Legal Question?

A legal question concerns the legal consequences of actual events or supposed events. A legal question is rarely about law in general, but rather is about some specific aspect of the law of some jurisdiction as it applies to specific events. If a law school professor tells a student she will raise his grade, but only if he buys her season tickets to the symphony, we might ask whether the professor has acted tortiously or violated some statute providing civil recovery, whether she has breached her employment contract, and whether she has committed a crime. We would concentrate mainly on state law but might also look at federal statutes.

For criminal liability, we would raise separate questions about different offenses because penalty structures vary and, even when identical penalties are available, it may matter whether someone is guilty of one or many offenses. One answer to a legal question, of course, is that behavior does not violate a legal norm. Practicing lawyers spend a lot of time figuring out what actions are legally permitted.

It is important here to draw a critical distinction that can be obscured by the phrase "a legal question." The legal questions that people are mainly interested in concern the legal consequences of their actions or the legal status of claims made on their behalf during the legal process. "Is inducing the student to buy tickets to the symphony the crime of criminal coercion?" "Is my claim that I am protected by the privilege against self-incrimination valid?" People are not ordinarily much concerned with the precise *formulation* used to assess legal consequences. Any narrow legal rule or broader principle may be stated in many different ways. Once a judge or lawyer departs from actual constitutional or statutory language, the best way to formulate a legal standard is open to debate. There will be no precise, single formulation that virtually all lawyers will agree is superior to every other possible formulation. If agreement about formulation were taken as the basic criterion for a determinate answer, there would be no determinate answer to the phrasing of a legal standard. With rare exceptions,[3] different formulations will have somewhat different implications for the treatment of certain situations, but many activities will be excluded or included under all plausible formulations. For instance, no plausible formulation of the statutory crime of theft, under present social conditions, will include the ordinary act of scratching one's nose. Every plausible formulation includes the intentional taking of someone else's valuable painting for one's own permanent use. My claim about determinacy is not a claim about the precise *formulation* of legal standards;[4] it is a claim about legal consequences attached to acts and claims.

Invariable Indeterminacy?

Once the question about the determinacy of law is understood in this way, we can see how ridiculous would be any suggestion that no or few legal questions have determinate answers. Legal questions are about subdivisions of law in particular jurisdictions and how they apply to specific persons or entities. Pushing someone during an argument is not larceny, or a taxable transaction, or acceptance under the law of contract, and it is not a tort (civil wrong) against a stranger who witnesses the pushing on the television news. If a citizen of Poland pushes another Polish citizen in Warsaw, that is not a crime in Vermont. The criminal law of every jurisdiction is determinate in its nonapplication to most distant events,[5] and many modern criminal codes begin with a statement of jurisdictional limitations. Moreover, life is filled with acts, like scratching one's nose and putting on one's socks that patently do not give rise to legal liability.[6] The norms of any legal system are determinate in their nonapplicability to countless human activities.

Is a thesis of invariable indeterminacy plausible if the universe of inquiry is restricted to questions that actually arise for someone about the application of legal norms? The answer is no. Given wide misunderstanding about basic features of law, some questions that actually occur to people are bound to have determinate answers. As they were growing up, my children often supposed that annoying behavior of others must be some kind of punishable crime, when at most it was a civil wrong. Such misconceptions are common. The percentage of determinate answers may decline as we move from the multitude of instances when an individual thinks about possible liability, to instances when such thoughts lead to discussion, to instances when an expert (or a published guide)[7] is consulted, but even in the last category many answers to legal questions will be indisputable.

A thesis of invariable indeterminacy may seem more plausible if it is limited to legal *cases*. Skeptics have focused mainly on cases, as illustrated by the use of that word in the second sentence of the quote from David Kairys. Careful thinking about this thesis requires us to consider what constitutes a case[8] and what specifically might always be considered indeterminate. What are "cases?" Every instance when someone makes a claim, including, for example, a letter from one party to a contract to another party asserting that the contract has been breached? Every instance of a formal claim, including disputes settled before a court actually does anything? Every instance involving some judicial determination, say about admissible evidence? Every dispute decided by a trial court? Every case addressed by an appellate court? If we are interested in the determinacy of law, limiting inquiry to cases actually decided by courts would be highly arbitrary, but that focus is a helpful beginning.

We need first to distinguish complete disposition of a case from determination of each legal question in the case. The answers to some legal questions in a case might be determined by the law even if indeterminacy in other aspects renders the result indeterminate.[9] Plainly some legal questions that arise in some cases have determinate answers.

David is a defendant charged with armed robbery. Prosecution witnesses say the robbery was committed by a single person and that David was the robber. His defense is an alibi; his witnesses say he was one hundred miles away when the crime was committed. No other evidence besides eyewitness testimony connects David to the crime. David's lawyer asks the judge for an instruction that makes clear that if the jury believes his witnesses, it must return a verdict of "not guilty."[10]

In giving this instruction, the judge "answers" a legal question in the only way that would occur to anyone; she determines that one is not guilty of robbery if he did not commit the robbery and had no connection with the robber but happens to bear a physical resemblance to him.

When trials take place and questions are asked of witnesses, lawyers occasionally ask questions that they know are improper because of a hoped-for effect on the jury, and lawyers occasionally object to questions of their opponents without any basis in law for doing so. Judges ruling on these evidential issues are also deciding questions as to which the law apparently dictates a single answer.

Is it possible that if some legal questions in cases have determinate answers, no *cases* that reach courts have such answers? If a case as a whole did have a determinate answer, why would a lawyer contest it? A suggestion that no case has a determinate answer founders on the fact that *cases* sometimes do not involve significant dispute over legal questions, only over the facts. The trial of the robbery defendant who claims he was elsewhere might be such an instance. That a robbery occurred and that this violated the law might not be contested. The only dispute might be the factual one whether the defendant was the robber.

I shall subsequently discuss factual uncertainties as they bear on claims of indeterminacy. Here it is enough to mention that in some cases turning on the facts, no doubt may exist about how the relevant law applies. Another problem with the claim that no *cases* have determinate answers is that lawyers sometimes have reasons, such as publicity or delay, to pursue legal claims they know are extremely flimsy.

The significance of another reality is harder to assess. The percentage of agreement on routine cases among appellate judges is remarkably high. While he was sitting on the New York Court of Appeals, Benjamin Nathan Cardozo estimated that nine-tenths of the cases before that court, New York's highest, could come out only one way.[11] Studies suggest that dissents are filed in only four percent of the cases brought before federal courts of appeals.[12] Some federal appellate judges, as I have learned from conversations, do not always dissent, even when they would decide the other way were the decision left to them. But this apparently occurs fairly rarely, mainly in unimportant cases. Usually agreement in vote does mark agreement about the right result. It appears that a rather high percentage of cases that lawyers think are worth pursuing, judges find to be "easy." Does it follow that the answers in such cases are determinate?

Were the test of a determinate legal answer an answer that would be recognized as correct by a substantial majority of those familiar with the law, then broad judicial agreement poses a serious problem for a proponent of the indeterminacy of law. But my standard at this stage is stricter; the answer must be one that virtually all lawyers and others familiar with the issues would recognize as correct.[13] If the standard involves what virtually all lawyers think, a lawyer's taking of the case to an appellate level may be more significant than the judges' agreement in rejecting her argument. Lawyers sometimes pursue issues they think they will and should lose, and lawyers litigating for clients may lose sight of how substantial their arguments are, but lawyers who appeal, frequently believe that they have a fair chance of winning and that they should win. The taking of an appeal is often some indication that a lawyer thinks the result below was mistaken.[14]

I emphasize that a lawyer's *prediction* of a likely result is not necessarily the lawyer's reasonable judgment about what a result *should be*. Some writers have suggested that if a decision is highly predictable, then the relevant law is determinate in the sense that matters.[15] Proponents of extensive indeterminacy, however, are making a claim about the imperative significance of legal materials and institutions, not about predictable outcomes.[16] And that is what I am addressing. If judges of all different political persuasions agree, that may be significant evidence of the strength of competing positions about the legal materials, but conceivably judges, because of common background and high position, might agree on answers not required by the legal materials. Judicial answers *might be* highly predictable but not determinate in the sense that counts here.[17] It is to meet the objection that wide agreement by itself, even among lawyers and judges, does not establish the determinacy of an answer that I have added the second of my criteria: that no powerful argument for a contrary result be consonant with the premises of the legal system. (Whether a powerful argument of this sort exists is a judgment that must finally be made by the person trying to decide if the question has a determinate answer, not by the judges and lawyers who think the question does have a clear answer.) If a powerful contrary argument can be mounted, I concede that an answer is not determinate in my strict sense, even if virtually all lawyers agree upon the answer.

A slightly different possible claim of indeterminacy than any discussed so far is that any legal issue requiring "interpretation" or "legal reasoning" is indeterminate. Everything here would depend on what counts as "interpretation" or "legal reasoning." If any construction and application of legal language counts, the claim is false, for reasons already suggested and for reasons I develop in what follows. If interpretation by definition[18] involves something more than straightforward application of norms, then all or almost all[19] of the issues requiring interpretation or reasoning may be just those issues for which the law as it stands provides no determinate answer in the narrow sense I employ here.[20]

A thesis that the law is always indeterminate is hard to understand; in any comprehensible and significant formulation, it is incorrect. I will later discuss some other possible defenses of the "indeterminacy" thesis, but they do not alter my conclusion that answers to legal questions are often determinate. A more important inquiry is *how often* the law is indeterminate.

Pervasive Indeterminacy?

The claim of indeterminacy is sometimes cast as a thesis that the law is much more often indeterminate than traditional legal scholars believe. Accompanying this claim may be an assertion that pervasive indeterminacy undermines the legitimacy of existing law and the courts.[21] Even if we begin with the strict criteria for determinate answers I am using in this part, we have no simple or single way to calculate the extent to which the law is determinate. One might put the issue in terms of some range of logically possible legal questions. The percentage of determinacy would then be very high, because of the wide range of acts and events that do not carry particular legal consequences. However, for any helpful relevant percentage of determinate answers, it should not count that an Italian's scratching of her arm in Rome does not constitute murder in New York. To be useful, an estimation should encompass only acts that are or might plausibly be within the domain of particular legal standards. What should be addressed is the frequency with which legal materials give definite answers to questions about coverage of law that might actually arise.

In this inquiry, focusing only on issues or cases that reach the courts would be a grave mistake. A steady dose of opinions, especially appellate opinions, highly distorts one's views about the determinacy of law. The percentage of questions that have easily determinate answers is greater than the percentage of questions that courts discuss that have such answers because many straightforward questions and answers are not tested in litigation. Suppose (to pick an absurdly high figure) that 99 percent of all legal questions with which people concern themselves have readily ascertainable determinate answers, but that only 5 percent of questions that are seriously litigated do. Focusing on the courts would give a very misleading picture of the law's determinacy overall and, therefore, perhaps a misleading picture of whether the legal system as a whole enjoys some kind of legitimacy.

Could someone respond that figures like these might indicate legitimacy for aspects of the system, but not for decisions by courts, since the answers courts give are so often not required by the law? A common defense of the legitimacy of courts in light of substantial indeterminacy for the questions that occupy them is that their relative detachment from power politics, their deliberative techniques, and their methods of justification make them better suited than other organs of government to resolve the legal questions that lack determinate answers. But another powerful defense made less frequently views the role of courts more broadly. A court system may be necessary to stand ready to declare on the questions that do have determinate answers. The threat of court enforcement by one party may induce the other party to accept what the law provides.[22] When questions without determinate answers are intertwined with questions that have determinate answers, resolution by one body may be needed. It may not be feasible for courts to identify questions without determinate answers and turn them over to minilegislatures or executive officers. Thus, the appropriateness of courts deciding questions without determinate answers must be viewed not only in light of their comparative ability to deal with these questions, but also in light of how these questions fit in a context of disputes that also raise questions with determinate answers. Once this is understood, even a conclusion that a rather high percentage of questions that courts actually consider lack determinate answers would not necessarily undermine either the legitimacy of the law in general or the function of courts.

Statutory Formulations and Determinate Answers

I now turn from these general observations to a legal example analogous to the nonlegal illustrations in Chapter 2. Having just emphasized the obvious *nonapplication* of legal standards to many acts and events, I now concentrate on a rule that apparently does apply. I ask, in light of the last chapter, what analytical steps and social assumptions allow us to say that a legal standard applies to yield a result? I consider a statutory rule. Since the standards of the common law are harder to formulate than statutory rules, and critical constitutional clauses tend to be open-ended, the way in which these might yield determinate answers on which virtually all lawyers and others familiar with the law agree is more complicated. That discussion is reserved for the next chapter.

The claim that the law can yield determinate answers is most straightforward with respect to simple statutory texts.

> The city council has recently adopted an ordinance that says, "Persons walking dogs in public parks must have their dogs leashed." Violations are punishable by a fine. The ordinance has been widely enforced by police and judges. Observed by a police officer, Olive, upon entering the park, lets her dog Angus run free without a leash. Paul maintains one end of a firm five foot leash in his hand with the other end attached to his dog's collar. Quentin has a similar leash on his dog, but the leash breaks and the dog runs free.

Which, if any, of the three dog owners has committed a punishable offense? We need first ask if the specific provision has been "violated." That question is the primary focus for this chapter. If the answer is yes, we must then determine if the "violation" is somehow cancelled by an overriding norm.[23] All other norms of our legal system are subject to principles of constitutional law, and applications of specific provisions of criminal law are subject to claims of justification. In the next chapter, I consider whether application of the leashing ordinance may be overridden by a constitutional right or the general justification defense.

Paul's case is the easiest. Whatever vagueness or ambiguity lies in the words of the ordinance, Paul has complied with it. Under the American system of law, courts are not free to create new crimes. Indeed, many states provide in their own penal codes that all crimes must be statutory. The law provides a determinate answer to the question of whether Paul has committed an offense by walking his dog with a leash. He has not violated this ordinance, and if no other relevant statutory language exists, he has not committed any crime.

Quentin's case is the hardest for a court. There is a period of time during which Quentin does not "have [his dog] leashed," but perhaps accidental unleashings should not be considered violations. Quentin's state of mind and the reasonableness of his behavior might be relevant to his possible offense. We would need to know more about Quentin and the law to decide if Quentin's case has a clear answer, but here I will assume that the law may be indeterminate as applied to him. The application of language may be indeterminate for some instances and determinate for others. Indeterminacy as to Quentin does not establish general indeterminacy.

Olive's case requires more analysis than do the other two. It poses the question whether a legal rule can ever impose liability that derives in a determinate or objective way from the rule. If Olive intentionally let Angus run free for their entire time in the park, Olive appears plainly to have violated the leashing provision. However, we can imagine at least two sorts of arguments Olive might make as to why she has not committed a violation. One argument is that the words of the ordinance are unclear and that she complied with their literal import. A more promising argument is that the import of the language, construed purposively, does not apply.

The language of the ordinance says that persons walking dogs in public parks must "have their dogs leashed." Olive might claim that she has had Angus leashed on other occasions, and that the ordinance does not specify *when* the dog must be leashed. If we divorce the language from this particular social context, this argument is not absurd. Suppose the ordinance had read, "Persons walking dogs in public parks must have their dogs vaccinated." We would not expect owners to be vaccinating their dogs as they walked with them in the park. A prior vaccination would be sufficient. How can we be sure leashing is different? The purpose of leashing is to prevent dogs from running free; prior leashing does not serve that purpose. The meaning, even the literal meaning, of this language depends on social understandings not only about what particular words mean but also about the point of using the words in context. The reason why we know that a prior leashing does not satisfy the ordinance is the same as the reason why we know that Sam is not supposed to cross over to Beth's desk and shut a cabinet door if what Beth says is, "Please shut the door." No reasonable person could think that the leashing referred to is other than at the time the dog is walked.

Olive might argue instead that although she did not comply with the literal language of the ordinance, nevertheless something in her situation calls for a judgment that she has not committed a violation. It is helpful here to draw a distinction. Olive might contend that although her leaving Angus unleashed did raise some of the risks that the ordinance was meant to reduce, the reasons for her action were so strong the ordinance should not apply. Such a claim falls clearly within a general justification defense (treated in Chapter 4), but it might also bear on how the ordinance itself should be understood. If, for example, an ambulance enters the park to rescue a stricken person despite an ordinance barring vehicles from the park, the ambulance does generate the harms and risks that led to the ordinance, but the reasons for its entering are so powerful that a court might properly conclude that the ordinance does not apply. Olive might similarly advance claims that the purposes underlying the ordinance were overridden. When a general justification defense is available, it is the natural repository of such claims; I reserve discussion of them for the next chapter.

Olive might argue instead that she and Angus simply do not pose the danger the ordinance was meant to avoid and that therefore the ordinance should not be applied to her. She might say, "The ordinance aims to assure control over dogs, so they don't bite people, fight with other dogs, and make messes in the wrong places. Angus is well controlled and behaved, and therefore he should be considered effectively 'leashed.'" This argument has broad significance, since many dog owners can offer similar claims.

A full answer to this argument is not simple. Although the words of the ordinance talk about leashing, not control, fictions are part of our law, and saying that an effectively controlled dog counts as being leashed would not be ridiculous. However, this sort of minor offense needs simple enforcement. Police and park officials can see if dogs are unleashed; control is more subtle. Were Olive's argument to win, probably only dog owners whose dogs cause serious trouble would end up being treated as offenders. The city council could have chosen words referring to effective control, and it has acted recently. The ordinance has been actively enforced and other courts dealing with it have assumed a literal interpretation of the word "leashed." A judge who views all these factors in combination[24] is bound to conclude that Olive's argument fails in our legal system. The legislature recently established a relatively literal rule, and courts here lack authority[25] to substitute a much less literal approach.[26] The question whether Olive has violated the provision itself has a determinate answer: she did. It now remains to explore this conclusion in greater depth.

Factual Uncertainties

Against my suggestion that the law provides a determinate answer to whether Olive violated the leashing ordinance, one might argue that doubts about facts render all such applications indeterminate, that neither language nor legal rules can determine anyone's actions, or that, whatever the apparent clarity of legal language, uncertainties about the role of courts undermine determinate applications.

I begin with the first objection: the law is never determinate because relevant facts—facts about the immediate case or deeper facts about the usage of language or social convention—are uncertain. For the most part, I employ a simple approach to what "facts" are, but I explain why my conclusions are not dependent on this approach.

That the facts conceded by both parties in negotiation or determined in judicial proceedings sometimes vary from what actually occurred is an obvious truth. For any case, the likelihood of the facts being correctly found is less than 100 percent. If factual uncertainty were the only basis for doubt about an appropriate result, we could speak of the law as being determinate given the factual findings of a court or given a different state of facts supposed to be true. Contrary to the intimation that the only useful way to speak is about applications or predicted applications of rules to facts as they are found, our ordinary discourse is rich enough to include more than one possibility. Suppose in a tennis match Steffi Graf hits an unreturnable ball to Monica Seles. The lineswoman, supported by the umpire, calls the ball "out"; a television replay shows it was definitely "in." Simone, returning from the kitchen, asks Rich, "Who won the point?" Rich would have to be extremely simple-minded if all he said was, "Graf," or, "Seles." He will say, "The instant replay showed Graf hit a winner, but it was called out so the point was awarded to Seles." We talk comfortably both about outcomes according to officials' decisions *and* outcomes according to correct applications of rules to facts.

To vary the hypothetical a bit, suppose that the lineswoman had fainted and missed the shot altogether. The umpire considers what to do. Before she decides, Rich has witnessed the television replay, which is unavailable to the umpire, and Simone asks about Graf's shot. Rich may say, "Yes, it was definitely good though very close." Rich's comment here is not fundamentally a prediction of what the umpire will decide; it is a statement of what the result should be given an application of the rules of tennis to the actual facts.

If doubt about how a legal rule would be applied rested exclusively on doubt about accurate determination of facts like these, we, like Rich, could say: "There is a determinate answer to how the legal rule applies to the facts as they occurred; there is a determinate answer to how the legal rule applies to the different facts a court might find; the uncertainty about the result concerns whether the facts as found will sufficiently coincide with the facts as they actually occurred." (What I have said does not, of course, cover legal characterizations of facts, like decisions whether behavior under undisputed pressure is "coerced." For purposes here, these count as legal conclusions, not factual findings.)[27]

Occasionally people resist the claim that the law is determinate with respect to an assumed set of facts in the following way: "It is possible that some yet unrevealed fact would alter the conclusion; therefore, the result on *these facts* is not determinate." Take, for example, an assertion that Nick's scratching of his nose is not murder. *If* Nick's scratching of his nose were a signal to someone else to set off a bomb, the scratching *could* make him liable for murder. It is true that for any state of facts of which we are aware, it is *possible* that some other facts unknown to us could alter the legal consequences of actions. When we say that the legal consequences of certain facts are determinate, we mean the consequences are determinate, barring the existence of yet unrevealed facts of legal importance. The chance of newly revealed facts functions here like the chance of misfound facts, as something that could alter the outcome. In a multitude of circumstances, confidence that no relevant facts remain to be discovered is very great. As a percentage of nose scratchings, the instances when someone's scratching his nose might amount to murder are exceedingly few. To say that the law is determinate as applied to facts is to say that it is determinate in the absence of additional legally relevant facts that could alter the outcome.[28] Something closely similar is involved when conclusions are based on hypothetical facts rather than events that have occurred. A statement of *hypothetical facts* implicitly assumes that all facts relevant to the legal problem have been indicated. A claim that the law is determinate as to those facts supposes that no further relevant facts remain to be stipulated.

That the legal system often fails to yield correct results because the basic facts are not reliably discovered is a highly significant truth, and the study of pitfalls that lie between events as they happen and a corresponding legal determination to that effect is important. That more *fully developed* facts can alter the legal conclusion that seems appropriate is also significant. But a substantial thesis about the indeterminacy of law must rest on more than such uncertainties of fact-finding or the inevitable gaps in fact statements.

What I have said about facts and legal determinacy does not depend on what may be considered by some to be a naive and misconceived realism about "facts." Suppose that we give up the ordinary commonsensical view that events actually happen "out there" (a leaf falls from a tree, a dog runs without a leash), that these things have happened whether anyone perceives them and that when a person asserts they happened, he implicitly claims that what he says happened corresponds with what took place, independent of any human perception. In its place we substitute the view that worrying about whether any world outside human perception exists is not useful; that the only facts, or the only facts to which human beings can relate, are facts perceived by human beings. Since the events we witness are filtered through our consciousness, and no one person's consciousness is exactly the same as another's, there is no factual truth that somehow transcends the consciousness of individual human beings, no "facts as they actually occurred." Our only test for truth is how well an asserted proposition coheres with other propositions we accept. Furthermore, the *meaning* of assertions of truth amounts to no more than claims about coherence with other beliefs.[29]

Even if we grant *all* of these propositions, no nihilistic conclusion is warranted. Substantial correlations in individual perceptions will still give human beings a strong interpersonal truth. Presented with clear conditions of observation and precision about what is to be observed, virtually all people who pay attention will be able to say whether a particular leaf falls or a particular dog runs without a leash. Some legal cases will come down to facts that are observable in this way. If the police officer says Angus was running free and Olive says he was on a leash, one or the other, in all likelihood, is not accurately reporting his perceptions as they were at the time of the event. We might reformulate my notion of the facts as "they actually occurred" into a more complex idea of facts, perhaps as "they were perceived by those present or would have been perceived by virtually any sane adult in our culture[30] who was present."[31] A degree of subjectivity or indeterminacy is interjected by the reality that events only have meaning for human beings through their own consciousness. But there are still many assertions about ordinary factual events that we make with a very high degree of confidence: "Rain fell in New York yesterday"; "John F. Kennedy was killed in 1963." If the indeterminacy or nonobjectivity of law amounted to nothing more than the "nonobjectivity" of factual claims like these, a claim of nonobjectivity would have no disturbing practical implications.

Our understanding of facts usually (or always) includes a component of assumptions about scientific generalizations as well as belief about what is observable.[32] We think that phenomena involving a brain and nervous system cause a dog's legs to move; we assume that a bullet through the heart causes death. Scientific generalizations are subject to continuing revision, and the work of Thomas Kuhn has suggested that the choice of broad scientific theories is partly determined by matters other than the persuasiveness of evidence.[33] Further, the assurances that what has occurred regularly in the past has occurred on a particular occasion and will occur in the future are not ones that science can establish. Perhaps on this one occasion the bullet, though damaging the heart, did not cause death, which instead occurred at just a split second later for a reason so far wholly unfamiliar to scientists. Still, there are many practical scientific generalizations—about gravity, about the need of ordinary human beings to have functioning hearts if they are to continue living—about which we are very confident. Again, if a claim about the indeterminacy or nonobjectivity of law were thought to be nothing more than a facet of this indeterminacy or nonobjectivity of scientific theories, it would be of little significance for understanding law. Skeptical theories about the nature of "ordinary facts" and scientific generalizations, even if accepted, do not undermine the idea that the law determines many outcomes.

Factual skepticism might be directed toward what I say about language and social practices. My claims about determinacy rest on the presence of shared assumptions about linguistic meaning and social practices. It may be logically possible that virtually all lawyers might somehow be wrong about these *or* that formerly correct assumptions will suddenly become wrong, for example, that in a moment "dog" will be taken to mean what up until now has been called a "horse." It is hard to conceive how all lawyers could be mistaken about linguistic meaning or social practice, and broad instantaneous changes in assumptions do not occur among human beings in society. These logical possibilities also do not threaten the idea that legal questions often have determinate answers.

Law as Guiding, Not Determining

Some writers have preferred to speak of the law as guiding rather than determining behavior. In one sense imperative language does not determine anything; the person to whom the language is addressed must decide whether to do what is asked for or demanded.[34] This element of choice exists for a person responding to a legal rule as well as one responding to an informal individual directive. It exists for judges as well as ordinary citizens. In this respect legal rules can only guide, not determine, behavior.

But the capacity of an imperative to indicate a uniquely correct or incorrect course of action for someone who is attempting to comply is another issue. In *this sense*, I have urged that both individual imperatives and legal rules can yield determinate answers. Beth's directive to Sam was not just a pointer about preferable actions, it required Sam to close the door.[35] The leashing ordinance directed Olive *not* to walk in the park with an unleashed dog. Combined with other legal institutions and rules, it directs a judge to decide that Olive's actions constitute a violation. Sometimes legal standards may only guide officials toward one among a number of actions. My contention is that the leashing ordinance does more than that for a judge faced with Olive's action. It *instructs* the judge to count her acts as a violation. It provides the judge with a determinate answer, one that is objectively correct under the law.

The Role of Courts

Uncertainties about the role of courts present a more complex challenge to the thesis that law has many determinate answers. A legal rule is more than imperative language. Saying that Sam was subject to a *company rule* to keep his door closed implied something about what a company is and what authority was within Sam's company. Saying that a judge must decide in a certain way is to accept certain ideas about the nature of a legal system. The half-court basketball example showed that practice may render application of a rule clear even though its verbal formulation may not be clear. Similarly, practice can make application unclear even though the language itself seems clear. The rule about leashing dogs *might* be construed in a nonliteral way, as demanding only effective control. Why can it not be argued that since courts might decide in favor of a nonliteral application,[36] application of the rule is not determinate even in the case of Olive and Angus?

Simple Approaches to the Role of Courts

The relation of courts to legislatures and other officials might be viewed in various ways. I mention briefly three simple approaches. The first focuses on legislative intent. Gerald Graff has suggested:

> Any sophisticated theorist of language would point out that the meaning of an utterance isn't a function of the words themselves or even of the sentence, but of the *use* to which the words and sentences are put by speakers and writers . . . . Guessing the meaning of a text or utterance is inferring what a writer or speaker was or is *doing* with language and not what some linguistic object essentially was or is.[37]

Under this approach, a distinction between sentence meaning and speaker meaning is unwarranted; all depends on the speaker's meaning in context.[38] Were judges to follow a speaker's intent approach in applying statutory rules, their job when an intent was clear would be to use it. It is often said that the language of statutes is canonical, that courts must take it as authoritative, but under this approach perhaps the language would become merely a highly reliable guide to what the legislature intended. This approach is subject to major objections. One is that the idea of a collective legislative intent is troublesome when most legislators have little or no conception of a range of applications for most statutory provisions.[39] Another is that no one has yet suggested a persuasive way to combine intents when disagreement exists.

A second approach would emphasize what a reasonable reader would conclude about how a legislature would want the words of a statutory rule to be applied. Some avenues of inquiry available under the first approach, such as statements by legislators after a law was adopted, and perhaps even comments during the legislative process, might be barred. The second approach could be sustained even if it were recognized that for most relevant subjects of lawmaking,[40] no subjective collective intent exists. It could be recognized that any "intent" referred to is a legal construct, one that, for purposes of application, treats a collectively adopted rule more or less as if it were issued by an individual who thought about the provisions.[41]

A third approach asks what it *now* makes sense to enforce, given the legislation's language and history and the acts and expectations of citizens and other relevant officials. I suggested in the last chapter that a major league umpire in the summer of 1987 rightly called a pitch just below the level of the armpits a ball although according to the language of the rule and the intent of those who wrote it the pitch should have been called a strike. Under this third approach, eventual adoption of a non-literal application of the leashing rule might be appropriate. What a court should do under this approach in any particular case would rest on a complicated theory of its role in respect to legislatures, enforcement officials, citizens, and other courts. Does that mean application is inevitably indeterminate? The answer is no because the conventions of legal practice limit what positions are at all reasonable, and the result under every reasonable position may be the same. At least when the same answer to a legal question would plainly be reached under all plausible accounts of a court's role,[42] the answer is determinate.

Reasonable Understandings of a Court's Role

Who is to say, and by which criteria, what are reasonable understandings of a court's role? A more detailed examination is needed to see whether the complexities of law undermine any claim that all reasonable observers will agree on some applications of rules. Matters were fairly simple for the rules of informal games; the understandings of voluntary participants controlled. Participation under legal rules may not be voluntary, and how much the understanding of various groups count is much more difficult to assess.

THE RELEVANCE OF VOLUNTARY PARTICIPATION

Those subject to legal orders have not agreed to the authority of officers of law for that occasion, and despite traditional social contract theory, most citizens have not voluntarily agreed in general to accept the legal system and obey its orders.[43] Sometimes voluntary acceptance of specific substantive law and official power will be present.

Joan and Keith enter into a contract. Familiar with contract law, they agree that they want the contract law of Illinois to govern terms that are not specified. They appoint an arbitrator to decide all disputes arising under the contract. An issue arises. A decision favorable to Keith is the one clearly indicated by the literal language of the relevant statutory provisions of Illinois, given the presently shared understandings of the meanings of the relevant words and phrases; it is the result assumed by those who have entered into contracts in Illinois and thought about the issue; it is the result reached by all courts and arbitrators applying Illinois law; it is the result that was envisioned by Joan and Keith, and, as they initially informed the arbitrator, one reason they chose Illinois law was that were either party to be found in Keith's present situation, that party was to win.

If Joan has the bad sense and lack of grace to urge a contrary interpretation, the arbitrator is bound by everyone's shared understanding to decide in Keith's favor.

What if someone has never agreed to the intervention of the legal system for some matter, say his possible punishment for taking a neighbor's valuable vase? The absence of voluntary participation by all those directly affected is not crucial for what counts as the law. If the great majority of those involved in some enterprise are satisfied with relevant rules and understand a rule in a certain way, if those who adopted the rules understand the rule in this way, if all of those who apply the rules understand it in this way, then we can say that interpretation within the norms of the enterprise yields that result, even if the person who loses by an interpretation would rather not be part of the enterprise at all, or would prefer to have a special exemption on this occasion.[44]

SHARED UNDERSTANDINGS

How do different groups count for determining relevant understandings about particular rules and about criteria for interpretation? Within a legal system one group of people adopts laws, another is subject to them, still other groups enforce and apply them. And since legal rules exist over a period of time, the group of people who adopted a law is different from the group that now has the power to repeal or alter it. (Of course, a single individual may be in two or more of these various groups.) As I have already mentioned, much of the debate over proper techniques of statutory interpretation can be seen as disagreement about which understandings of which groups count the most. My main point here is that when the groups are in ascertainable agreement as to what the language of a rule means, a judge, who has voluntarily assumed his or her position, is ordinarily constrained by these shared understandings.

It is worth noting that an interpretation can depart from a shared understanding even though it is not blatantly inconsistent with the literal language of the rule and, until proposed, has never actually crossed the minds of participants and officials. A novel interpretation, say that having one's dog leashed at some time prior to entering the park is sufficient to satisfy the ordinance, can be measured against the language of the rule and shared interpretations of what the language does reach. *If* the new proposed interpretation would evidently defeat the main underlying purpose of the rule, as would this claim, *or* the new proposed interpretation would render incongruent much of what is agreed upon in the shared understandings, *or* the proposed interpretation would require a kind of activity by the official applying the law that is understood to be inappropriate, then we can say that the result proposed by the interpretation is objectively wrong, even though the precise interpretation has not yet been consciously rejected by those who are involved in the social enterprise.

When we consider disagreements in understandings of the particular language of a rule, or about the role of courts, we face genuinely troublesome questions about law's determinacy. One kind of disagreement is within relevant groups, another is between relevant groups. The first is subject to relatively easy analysis. In my basketball example, I assumed unanimity of understanding about the meaning of the relevant rule. Were understanding completely divided, half the players thinking the rule meant one thing and half that it meant the opposite, no relevant shared understanding would exist. (Any claim that the rule was still determinate in application would have to rest on richer standards of evaluation than I have yet explored.) If, instead, there is only slight dissent from the prevailing understanding—one person out of a hundred takes a view different from the other ninety-nine—we can still speak of a shared understanding. Something less than unanimity is required. Once this is granted, we must recognize that no sharp line will indicate when a shared understanding is *broad enough* so that the rule in context, read in light of conventional understandings, determines the result.

The dilemma is more serious when disagreement is mainly between groups, for example, most legislators suppose one thing (or the most plausible account of what the legislature has done would indicate one thing), but most judges and participants suppose another. Application of a rule may not be determinate then unless some clear hierarchy of sources is supposed. As far as judges are concerned, some clear hierarchies do exist in the common law system. One aspect of our law is that lower courts are bound to apply rules of law in a manner established in precedents by the highest court that decides such questions. Thus, if the Illinois Supreme Court has decided a case that is not plausibly distinguishable from the dispute between Joan and Keith, and nothing has occurred in the meantime that alters the relevant statute or suggests that that court is likely to change its mind, a lower court in Illinois would have the law determined as far as it was concerned, as would an arbitrator. Since the Illinois Supreme Court is free to overturn its own precedents, we can imagine a case, one in which the arguments for overruling are substantial, in which the statutory rule as presently understood might determine an outcome for a lower court but not for the state Supreme Court.[45]

Levels of Authority and Discretionary Noninvocation of Legal Rules

The last point about the hierarchy of courts suggests a more general and subtle problem. The actions of various individuals and official organs affect the application of law. Perhaps what is determinate for one person applying the law will not be determinate for another. So long as one crucial official does not have his action determined by the law, can we say that the law is determinate in application to behavior? If police sensibly regard themselves as able to "overlook" some violations of the leashing ordinance that resemble Olive's, does the law, or the legal system, really give a determinate answer to whether her behavior is wrong under the law? A proponent of indeterminacy might claim that some official or person will always have latitude not to apply the law, so its application is never objectively required.[46]

Initially we need to untangle threads of this question. What are persons who may apply the law normatively constrained to do? How will they act? How are we to conceptualize the conclusions? The more difficult problems of the criminal process can best be addressed after we consider a simple breach of civil law obligations.

Suppose that Joan has clearly breached a contract with Keith, and the damages are $200,000. The instance is one in which the law of contract plus the language of the contract itself would yield a determinate answer for a judge. In our system of law, the damaged party must initiate an action before officials are involved. It is not assumed that damaged parties must, or should, bring actions; that choice is left to them. The law, then, does not determine whether Keith should sue; it also does not determine what the parties should settle for if the suit one initiates is not pursued to a court decision.[47] As far as substantive resolution of the dispute is concerned, the law mainly determines what judges, or jurors, should do about the case if it is tried. Since Keith is free *not* to sue, we might say that the law overall does not determine that Joan should be *held* liable because it does not determine that the case should ever reach a court. It does not overall determine how she *should be treated* because Keith is free not to invoke remedies the law provides. One can argue about how to conceptualize this conclusion, but the most comfortable way is to say that Joan violated Keith's legal rights and is liable under the law, but that a finding of liability and the invocation of legal consequences depend on Keith's initiative. In any event, were this all that a thesis of indeterminacy amounted to in civil cases, it would not be very striking.

Matters become more complex when the institutions of the law themselves make it unwieldy to establish one's theoretical legal rights. Suppose Joan's "clear breach" relates to a transaction worth a few dollars over which no sensible person would sue. As a prediction of consequences, we can now say that the law is highly unlikely to be used to determine liability, although Keith is permitted to sue if he is upset enough.[48] A judge or juror is still required to decide in favor of Keith if he sues, a choice the law gives him, but the institutions of the law are set up in a way that makes that course of action unwise.

When we turn to the criminal process, we know that a common discrepancy exists between the law on the books and the law as it is brought to bear in relatively trivial matters. In some cities in which an ordinance forbids pedestrians crossing streets in the middle of blocks or "against" lights, police act on "violations" with extreme rarity. If one is virtually certain no enforcement official will act, does the law *really* prohibit "jaywalking"? Comparative triviality typically results in non-application of norms that would seem "on the books" to apply and that would be applied if a case went to court.

The reverse situation can also occur when norms broader than those "on the books" are applied in practice. I recently came across a possible example in New York law. A close acquaintance's son, fighting with a schoolmate in a secluded part of a public park, was arrested for disorderly conduct. The lowest level of disorderly conduct is only a violation, less than the lowest category of misdemeanor. It can be committed by fighting when one has an "intent to cause public inconvenience, annoyance or alarm, or recklessly creates a risk thereof";[49] recklessness in New York requires awareness and conscious disregard of a substantial and unjustifiable risk. The boys, accompanied by a few friends, chose the spot for the fight as one out of the way, and they neither saw other people nor supposed others might be bothered. The boys lacked the required intent or recklessness to violate the law. Further, a decision by the highest state court, involving a dance hall fight with seventy-five to one hundred onlookers and accompanied by shouts of "fight, fight" that led others to run toward the fight for a look, indicated that foreseeable public disturbance must be substantial indeed before it qualifies under the statute.[50] Given the statute and the judicial decision, I concluded that if the facts were found accurately, the boys were clearly not guilty of the offense. A knowledgeable colleague suggested to me that for the police and some judges in the summons part of criminal court that handles these cases, any voluntary fight in a public park may count as disorderly conduct. The vast majority of those charged simply plead guilty, knowing that they face only a small fine, and virtually no one convicted after an informal hearing bothers to appeal. If this possibility were realized, the law as it is administered would cover much more than "the law on the books."[51]

Another kind of divergence between the law "in practice" and the "law on the books" reaches serious offenses as well as trivial ones. Prosecutors have authority to charge a lower offense than the most grave one committed, and occasionally, in exchange for a guilty plea, they charge a defendant with an offense that really does not make sense given the actual facts of the case.

Any examples in which the "law as applied" is more severe than the "law on the books" raise serious questions of appropriateness, but it is almost universally assumed that prosecutors and police act properly in treating behavior more leniently than the substantive criminal law seems to require. It is *logically* possible that for different officials at different levels, there could be determinate but contrary answers about what the law provides, or that what is determinate for officials at one level would be indeterminate for officials at another level (as I have suggested may be true for well-established precedents that a lower court must accept but that a higher court may oveturn). But that is *not* how prosecutorial and police latitude is conceived. It is conceived as a discretion over whether to invoke the full force of the law. In principle it is not unlike Keith's discretion, although here discretion should be guided by considerations of public welfare. Some offenses are so serious that failures to proceed with the full force of the law may be criticized, but prosecutors "charge down" even for terrible murders in exchange for information and testimony about other participants. Although what courts interpreting the law may decide about many actions may be objectively determined by the law, how those actions should be treated by legal institutions altogether is not determinate because of discretionary enforcement elements. This conclusion applies to Olive's situation.

It is important that the law's treatment of situations in this broader sense is not fully determined even when application of the law is clear. A proponent of invariable indeterminacy might say that dividing the substantive law from discretionary elements is arbitrary; without such a division, discretion would undermine a claim that positive application[52] of a legal rule is determinate. I think this attack should be resisted, since in civil cases it makes good sense to distinguish the law from a party's decision to invoke the law, and the same is true of criminal enforcement. In any event, the conceptual point is not critical. I could revise the thesis of frequent determinacy to talk about particular officials and particular choices. I could say, "For a judge faced with the legal question whether Olive is liable under the ordinance, the law provides the determinate answer that she is." Similarly, for a police officer, prosecutor, or judge faced with the legal question whether Paul (who kept his dog on a leash) violated the ordinance, the law provides a determinate answer that he did not.

Disobedience and Normative Authority

It remains to ask what relevance a legal rule has for what a judge or other official should do overall, assuming that the law itself confers no discretion to disregard its terms. The rule's application, or the rule, or the system more generally may seem unjust.

As with my nonlegal examples, the question of what a legal rule requires is not the same as the question of whether either a citizen or official should comply. In law, the dichotomy between the two questions is not always sharp. Since there may be dispute as to who has the authority to determine what legal norms mean, an official may reject dominant understandings about some matters and still be faithful to his, defensible, view of the law. But there are limits. A trial judge who makes up a wholly new form of criminal liability without statutory support has failed to observe the law, whatever his state of mind. And I have argued that in Olive's case a lower court judge is not free to substitute a nonliteral interpretation that focuses on control for an explicit requirement that a dog be leashed.

Someone who agrees that the law provides an answer need not conclude that an official, even a judge, should follow it. The law of 1840 may have required return of a fugitive slave, but a judge might have decided he should free a slave before him by making an erroneous finding about her identity. Imagine that Judith is a modern judge who is radically dissatisfied with the overregulation of legal norms. She thinks judges should be explicitly allowed to reject legislative forms of regulation they believe are undesirable. If Olive argues to Judith that the value of having dogs run free outweighs any interest in leashing, should Judith disregard present law and try to create better law?

No absolute general principle of morality bars Judith's deciding contrary to what she understands the law to provide. However, significant reasons oppose that course. In taking office, Judith has sworn to uphold the law. She has agreed to perform a job as conceived in a certain way. If she wanders too far away from the widely understood job description,[53] she has failed to keep her promise to perform *that* job. Moreover, people in a society base reasonable and justified expectations on the law's provisions. When private rights are contested, a radically innovative decision defeats the expectations of the losing party. Nothing quite so direct occurs if Judith employs her novel version of who makes law to excuse Olive, and the practical importance of this one incident is trivial. But other park users may have depended on the ordinance being enforced, and the ordinance may even represent a conscious compromise between excluding dogs from the park altogether and allowing them to run free. Judith's ruling will deny other users of the park the fruits of what has been agreed upon in the political process. Were Judith's approach to legal norms generalized, the law would yield much less stability in social relations. Shared understandings not only constitute an aspect of the law, they exert a broader normative force on those who interpret the law in favor of compliance rather than disregard.

4

Determinate Answers
Under General Statutory and
Constitutional Standards
and Principles of Common Law

Chapter 3 has established that the nonapplication or application of specific statutory rules is often determinate. Many answers to questions about those rules are objectively correct in the sense of being understood to be correct by virtually all lawyers and others familiar with the law and of not being subject to a powerful contrary argument that is consonant with the premises of the legal system. I now examine standards whose general language does not yield answers so straightforwardly or whose own status may be subject to challenge. If the application of such standards is invariably indeterminate, that will sharply limit the practical significance of what I have shown thus far. I first treat broad statutory and constitutional standards, and then briefly discuss the force of common law standards.

Applications of legal rules are subject to traditional privileges and excuses and to constitutional challenges. A narrow rule like the leashing requirement will finally apply against Olive only if any claims by her on those bases fail. If the answer to those claims is always indeterminate, we could never conclude that application of the ordinance is determinate. *Nonapplication* of the specific rule could be determinate, as in the case of Paul whose dog was leashed, but with respect to Olive, application would always depend on how the broader claims are evaluated, and the outcome of these evaluations would not be determinate.

Nonapplication of the General Justification Defense

American criminal codes contain a number of justifications, like self-defense, and excuses, like insanity. When the criminal codes themselves are silent, similar defenses derived from the common law are effective.

I concentrate on the broadest justification, what is called the necessity defense or general justification. The formulation in the Model Penal Code, an important model for actual legislatures, is:

> (1) Conduct that the actor believes to be necessary to avoid a harm or evil to himself or to another is justifiable, provided that:
>> (a) the harm or evil sought to be avoided by such conduct is greater than that sought to be prevented by the law defining the offense charged . . . .[1]

Further subsections make the defense inapplicable if other provisions, such as self-defense, specifically deal with the situation, or if a legislative purpose to exclude the justification plainly appears.

The language of this standard is so broad and open-ended that an argument that application is always indeterminate appears more promising for it than for other defenses.[2] If application of the general justification defense is never foreclosed, *positive application* of any specific provision of the criminal law is always indeterminate because no action will both be plainly in violation of the particular provision *and* be unwarranted under the general justification defense. More concretely, if Olive raises general justification claims whose resolution is not determinate, final application of the leashing ordinance to her is not determinate.

What claims might Olive make for letting her dog run free? Olive's arguments might be about dogs in general, about Angus, or about her own status. Suppose Olive claims that the value of having dogs free outweighs the benefits of leashing.[3] The conclusive argument against this claim is that if it were accepted, it would effectively eliminate the leashing ordinance. Were dogs generally able to run free because of this defense, no dogs, except perhaps a few demonstrably dangerous ones, would have to be leashed under the ordinance.[4] That is not what the city council was aiming for in adopting a broad rule requiring leashing. The general justification defense is not now understood as authorizing the judiciary to overthrow legislative judgments. Further, this particular version of the defense forecloses its use when a legislative purpose to exclude the justification plainly appears. Adoption of the ordinance evidences a legislative purpose to exclude a justification so broad that it would effectively eliminate the ordinance.

A counterargument by Olive might challenge the assumption that the court should defer to the legislative judgment that dogs generally should be leashed.[5] One possibility would be to concede legislative power to restrain judges, but deny that the legislature had exercised it here. Olive might say:

> The judiciary in a legal system might operate as a general check on legislative decisions about criminality, especially decisions by inferior legislatures like city councils. Under such a scheme, invocation of the general justification defense would be appropriate for courts that deem particular legislation unwise. A legislature might be able to block the use of the general justification defense, but only by stating a specific intent to do that. Our system should be so understood. The simple passing of the ordinance should not be conceived as a plain indication of a legislative purpose to exclude the justification, and the general claim that the ordinance is misconceived for most dogs should be open to judicial examination.

Up to a certain point, Olive's argument is plausible. A legal system could operate in this way, and a general justification defense in that system might have the language of this general justification defense. Thus, the language of the defense alone, assigned its ordinary significance in English, does not preclude Olive's winning on her claim that the legislative judgment about leashing dogs is unsound. But the system she presumes is not ours. The general justification defense is not understood by legislators, lawyers, and scholars who think about these matters as authorizing such judicial power. In the context of the assumptions of our system, the ordinance itself, supported by the portion of the general justification defense that excludes its use when a legislative purpose to do so plainly appears, forecloses this general argument of Olive's.

Olive might explicitly grant that existing premises of legislative supremacy would defeat her, but urge that the judge should acquit Olive because our system would be better if judges interposed their judgments about desirable criminal liability much more freely. As I have suggested about Sam's carrying out the responsibilities of a subordinate, a judge who acted upon this argument would not be playing by the rules of the enterprise. Olive is asking the judge to reach an answer different from the one the law, including basic assumptions of the system, now requires.

If Olive relies on special features of Angus or herself, she calls for the kind of individuation and equitable qualification of legislative classifications that the general justification defense evidently demands. She might say about Angus that (1) he is so well trained he poses no danger if unleashed, (2) he is specially in need of exercise, or (3) he is intrinsically more valuable than other dogs, so his physical and emotional well-being are more important. Unfortunately for Olive, none of these claims presents the right *kind* of exceptional circumstance. Many dogs are well enough trained not to present dangers in the park; as Chapter 3 indicates, a legislature would write a different ordinance if it wanted courts to assess the exercise needs of particular dogs or the risks they pose. Moreover, practical administration of this minor ordinance could be compromised if police and courts had to assess these matters.[6] The response to Olive's claim that Angus is simply more valuable than other dogs is that much of the law reflects the view that privileges for dogs do not depend either on their market value or their owners' subjective valuations. Unless Olive can come up with some feature that singles out Angus more distinctively, a judge who complies with the rules of his enterprise must reject the defense.

The same conclusion applies for most claims Olive might make based on her own status. Suppose she argues that Angus gets exercise twice as fast when he is off the leash, and this allows her more time to study for her law school courses, which is of tremendous importance to society. Neither our law nor our culture recognizes legal study as of such pre-eminent importance that those engaged in it should be relieved of ordinary legal restrictions when freedom from these restrictions would save them time. Rejection of this claim, therefore, is also required.

Lurking in the background of my conclusions are some troublesome questions about the general justification defense that receive consideration more generally in Part III. Is a judge to rely on (1) judgments of relative value derivable from the legislature and from broader legal materials, (2) judgments derivable from community morality, or (3) judgments based on attempts to make correct moral assessments? Here, it suffices to say that so long as a judge defers to the specific legislative judgments about leashing dogs, he must reject Olive's claims if he gives substantial weight to values derivable from law or culture and gives no greater scope to efforts at correct moral assessments than the maximum the existing system plausibly allows. Our system does not widely grant judges authority to rely on positions about comparative values that are directly at odds with sentiments reflected in the law and shared almost universally in the community. If judges properly rely on their own moral assessments, as contrasted with those reflected in law or accepted by the community, it is generally only when the latter sources fail to give clear guidance or when the difference between those sources and the judges' assessments is marginal. Nothing of this sort could be said for adopting any of Olive's claims, even if one conceded that they *might* represent correct moral assessments.

In sum, when the purposes of the leashing ordinance, the need to administer it in some comprehensible fashion, and the values of dogs and people reflected in the law and in the culture are considered, Olive's arguments for applying the general justification defense are not only unconvincing, but highly implausible and even silly. In another society sometime and someplace, with no linguistic alteration in the general justification provision, one of these arguments might persuade, but for the society of this time and this place, the result these arguments urge is objectively wrong. It is wrong because interpretation within a system requires reference to the values embodied in the system and to the understandings of those participating in and subject to the system. Despite the open-endedness of the general justification defense, the law determines that it does not cancel the application to Olive of the more specific language of the leashing ordinance.

Nonapplication of Constitutional Limits

Since the analysis is closely similar to that of the general justification defense, I shall be very brief in considering the possibility that application of the leashing ordinance to Olive is indeterminate because it could be overridden by the indeterminate application of some federal or state constitutional standard. For the sake of convenience, I concentrate on the equal protection clause and the due process and privileges and immunities clauses of the Fourteenth Amendment of the federal constitution.

Olive might claim that the classification improperly discriminates against dog owners in comparison with other users of the park, owners of monkeys, bicycle riders, parents with children, or some other collection of people not subject to similar regulation.[7] The constitutional language is open-ended enough to lend itself to invalidation of the ordinance on one of these grounds, but now firmly settled constitutional doctrine is that legislatures have wide room to adopt rules that implicitly distinguish along any of these lines. Conceiving any argument for altering this position that is tied to other basic premises of our constitutional order is difficult. The group that is "discriminated against" lacks the characteristics of disadvantage that might lead a court to expand protection to it without drastically shifting the whole landscape of equal protection doctrine. Even for judges not restricted by precedents of a higher court, finding a denial of equal protection here would be objectively wrong because it would be at odds with any basis for judgment that the legal system countenances.

An argument that the ordinance violates due process or privileges and immunities would have to rely on some claimed fundamental right of Olive's. Since a right to have dogs unleashed in public parks is hardly a traditional basic right, the right would have to be found in a category of rights that is expandable in light of fundamental cultural values. The right Olive claims is so far removed from fundamental cultural values and from rights that now enjoy constitutional protection a judge would depart from the rules of the enterprise in declaring such a right. In the future our law and culture may value dogs and other higher animals much more than they do now, and a leashing ordinance may appear to be unwarranted cruel treatment of dogs that deserve protection through the claims of owners' rights. However, until some movement in that direction takes place, a judge would be unjustified in declaring such rights. Despite the open language of relevant constitutional provisions, their nonapplication to Olive and Angus is determinate.

Positive Application of the General Justification Defense and Constitutional Limits

In the last two subsections, I have suggested that *non*application of justifications and constitutional rights is sometimes determinate. Do general standards of this type ever plainly apply, leading to a conclusion that despite the evident application of a more specific provision, the law objectively does not forbid the behavior involved? My unsurprising answer is yes.

> Angus is a big dog who has been trained to save young children from the water. Olive is walking in the park with Angus on a leash and sees a small baby fifty yards away who has fallen into a pool three feet deep, while her parents are chatting with friends. Olive releases Angus who runs to save the baby, and does so. A police officer whose vision is obscured by trees sees only Olive's release of Angus; when he comes upon Olive twenty minutes later he issues a summons. He does not then believe her story, and the parents have departed with their baby. Olive manages to find the parents who testify to the accuracy of her account in court.

In this circumstance the general justification defense undoubtedly applies. Given the high value placed on human life in our law and culture, and the slight risk that Angus will do serious harm in the brief time he is unleashed, a judge who believes Olive's account is required to find that the general justification defense applies.

My constitutional law example departs from variations on the theme of Olive and Angus.

> The council of a town most of whose working residents earn over $50,000 a year votes that no resident who is not a member of a family earning $25,000 or more will be eligible to use the public swimming pool. The reason for the ordinance given in the preamble is that the well-to-do-residents will feel more comfortable if they can use the facility without having to associate with poor residents.

No Supreme Court case has presented quite this issue, and I do not think any rules drawn from cases that it has decided directly preclude this strategy, but the swimming pool regulation is nonetheless a blatant violation of the equal protection clause, as it is now conceived. The sense of equal protection jurisprudence is that any explicit effort to limit community services on the basis of family income would be "suspect" or "disfavored," and the reason of preserving the pool serenity of the well-to-do would be patently inadequate to justify the classification.[8] One can comfortably say that constitutional law as it presently exists determines the unconstitutionality of this strategy. At least for a judge who is not on the Supreme Court,[9] "the law" yields an objective answer that the ordinance is unconstitutional.

The Determinacy of the Common Law—The Absence of Canonical Formulations and Possibilities of Overruling

Once it is understood that answers to some statutory and constitutional questions may have determinate answers, doubt may still be raised whether the answer to a question of common law can ever be determinate in the sense that I have spoken of. One possible doubt concerns the formulation of standards of common law; it is often said that no formulation is canonical. The other possible doubt concerns the authority of courts to overrule their own precedents. If courts can alter the law, how can the answer to any question be determinate? I should note at the outset that insofar as these aspects of the common law are threatening to any thesis that some cases have determinate answers, the threat extends to statutory and constitutional conclusions whose authority depends on prior judicial decisions. A judicial formulation of a relatively precise standard governing freedom of speech under the First Amendment has itself no more of a canonical status than a judicial formulation of a common law rule. I shall deal with both doubts about determinacy relatively quickly.

NO CANONICAL FORMULATION

The idea that common law rules do not have canonical formulations is that the scope of a rule may be cast in different ways. A contrast may be drawn between the common law, on the one hand, and statutes and constitutions on the other. The language of a statute or constitution is the language to which a court must refer; that language represents an authoritative formulation. But when courts offer formulations of rules of common law in their opinions, those formulations, at least typically,[10] are not uniquely authoritative in the same way. A future court may accept or offer an alternative formulation as capturing the existing rule as well or better. The different ways in which a rule may be cast may have different implications for the resolution of some situations. If alternative formulations are always possible, can any case be resolved definitely by a common law rule?

The answer is fairly simple. Ordinarily the various formulations are cast with certain core situations in mind, those resolved by the courts in one way or another. Suppose "hearsay" evidence is to be excluded. Witness *A* is to testify that *B* told him that she (*B*) saw *C* steal money. If *A*'s testimony is to be used to show directly that *C* stole money, that is hearsay evidence and, barring some exception,[11] is not admissible. More generally, *some* cases will come out the same way under any plausible formulations of common law rules that remain faithful to the rules as they then exist. Put differently, all plausible formulations will have some overlapping content.

Certain common law formulations lack the precision associated with rules. These broader standards call on judges or jurors to make an assessment of proper or reasonable behavior. Rules so formulated may still yield determinate answers, as does the general justification defense, when values drawn from the law or culture leave no doubt about the proper outcome.[12]

OVERRULING

If courts may explicitly overrule existing common law cases, or drastically alter the coverage of common law rules, does that undermine the determinacy of applications of common law? Since lower courts may be required to stick more closely to existing rules than the court that has established them, this worry about determinate results is particularly great for the latter court. For cases as to which overruling is appropriate, one cannot say a decision that follows the narrow existing law is objectively required. But not every case falls into that category; shared understandings limit the appropriateness of overruling.

> A rule of common law dealing with real property is challenged before the state supreme court that established it. The rule concerns an aspect of property law as to which having a settled rule is very important. The rule has been followed by all the courts in the state for thirty years since the original decision, and has been relied upon heavily in many property transactions. The argument offered for overruling is that when the rule was initially laid down, the reasons for a contrary rule were marginally stronger.

As hard as it is to say when our traditions permit overruling,[13] this is not such a case. This situation is one in which any court would say that even if the initial decision might better have come out the other way, the rule is too firmly settled to be disturbed, absent some serious claim of present injustice or importantly changed circumstances. The law, that is the old rule plus the vague traditions controlling overruling, determines that the rule should be applied to the new case.

Whether this analysis of common law cases can be extended to constitutional and statutory ones is debatable. Although our dominant and sound tradition gives precedents weight in both statutory and constitutional cases, it is even harder to formulate when overruling is appropriate. The suggestion that precedents should always yield to original legislative intent or some other standard may not be "off the wall."[14] For my very strict standard of what counts as a determinate answer, an answer for a statutory or constitutional case that might otherwise be appropriate possibly is not foreclosed for a "highest court" by precedential decisions to the contrary.

5

Law's Determinacy in Light of General Theories of Prediction, Rule Following, and Interpretation

The preceding chapters have explained why many legal questions have determinate answers, in the sense of answers (1) that virtually all lawyers and others familiar with the legal system would reach upon understanding the legal questions, and (2) that are unopposed by any powerful contrary arguments consonant with the "ground rules" of the legal enterprise. Although I have more confidence in the nonlegal and legal illustrations I have provided than in any abstract formulation, the conclusions of the last chapters can be summed up in this way.

The application or nonapplication of an authoritative rule or broader standard can be determinate if

1. that outcome is indica ed by the literal meaning of the standard and no serious reason for different treatment appears in (a) other relevant authoritative standards, (b) the relevant purposes of those involved in the system of which the standard is a part, or (c) the understandings of those who adopted the standard,[1] those who now apply it, or those who are now subject to it;

or

2. despite the absence of a relevant literal meaning, the import of other standards and/or the relevant understandings of those involved in the system of which the standard is a part plainly indicate a result, and no serious relevant reason appears to the contrary.

In this formulation, rules are one kind of standard, the kind that is relatively precise in its coverage. The application of the formulation to common law standards and other judicially established rules or broader standards of law[2] requires that the outcome be the same under each plausible formulation of the standard.

Thus far my analysis has been uncluttered by many references to broader theories that might be relied upon to support the thesis that applications of law are invariably indeterminate. This chapter comments on some of those theories and their relevance. Readers uninterested in this theoretical digression may skip this chapter, although it clarifies further the manner in which aspects of a legal system help yield objective answers. My attention is devoted mainly to the argument that applications of law depend upon interpretation, that legal interpretation is a species of interpretation in general, that all interpretation depends on the subjective attributes of the interpreter, and that, therefore, no interpretive question has an objectively correct answer. Theories of interpretation will also figure in later chapters of the book; here I discuss them primarily to deal with the claims of invariable or pervasive indeterminacy. Before embarking on that task, I briefly consider whether scientific indeterminacy or uncertainty, or a general indeterminacy of rules, somehow supports indeterminacy of law. Although I do not deal with every skeptical account of human understanding or external reality that might challenge the determinacy of some legal outcomes, the ability of my account to deal with those that I do discuss strongly suggests a capacity to withstand other grounds of attack as well.

Scientific Indeterminacy

In an earlier era, the regularity of the physical world was held out as an aspiration for law, a regrettably messy human endeavor. But in recent years, it has been suggested that there are inherent limitations on the regularities of physical movements or on the ability of human beings to predict them, and that these limitations bear on legal determinacy. Most often trotted out among the complexities of quantum physics is Heisenberg's "principle of uncertainty," and it has been proposed that modern chaos theory had a strong bearing on legal development.[3] Also seeming to support indeterminacy may be the status of the principle of induction (mentioned in Chapter 3): we have no complete assurance that physical regularities of the past will continue into the future.

I have argued that the determinacy of particular outcomes is not fundamentally a matter of prediction, much less absolutely certain prediction. No doubt if virtually all lawyers agree, the outcome they agree upon is highly predictable, but my use of that standard does not concern prediction but rather an indication of the plain normative implications of existing legal materials and institutions. I shall consider this perspective shortly, but let us for the moment consider a claim of legal determinacy as a claim of certain predictability. (After all, *some* claims of determinacy do concern prediction.) What is the import of scientific indeterminacies?

Whatever indeterminacies and uncertainties exist about certain aspects of the physical world,[4] they do not undermine fairly precise predictability about movements of many objects on this earth. If someone releases a stone from his hand during calm weather, the stone is very unlikely to move up toward the sky rather than down toward the ground. If the predictability of a legal outcome can be as certain as the downward movement of the stone, that is sufficiently certain for any purpose relevant to a philosophy of law. The uncertainty introduced by doubt that past physical regularities will continue into the future is present for every human prediction[5] and has no special bearing on prediction of human choice.

Chaos theory, which concerns highly complicated causal relationships that do not repeat themselves exactly, as with weather patterns, may have more obvious relevance for problems of human choice, including legal choice. The way legal doctrines develop by incremental decisions, themselves affected by a wide range of variables, may resemble other patterns described by chaos theory.[6] Shifts in social conditions, attitudes, or legal materials not closely related to the issue to be decided can alter prediction of outcomes. But when those changes occur and render prediction uncertain, the legal questions would no longer be determinate according to the criteria of the previous chapters. Thus, chaos theory has little bearing on simple cases of guidance by rules. In sum, indeterminacies and uncertainties in predictions of the movements of natural bodies have scant relevance for any thesis about practical certainty in human decision.[7]

In any event, as I have said, my thesis about determinate outcomes is fundamentally about what outcomes are appropriate, not what outcomes will occur. The indeterminacy or unpredictability of a specific physical movement is far removed from the question whether authoritative language in context *requires* a particular conclusion. But one can draw connections between descriptive uncertainty and normative uncertainty. As I suggested in Chapter 3, one who asserts that a rule requires a particular result may be wrong because one is mistaken about what words mean; consequently no one can ever say with absolute certainty that a particular outcome is correct. One might also make a more complex sort of mistake. My argument for determinate outcomes depends on social assumptions about practices and roles, such as the relations of legislatures to courts. One could be badly wrong about these. It is also logically possible, as I said, that assumptions could change radically *and* instantaneously, although that has apparently never happened in human history. If someone says what a correct outcome is, and implies that that correct outcome will not change in the next five minutes,[8] his claim is subject to invalidation by a radical shift in social assumptions within those five minutes. These possibilities of simple and complex factual mistakes mean that a statement about a normatively correct outcome within an enterprise is never certain without any glimmer of doubt. But none of these possibilities undercuts practical certainty in human affairs. Practical certainty about language and social practices is sufficient to sustain the claim that answers to legal questions are often determinate.

The Possible Indeterminacy of Rules in General

A different possible ground for skepticism focuses on what it means for human beings to follow rules. This inquiry seems more apt because it focuses on human activity and enjoys a much closer tie than does quantum physics to the theories of interpretation I shall shortly discuss. Doubt may be raised whether human beings can ever be wholly confident that they are following a rule: a rule of language, a rule of arithmetic, or a rule of law.

This problem is examined in a book by Saul Kripke attempting to develop Wittgenstein's account of rules and private language,[9] a book which has been said to be "relevant and important to contemporary lawyers . . . . a powerful philosophical argument about the indeterminacy of rules and all forms of rule interpretation."[10] Kripke suggests that even with respect to a rule of addition, our past instances of addition and our learning of an abstract method of addition will not guarantee how a new problem should be treated. This skeptical judgment does not concern psychology but what rule past behavior exemplifies and whether any particular result is required in a novel case. As Dennis Patterson explains the position, "one can never know whether one's current use of a word coheres with one's past use, for one's current use of a word (or calculation of a sum) can always be shown to be in accord with any number of rules."[11] Whether Kripke's account offers the best interpretation of the passages in Wittgenstein's *Philosophical Investigations* and, more importantly, whether it provides an appealing account of the relationship between rules and their applications have both been sharply challenged. In particular, G. P. Baker and P. M. S. Hacker have claimed that Kripke (presenting Wittgenstein's argument as it struck him) fails to see that adopting a rule involves more than envisioning how it deals with particular instances; there is an internal relation between a rule and acts that conform with it, and knowing how to apply a rule to a problem does not depend on having conceived that discrete problem before.[12]

I need not explore the intriguing intricacies of this issue in its broad form as concern about all rules. Whatever is the correct view, the issue is centrally about human language. If general skepticism is warranted, it is a skepticism that extends to rules of arithmetic and to rules for distinguishing "doors" from "windows" or "dogs." No one denies that for ordinary cases, human beings have practical rules for adding and for describing standard instances of doors. If legal applications can achieve that degree of certainty, they are certain enough. Whatever the merit of Kripke's account in revealing some philosophical dilemma about the nature of following rules, it alone does not cast doubt on the possibility of practical certainty in human affairs; if certainty does not flow from an internal relation between rules and applications, it can flow from community practice.[13] The general skepticism about rules offers no basis, because it does not consider the question, for saying that legal applications are subject to some uncertainty that does not beset standard instances of addition and naming objects.[14]

Margaret Radin urges that there is broader significance in Wittgenstein's fundamental idea that rules are constituted by social practice.[15] If that idea is accepted, one must reject the claim of traditional formalism that answers can be deduced from the words in which rules are formulated. Radin suggests we must accept the following philosophical consequences if we accept the pragmatic Wittgensteinian view of rules: "the tendency of 'applying rules' to coalesce with 'making' rules; the tendency of the 'rule' to coalesce with the 'particulars' falling under it; the idea that rules are contingent on whole forms of life and not just specific acts of a legislature; and the essential mutability of rules."[16] Professor Radin does not propose that the "social practice" account of rules undermines the claim that there are *some* determinate answers to legal questions, answers that judges and other officials are obligated to reach.[17] And the reader will note that the account I have presented in the last three chapters is, indeed, one that relies on social practice. One's overarching view of the nature of social rules will affect one's understanding of what constitutes determinate answers, but no plausible view yields a total absence of determinate answers.

Theories of Interpretation

The last decade has seen a proliferation of writing about the manner in which legal interpretation relates to other forms of interpretation, and enlightened views about interpretation in other spheres are sometimes thought to teach lessons about indeterminacy in law. One would be foolish to deny the fruitfulness of such comparisons, but one must also be very cautious in assimilating insights from other exercises in interpretation. No relevant insight supports invariable indeterminacy.

We can identify at least five varieties of interpretation that involve constructive understanding: legal interpretation, religious or theological interpretation, literary interpretation, reproductive interpretation (as in producing plays and performing music), and interpretation in the human sciences (history, anthropology, etc.).[18] Interpretation may be of documents, of practices, or of something else, such as dreams. The aim of interpretation may be descriptive, to inform others of some aspect of reality, or normative, to indicate desirable action or to exhibit what is good, or a combination of descriptive and normative. The object of interpretation may be to answer a particular question or yield a much broader account of what is important. Various relationships of authority may exist between the interpreter and what is interpreted and between the interpreter and the community within which he interprets. Not everyone of these distinctions may turn out to be crucial with respect to indeterminacy, but each deserves examination. The attractions of fresh perspectives and weighty intellectual names is not a substitute for careful analysis of the importance of broader ideas about interpretation for the determinacy of law.

The Subjectivity of Interpretation

Much modern writing on interpretation, or hermeneutics, emphasizes the inevitability of an interpreter's reliance upon his or her own presuppositions in interpreting a text or practice. Further, since the point of interpretation is to ascertain something relevant for interpreters and those to whom they may communicate, this inevitability generally is not to be regretted, but welcomed; it is questionable whether the interpreters should even attempt to submerge their own particular presuppositions. As Hans-Georg Gadamer, one of the most profound hermeneutical theorists writes, "A law is not there to be understood historically, but to be made concretely valid through being interpreted."[19] He goes on to say that for a religious proclamation to be understood properly for its saving effect, it "must be understood at every moment, in every particular situation, in a new and different way."[20]

In a leading American comparison of legal interpretation and literary interpretation, Sanford Levinson talks about law as "the creation of willful interpreters . . . ."[21] He suggests that "the very multiplicity (if not promiscuity) of [Chief Justice John] Marshall's approaches to interpretation . . . calls into question whether interpretation for Marshall (or for anyone else) ever transcended a desire to achieve specific political results."[22] To counter the possibility that author's intent might provide a fixed standpoint for interpretation, Levinson emphasizes the absence of authorial intent in jointly authored documents.[23]

The inevitability of the interpreter's perspectives coloring an interpretive effort should give us pause before we assert that any single objectively correct interpretation of a law, or anything else, is always available. But lest we be overcome by skepticism, we need recall that language is, after all, a communal construction and that those who share a common language and culture often understand that the meaning of sentences in context includes some things and excludes others. A speaker's meaning and a reasonable listener's understanding often will converge on standard instances. The subjectivity of interpretation does not itself bar a conclusion that questions about meaning can often be answered with confidence, that an answer can be objectively right or wrong.

Of course, as I indicated in Chapter 3, someone might say that *interpretation* is required only when meaning and the application it requires are not transparently clear in the situation at hand, but the critical question is whether authoritative legal standards produce definite answers to questions in many circumstances, not what qualifies as interpretation. I shall assume in what follows, as do many of those writing on interpretation, that even deriving simple answers from texts involves interpretation, but that categorization is not important for my purposes.[24]

Descriptive or Normative Interpretation

When legal interpretation is compared with theological interpretation, literary criticism,[25] and interpretation in the human sciences (such as history and anthropology), a distinction that immediately comes to mind is between descriptive and normative interpretation. Theological and legal interpretation, and perhaps literary criticism,[26] may be regarded as mainly normative, because they seek to indicate what people should do and what things are worthwhile and worth achieving. Interpretation in the human sciences may be regarded as descriptive because it aims to reveal what exists and occurs. This dichotomy has some significance, but it is much less sharp than it appears at first glance, and it proves to have relatively little bearing on the issue of determinate answers.

A distinction between descriptive and normative interpretation could focus either on the *purpose* of the interpreter or the interpreter's *understanding* of what he or she interprets. A historian may consider ancient Greek texts to determine Greek conceptions of moral duty. The historian's purpose would be descriptive, to tell others how Greeks considered moral duty. But he would be seeking a normative understanding, that is, an understanding of normative outlooks of ancient Greeks. On the other hand, a person approaching the Bible as an aid to decide how to live finds a text that contains a good deal about human history and human motivations. Biblical interpreters with primarily normative purposes may engage in much interpretation that is essentially descriptive.

Matters are complicated still further. First, the purposes of interpreters often are mixed, and so are the understandings. Why would a historian be interested in how Greeks conceived moral duty? Probably he will suppose that increased knowledge about Greek conceptions will give us some assistance, in some way, in deciding how to live our lives now.[27] Second, the initial understanding that the interpreter brings to the subject to be interpreted will not sharply separate normative from descriptive elements. The interpreter typically will engage in some normative evaluation when aiming to provide a descriptive account, and his sense of empirical reality will influence whatever normative lessons he derives from what he is interpreting. Third, an understanding of a culture's norms is not easily separable from an understanding of its history and of other elements that are not obviously normative.[28] If legal interpretation is fundamentally normative, that is, if it deals with questions of what people should do, an aspect of much legal interpretation is construction of what people are like and what they aim to achieve. In sum, no identifiable normative interpretation stands neatly separable from descriptive interpretation.

Does it matter for the possibility of determinate answers whether normative judgments are subject to the same criteria of truth or falsehood as descriptive judgments?[29] At a simple level, a proposal that this possible difference demarcates *descriptive interpretation* from *normative interpretation* confuses two sets of criteria: the criteria for the validity of direct normative claims and the criteria for accurate interpretations. Normative interpretation concerns the normative perspective of texts or practices. A text may provide a *definite answer* to what one should do, even if there is no correct answer to the question of whether *one really should* do that, all things considered.[30] If Beth tells Sam that the temperature is 65° Fahrenheit and that he should shut the door, there is no reason to think that her normative directive is harder to understand, or is less definite in its implications, than her descriptive assertion.

At a deeper level, this problem that criteria of normative judgment may differ from those of descriptive judgment is more serious. Suppose a text or practice is being interpreted by someone who assigns a very high authority to it. This interpreter will be strongly disinclined to say that although the text he is interpreting indicates that he should do one thing, he should, all things considered, do something else. If the implications of the materials being interpreted are interwoven with other criteria of normative judgment, the interpreter may not wish to say that the materials yield definite answers of a kind that are not possible for final normative judgments. Thus, people who believe that what we should do is determined by time, place, and perspective, and who believe that the Bible has high authority, are unlikely to find that the Bible forbids every act of adultery in every social circumstance.

I have strongly urged, nevertheless, that normative interpretation is ordinarily not identical with judgment, overall, about the actions one should take. Certainly as far as the law of human beings is concerned, one may say that the law indicates that a person should act in one way, but that acting in a different way is better, taking everything into account.[31] In many instances one's view of the authority of a text may influence how one interprets or applies it, but that truth does not mean that all or most normative interpretation is indistinguishable from judgment about what one should really do.[32]

Legal interpretation is essentially normative. This matters. Comparisons are likely to be more illuminating between legal interpretation and other forms of interpretation that are essentially normative, in either the sense of seeking normative understanding or in the sense of being directed toward choice, than between it and forms of interpretation that are normative in neither sense. But the normative character of legal interpretation is not itself a reason to suppose that answers to legal questions will be more or less capable of definiteness than answers to other kinds of interpretive questions.

More important are the three other subjects to which I now turn: (1) the specificity of the interpretive inquiry, (2) the degree to which different answers to a single interpretive question are mutually exclusive, and (3) the relationships between the interpreter and what is being interpreted and between the interpreter and the community in which he is situated.

How Specific Is the Interpretive Inquiry?

The possibility of a determinate, objectively correct answer depends considerably upon the nature of the question asked. When comparisons are drawn between literary interpretation and legal interpretation, the questions in literary interpretation often involve how to interpret a work or character.[33] Given subtle differences and gradations, one might interpret a work in an infinite number of ways. If someone asks how the Constitution is to be interpreted and conceives the Constitution as embodying our public values, one might also find, including variations on major themes, an infinite number of ways in which to interpret the Constitution. But, as scholars have often pointed out, many of the structural parts of the Constitution are quite specific, and if someone asks, "Could an eighteen-year-old English rock star with no claim to American nationality permissibly serve as president of the United States?," the document yields a definite answer, no. Much of the same range of interpretation applies in an analysis of literature. Suppose these questions are asked about Dostoyevsky's novel, *The Brothers Karamazov*: "Does Fyodor Karamazov, the father, remain alive (in the literal sense) at the end of the novel?" "Is Dmitry Karamazov, the oldest son, one of the fifteen most important characters in the novel?" The answer to the first question is clearly no; the answer to the second is clearly yes. The answer to the first question requires only superficial attention to the events described. If one takes them at face value, it is as certain that Fyodor dies during the novel as that John F. Kennedy died during his term as president. For any actual historical event, it is always conceivable that people have been the victims of an incredibly elaborate hoax or that they have lost contact with reality; therefore, we *might* be wrong about John Kennedy's death. Perhaps it is also conceivable to interpret Dostoyevsky's novel as *really* involving an elaborate hoax, according to which the main characters of the novel, or the reader, are fooled about the death of the father. But such an interpretation is not just off the wall for present readers; one is hard put to imagine how people in the future would embrace it. As to whether Dmitry is one of the *fifteen* most important characters, a degree of judgment is involved, but again it is hard to imagine how one could rank fifteen other individuals in the novel as more important than he. If the position is taken that the answers to *these* questions do not really require *interpretation* (in the relevant sense), then that shows that literary *interpretation* builds on features of literary works as to which determinate, objective answers can be provided. If law is similar, the place of a significant number of determinate answers is secure.

My suggestions about literary analysis also apply to interpretation of theological texts. A recent book describes how small groups, invited to give free flow to their imaginations, can relate biblical passages to personal experiences in a helpful way.[34] In such a process, no specific narrow question is to be answered and the idea of a single "correct" meaning to a passage is antithetical to the kind of "interpretation" in which the participants engage.[35] On the other hand, if the questions are put, "Is Jesus of Nazareth the most important character in human form[36] in the account of the four gospels?," "Do many biblical passages indicate that concern for others is called for?," and "Does the Bible suggest that God cares about human beings?," the answer to each question is undeniably yes.

Many ordinary critical questions in law take an either–or form. One might object that many substantive legal doctrines, such as the degree of comparative negligence and the measure of punitive damages, do not take this form. One might also object that the competitive either–or aspects of law are undesirable features that should be scrapped. I shall touch on such problems in Part II, where I claim that no enlightened system of justice could eliminate all either–or questions. Here it is enough to say than *many* legal questions *now* are either–or. Does a particular court have jurisdiction to consider a case? May the death penalty be imposed? May a judge order a witness to testify about whether a defendant stole jewelry if the witness has not yet been tried or granted immunity, the theory of the prosecution is that the witness stood as lookout while the defendant stole the jewelry, and the witness invokes the privilege against self-incrimination? In most instances, a statute will clearly indicate whether a court has jurisdiction. No one asserts that a state trial judge can impose the death penalty in a state whose legislature has voted explicitly to permit only a range of penalties that does not include death. No one questions that on the facts recounted, the judge must accede to an invocation of the privilege against self-incrimination.[37]

It often passes unnoticed in discussions of these matters that the same legal standard may function in at least five ways: providing a determinate answer to certain legal questions, providing the basis for interpretation and application in borderline instances, contributing to a more general view of a document or legal system that influences legal judgments outside the sphere of the standard's own arguable coverage, contributing to understanding of the kind of society in which we live, serving as one among many guides for how citizens should act toward their fellows.

Consider, for example, part of the wording of the First Amendment: "Congress shall make no law respecting an establishment of religion or inhibiting the free exercise thereof. . . ." Can Congress establish a national church virtually identical to the Church of England in 1791? The definite answer to this question is no. Can Congress provide substantial direct grants to church schools for the education of ordinary school children? For this question the clauses, and the cases interpreting them, must be interpreted; the better answer remains arguable, but precedents over the last few decades indicate that the answer is no. May government give "preferences" in hiring to members of racial minorities which have suffered discrimination? This question is not addressed under the religion clauses, but they and their interpretation *may* help inform what is permissible treatment to deal with nonreligious social divisions. That the religion clauses may not yield one determinate, correct interpretation in respect to the second and third legal questions does not mean they fail to produce a clear answer to the first question. The three levels of legal interpretation of the clauses are supplementary, not mutually exclusive. The religion clauses also help to define an American tradition of religious freedom and toleration, and they may be taken by citizens as a kind of norm in favor of tolerance, even when personal intolerance is legally permitted. In these respects, the clauses have evidently no single correct meaning.

Mutual Exclusivity of Answers to an Interpretive Question?

I turn now to the second broad inquiry: are different answers to the same interpretive question mutually exclusive? Suppose the question is how to interpret a character in a novel, such as Alexey Karamazov, the youngest brother in *The Brothers Karamazov*. On the surface of the novel, Dostoyevsky's hero appears to be a very good person, one with few, if any, malign feelings and aims. One could imagine at least six different perspectives for interpreting his character. Which interpretation (1) makes his character as much like that of real people, or some real people, as is possible; (2) renders him most interesting as a human being; (3) makes him most appealing from an aesthetic point of view; (4) presents him in the most helpful way as a moral exemplar; (5) best fits with Dostoyevsky's own conception; (6) fits best with Russian thought at the time the novel was written? Further, each of these questions could be asked focusing on Alexey as an individual or on the novel as a whole (conceivably an interpretation that renders *him* less interesting makes the whole novel more interesting). Perhaps some of the questions I have put are now considered outside the domain of literary interpretation, but each might be of interest and value for people.[38] Different answers could be illuminating, and so long as the interpreter's standpoint was clear, they would not be mutually exclusive. A person reading various interpretations might conclude that taking Alexey as he appears on the surface makes him the most helpful moral exemplar and fits the author's intentions, but that a more complex "Freudian" reading, in which his caring attitudes and behavior are the result of repressed hostile feelings toward his father and brothers that frustrate his chances to develop as an individual, makes him and the novel more interesting and a deeper work of art. There is no reason why a novel or poem cannot be read like a piece of music can be heard, in many fruitful ways by the same individual.[39]

Essentially the same point may be true about much biblical interpretation. Suppose the effort is not to establish doctrinal truth but to illumine one's personal experience. Different ways of understanding a biblical story or parable may yield insight.[40] Perhaps the individual reader or participant in a study group need not decide which interpretation is most likely correct, but rather may welcome the value of various interpretations.[41]

Insofar as legal norms indicate cultural premises and possess broad educative value for individuals, people do not need to settle on a single correct interpretation, but practical questions bearing on legal results are different. The person who considers the legality of behavior is not seeking illumination about life. He or she wants to know whether it is all right to engage in a certain action. The judge deciding legal issues must resolve them. This insistent demand for a practical answer does not characterize literary interpretation or typical interpretation in the human sciences. It is a major aspect of theological interpretation of sacred texts only for those who think that definite concrete answers about what to believe and how to live can be drawn from particular texts.

In law, then, different answers are usually mutually exclusive. If one lawyer tells a judge that she has jurisdiction and the other tells her she does not, the arguments may enlighten the judge's views about jurisdictional practice, but at the end of the day she must assert jurisdiction or not. Not all narrow questions that must be answered will have determinate answers, but the need for an answer one way or the other undoubtedly has to do with what has been called by Thomas Grey the "presumption of literality" of legal materials.[42] The possibilities of determinate answers to questions are much greater when either–or answers must be given and materials are treated in a relatively literal way than when many different answers are compatible and nonliteral understandings predominate.

Relations of Authority

Relations of authority are the most complex variable for comparisons among kinds of interpretation. With some frequency, authority in one kind of interpretation is analogized to authority in another.[43] These illuminating analogies can mislead if salient differences are neglected. My fundamental thesis is that relations of authority are significantly different for law than for other major kinds of interpretation[44] and that the special character of authority in law enhances the possibilities for determinate answers. In making this argument, I will consider the authority of the text for the interpreter, the authority of the interpretive community for the interpreter, and the authority of the interpreter's "reading" for others.

LITERARY CRITICISM AND INTERPRETATION
IN THE HUMAN SCIENCES

In literary interpretation, the text of the work being interpreted is authoritative in the sense that it is what is being interpreted.[45] Critics are not free to make up different texts that they think might be better. The fact that the critic has chosen a particular text to interpret ordinarily shows that he thinks the text is valuable enough to warrant interpretation. That, perhaps, is a kind of authority for the text, although a critic might pick a text because he strongly objects to its style or message. Is anything else authoritative? Many texts will, of course, come preinterpreted, and preinterpretations of which a present critic is aware or that have affected discourse about the work will influence what the critic thinks. More generally, critics will be placed within a community of discourse about what things are relevant that will channel their views.[46] And if a critic strays too far from what is deemed acceptable interpretation, reputation and career may suffer. A critic's own interpretation may influence others, in turn, as prior interpretations have influenced him.

All these types of authority are significantly limited. The critic has chosen to interpret a particular text. Not only may he fault aspects of the work, he may change his mind about its significance. The preinterpretations of a text will affect how he comes to regard the text, but he is free to reject any particular interpretation in favor of others. There may be no single controlling interpretive approach at a point in time; rather a pluralism of approaches may coexist.[47] And instead of following the presently dominant methods of interpretation, a critic may revert to some older method or create a relatively original one. If he gets too far out of step with contemporaries, a critic will not be highly regarded in the discipline, but his ambition may be to reach a narrow section of the general public or to be read one hundred years from now. He may be willing to accept a lower present status. The concept of academic freedom and the practice of tenure in part reflect the view that academics should be permitted to pursue truth as they see it even if they are out of line with their fellows. The community of interpreters may have the authority of "inevitable influence" and the authority of "determining the critic's success" in the profession, but it lacks other authority. It does not have the authority to tell the critic how to interpret, and if the critic's views turn out to be bizarre, it will not be thoughtfully supposed[48] that his failure lies in a failure of duty toward the community, unless he has acquired a job under false pretenses, or has deviated from what he agreed to do, or has acted frivolously. Neither the text nor the critic's interpretation of it require that he behave in a certain way toward others in everyday life. Nor does his interpretation require anyone else to take any specific action.

I shall devote only a few words to the interpreter from the human sciences who is trying to understand the significance of a text or social practice. For the historian, anthropologist, or sociologist, the text or events have an authority in the sense that they are the subject of interpretation. Like the literary critic, however, each may choose what he wants to interpret, though he may be subject to criticism if he does not choose a subject that has importance for the purposes of his field. A serious historian would not be expected to analyze with great care the evolution of the rules of baseball; a serious literary critic would not be expected to devote concentrated attention to *The Wife-Swappers*.[49] The facts will often be preinterpreted, and the interpreter's perspectives will inevitably be influenced by his environment. The relationships between the particular interpreter and interpretive community and audience will be closely similar to those I have described for literary interpretation. A social science interpretation, if credited, indicates something about the external world, but does not, by itself, require action by the interpreter or his audience.

THEOLOGICAL INTERPRETATION

Some matters are different for theological interpreters; exactly how different will depend on basic theological assumptions. The theological interpretation I concentrate on here is that of an interpreter who seeks to discern religious meaning of texts with some special religious significance. I omit both religious interpretation of an ordinary novel, like Graham Greene's *The Heart of the Matter*,[50] and an interpretation of religious texts like the Bible "simply as literature" or for historical purposes.

The Authority of Text   For Christians the primary, if not exclusive, text with special religious significance is the Bible. (I restrict myself to Christians here because of my limited understanding of Jewish scriptural interpretation.) There are variations in the exact status the Bible is accorded. Some think that on a question that does not permit multiple correct answers, an accurate interpretation of the Bible yields unquestionable guidance for what to believe and how to live; for example, "If the Bible forbids adultery, then one should never commit adultery."[51] One might believe this about each and every part of the Bible or one might think this about the Bible as a whole but nonetheless believe that some of its parts do not have that status. A Christian, for example, might assume that some Old Testament stories in which God commands the killing of men, women, and children must not reflect God's true will or that the book of Ecclesiastes reflects a despairing, atheistic view of human life that does not correspond with the true account in the rest of the Bible. Alternatively, someone might think the Bible is an important and special source of guidance, but that other criteria of what to believe and how to live must be measured against even correct interpretations of the Bible. Since many Christians believe that in some sense the Bible is the revealed word of God, the pressure is great to render interpretations that do not deviate from what they believe overall is correct. A person may feel quite comfortable saying, "This is what Tolstoy's essays claim about pacifism, but he was wrong in that respect"; many Christians will feel much less comfortable saying the same thing about the letters of St. Paul that are included in the New Testament.[52]

A critical point of disagreement among Christians is whether other writings or sources of authority have a status like that of the Bible. The long-standing Roman Catholic view is that the tradition of the Church and the authoritative statements of the Church hierarchy have a similar authority, that indeed for the ordinary believer the Bible itself is to be understood in light of those sources. The common Protestant view is that the Bible has a unique status, though various Protestants may give more or less significance to the judgments of those within the believing community.

With these various positions in mind, we can understand the authority of the text and the theological interpretive community. On any view that accords special religious significance to the Bible, it is an important source of enlightenment and guidance about the nature of reality and how we should live. It has authority for the Christian interpreter and his audience that is qualitatively different from that of even the greatest work of literature.

The Authority of the Interpretive Community   The Bible comes to any contemporary interpreter preinterpreted, of course, and the perspectives of the community of believers through the ages are an inevitable determinant of the perspectives he brings to bear. If the interpreter occupies a position within a church or an academic theological institution, how he interprets may affect his immediate prospects. If he is too far out-of-line with dominant approaches, he may not advance. But this prospect *alone*, here we can see clearly, is hardly the kind of authority that exerts normative force. The interpreter is attempting in some sense to discern the nature and will of God and communicate that to an audience now and in the future. If his contemporary interpreters think he is crazy, he may assume that the problem is theirs; the interpreter, as theological interpreter, responds to a higher obligation.[53] Often, however, the interpreter will accord an importance to the community, or a particular subset of the community, that is greater than its roles as inevitable influencer of perspectives and determiner of his vocational advancement. To take the extreme, if one believes that another interpreter, say the pope or the head of the Mormon church, cannot err in certain of his statements, then one would never in a full sense reach an interpretation contrary to that interpreter's positions when stated under conditions that guarantee correctness.[54] Short of this deference, one may accord heavy weight to interpretations within the church community, believing that the community is strongly guided by the Holy Spirit. One may doubt one's own judgment if it is opposed to those prevailing in the Church; because of this, or for reasons of church loyalty, one might choose not to publicize one's views. Thus, the interpretive community, or parts of it, may have an authoritative significance for the theological interpreter that is qualitatively different from the authority of a community of literary critics. Just what this authority is will depend on theological perspectives that themselves are influenced by one's interpretation of the religiously authoritative text.

The Interpreter's Authority   One aspect of what I have just said is that some theological interpreters carry an authority for their audience that is not present in literary interpretation. A literary critic relies upon the force of his analysis, the depth of his insight, and the eloquence of his expression. No doubt, some critics get reputations as wise men or women, and a particular reader who has found a critic's past interpretations insightful may be inclined to credit a subsequent one. Therefore, a critic may have authority that does not derive solely from what he or she says on a particular occasion. But religious interpreters may have authority that depends on theological premises, not past success or individual character. Two notable examples are the original writers of books of the Bible and the pope. If someone believes that in the materials that have been collected in what he takes as an authoritative Bible each part correctly indicates God's nature, then the interpretations of Jesus's message by St. Paul in his biblical letters take on infallible authority (though they must, of course, themselves be interpreted). If one thinks the pope is infallible on the rare occasions when he speaks *ex cathedra*, and the pope renders an interpretation while speaking in this way, then his interpretation will be infallibly correct (though it must be interpreted). (I lay the stress I do on infallible authority not because I believe in it or believe that it plays a dominant role in much Christian faith, but because a difference between theological interpretation and other types of interpretation is presented in its most stark form by belief in infallible authority.) Among some Protestants, a minister or other interpreter may be viewed as nothing more than a kind of specialist about religious questions with no status intrinsically different from that of any other Christian. In that event, the authority of the minister's interpretation will resemble that of the literary critic. But there are many Christians, Protestant and Catholic, who believe that priests and ministers, or a community of interpreters, are inspired by God in a way they as individuals are not; in that event, interpretations by members of the clergy or by communities may carry an extra force that would not be accorded the same interpretation made by a gifted individual layperson.

The special status Christians accord a biblical text that is being interpreted affects the import of interpretations. Once people accept a particular biblical interpretation as correct on a question that does not permit multiple answers, the interpretation has very powerful implications for what they should believe and how they should live.

LEGAL INTERPRETATION

The Authority of Legal Materials and the Interpretive Community   The
subject of authority and legal interpretation is highly complex. The authoritativeness of many legal norms resembles the authoritativeness of the Bible
for those who take the view that all parts of the Bible reveal God's will;
but this assertion can be understood only with close attention to various
subtleties and to critical differences between authoritative legal norms
and that view of biblical authority.

I have noted that many rules of law lack a single authoritative formulation. Most working rules of the common law and constitutional law do
not have a single "canonical" formulation as do statutes and constitutional provisions themselves, and as does the Bible under the view that
every passage contains the infallible truth. An actor or court cannot always
point to an exact set of words as the test of whether behavior is legally
permitted.[55] And, as we have seen in connection with the ordinance about
leashing dogs in the park, a rule that is otherwise applicable can be subject
to cancellation in the particular instance if the conduct is privileged or the
rule is invalid under some higher legal standard.

Courts may in the United States overturn some rules without relying on
particular superior norms. A court that has established a rule of common
law can overrule it if it is judged to be misguided, and courts also may
have some authority to decide that statutes that have long lain unenforced
are no longer effective. Further, a court may have some discretion not to
penalize those whose conduct amounts to a violation of law. But in the
absence of exercising such discretion, a court considering Olive's case is
legally bound to apply the ordinance. It cannot say a recently adopted and
actively enforced rule requiring leashing is invalid. This conclusion rests
partly on the premise that courts are bound to apply legislative directives
that have no defect and are actively enforced.

Not all standards of law are of the sort on which I have concentrated so
far. Some are simply reasons for a decision that weigh in one direction
but can be outweighed by other factors. Thus, the principle that "penal
statutes should be strictly construed" may figure in an interpretation of a
criminal provision, but strong reasons may lead a court not to interpret a
particular provision in the more strict of two plausible alternative ways.[56]
Indeed, the same standard could be the source of both ordinary rules and
factors to be weighed in decisions. As I have suggested, the Establishment
Clause may both forbid a nationally established church and be understood
to support a more general principle against government classification
for employment among groups defined in terms not directly relevant for

employment purposes.[57] This principle would be *a reason* not to allow employment preferences for blacks, but all sorts of countervailing reasons might lead a court (and should lead a court, in my view) to determine that such classifications are permissible.

Within the general parameters of what I have said, substantial disagreement may exist about *how far* present interpreters should be guided by the linguistic implications and value judgments of those who have established legal standards and how far they should be guided by the judgments of some contemporary interpretive community or by their own judgments about what is best. Such questions do not arise in this form for the person who thinks each passage of the Bible infallibly reveals the will of God. That person may wonder how much credence to give to prior or contemporary interpretations, and how much latitude to accord changing social conditions in figuring out God's will, but he will not self-consciously set up "God's judgment" as something that might possibly be overcome by "the judgments of contemporaries" or "my judgment." A judge who thinks a legislature was grossly ill informed or that events have rendered outdated its perspective of twenty years ago may think in precisely those terms. Law is a human and complex contrivance; disagreement exists over just how much latitude judges have.

Finally, to reiterate a point made earlier, for the citizen, the police officer, and the judge, the law is not the *final* word about what should be done. A person is unlikely to say, "This is what God wants but it's not the right thing to do when everything is taken into account." The law lacks *this kind* of authoritativeness. All may recognize that driving an escaped slave in a cart for two hundred miles across a state line violates laws against aiding fugitive slaves, but the citizen may nonetheless believe he should do just that, the law enforcement official may believe he should turn his head, and a judge might decide he should refuse to find the obvious facts that would lead to the citizen's conviction and to the return of the slave.[58]

In all the ways I have noted, legal materials may have an authority that varies from what someone understands as a biblical mandate. Still, they have an authority just by virtue of being part of the law that is quite different from any authority that exists in literary or historical interpretation.

The Authority of the Judicial Interpreter   Within a legal system the authority *for* judges of the interpretive community is woven with the authority *of* judges in our political system. Parts II and III return to this subject, so I shall limit myself here to some obvious points. A legal system is an order for regulating affairs, and the law of the state typically includes coercive force as a critical element. A legal system fundamentally concerns action, not enlightenment; reasoning within the law is a form of practical reason leading to narrow decisions, not reflection for the sake of understanding. In this respect, legal interpretation is notably different in emphasis from interpretation in the human sciences and literary interpretation. When judges interpret the law, they are deciding whether or not the coercion of the state will be employed for a particular objective. The judge thus has a type of authority that other modern interpreters lack; the individual who loses must act as the court indicates whether or not he is persuaded and whether he has any inkling of the content of the interpretive judgment.[59] Theological interpretation that leads to excommunication or shunning is somewhat similar in this respect, but the modern church cannot dictate imprisonment or fines. It has power in the human realm only to sever connections with those who seek to maintain them.

In our legal system, judges not only have the power to dispose of cases, their interpretations also become authoritative bases for future interpretations. General discourse about law, including the expressed views of teachers, scholars, and others who talk or write about the law but do not have on that occasion the power and authority to decide,[60] may function like historical writing or literary interpretation; but judicial interpretations in decisions have a special authority. Since what judges say and decide can be explicitly rejected in subsequent cases for good enough reasons, a judicial interpretation does not have the infallible authority attributed by some Christians to the interpretations of the life of Jesus in St. Paul's biblical letters. Nevertheless, strong reasons are required to reject a previous judicial interpretation. It has some force by dint of being expressed in a case that does not depend wholly on either its intrinsic persuasiveness as compared with alternatives or on the reputation or general abilities of the judges who made the interpretation.[61]

In a system in which so much rides on decisions and in which a judge's power is so considerable, it is not surprising that judges act under strong constraints.[62] Some of these, like the rule in the federal constitution that judges must enforce the Constitution and federal statutes against conflicting state law,[63] are reduced to canonical formulation, but most are not. The doctrine of precedent is, of course, a constraint on subsequent judges. So are notions that judges should not deviate too far from values and reasons reflected in the entire corpus of law or from the values of the community. As normative constraints on *how* a judge interprets, these conventions have two qualities that critically distinguish their influence from the way in which convention may restrain in literary or historical interpretation.

The most important quality is that individuals and organizations build up expectations on the basis of the system. These are not just subjective expectancies of which interpretations will occur, such as, "I imagine that if Yale hired her she's a deconstructionist"; they are the types of expectations on which people rely in planning their lives. Encouraging and satisfying such expectations is a powerful aspect of any legal system. Judges who disregard basic legal conventions *not only* surprise and disappoint fellow interpreters and reduce their opportunity for respect and advancement within the law; they fail to meet their institutionalized role to satisfy the justified expectations of those who are subject to the law's coercion.

There is, of course, a circularity to this analysis. If it were understood that judges were really *free to do* virtually anything, then however predictable their behavior might be, perhaps no one could justifiably rely on their acting in the predicted way.[64] But that system is not the system of law in the United States, which recognizes the value of having justified expectations and places considerable stock in their satisfaction. The achievement of that value has much to do with aspects of the law that render determinate answers feasible.

I turn now to a closely related quality of the restraining conventions mentioned in previous chapters. Since no one *has* to be a judge, those who assume official positions implicitly agree to perform the duties of those positions, and all judges I am aware of actually take an oath of office to this effect. Those oaths amount to a promise to perform somewhere within the broad realm of the powers that judges are understood to have in our legal system. As I have urged in previous chapters, a promise to fulfill a role carries weight for whether one should, overall, perform the acts that fulfill the role.

No doubt there is room for much argument about the best conception of a judge's role, and no doubt this conception can shift significantly over time. A judge may self-consciously act upon a conception that is in some respects accepted only by a minority. But there are limits. If, now, a trial judge in a courtroom in a state without a death penalty who is about to sentence a convicted murderer simply pulls out a gun, says, "Here is what you deserve," and shoots and kills the murderer, he has acted illegally. By failing to adhere to basic norms that define his role within the legal system, he has performed an act that is determinately, objectively wrong under the law, and he has violated his promise to fulfill the judge's role.

II

How The Law
Treats People

6

Standards of Judgment:
External or Internal,
Personal or Reasonable

This chapter introduces a different set of concerns about objectivity and law. In it and the next two chapters, I turn from the subject of determinate answers to criteria used within the law to judge people's behavior. What does someone mean by saying legal standards should be objective? Different issues are embraced by this question, and only confusion can result if the inquiry is not carefully focused. It helps to begin with some of the oppositions that need to be considered: (1) objective (external) versus subjective (internal); (2) objective (criteria based on reasonable persons) versus subjective (personalized criteria); (3) objective (dealing with many situations similarly) versus contextualized (using individualized approaches); (4) objective (dictating results) versus discretionary (leaving much to the judgment of officials); (5) objective (fair) versus arbitrary (or unfair). The simple idea that law is "objective" usually has a flavor of all these senses. Legal rules deal with external acts, they hold people to standards that govern reasonable people, they establish abstract general criteria that seem substantively fair, govern large classes of actions, and constrain officials reaching decisions.

A challenge to the objectivity of law may amount to a claim that law as it stands *is* much less objective than the prevailing ideology would have it, or that law *should be* less objective than it is or than others recommend. Whichever form a challenge takes, one must understand just which of the five features it addresses.

This chapter focuses primarily on phrasing legal rules in terms of reasonable people rather than an actor's personal characteristics. This analysis raises the closely related problem of how far rules are abstract and general rather than contextualized. The treatment of these topics is preceded by a brief discussion of the external aspect of law. The chapter assumes what I have demonstrated in Part I: general rules can dictate results. Chapter 8 asks whether there is something inherently undesirable about any system of governance that relies heavily on abstract rules established in advance. Chapter 7 explores a number of problems about arbitrary and unfair classifications involving differentiation by race and gender.

One important connection between this part and Part I is straightforward. The character of legal rules will affect the degree to which the law will provide determinate answers in the sense developed in the last few chapters. Another connection is more subtle. Some of the debate over whether legal standards should be objective is over whether liability should depend on the actual mental states of actors. In ordinary life, the primary way we determine the mental states of other people is by the language they use. Often the expression is direct—"I feel pain," "I want the door closed"—but we also infer mental states from other language. If Sam says, "Beth is an arrogant, mean-spirited boss, who has destroyed my prospects at every turn," we assume that Sam has unfond feelings toward Beth. Confidence that human beings are capable of discovering the mental states of others depends substantially on confidence about the intersubjectivity of language. Unless one believes that the meaning of language is often determinate in context, one could hold out little hope for the accurate discovery of mental states.[1]

In this chapter and the next I concentrate primarily on aspects of criminal law and administration, but my remarks have a broader aim, and the discussion wanders briefly into other domains. Treating familiar subjects of criminal law in this chapter, I show multiple facets of the problem about objectivity. Although I draw some subsidiary conclusions along the way, my main point, which will hardly surprise those who have thought seriously about the substantive criminal law, is that simple favoritism toward objective or subjective approaches does not resolve much. Some more subtle blend is needed. I do not try to present a full and systematic moral philosophy in support of either my general conclusion or my particular recommendations. Rather, I appeal to a sensitive appreciation of what I take to be widely held convictions.

One important aspect of the topic that I disregard, except for its mention here and in the discussion of a "pure harm" approach to liability, is the relationship between sentencing provisions and the substantive criminal law. For much of this century sentencing standards became more and more discretionary, a wide range of choice being left both to sentencing judges and to parole boards. In the 1970s highly discretionary sentencing was attacked as being unfair: it was said to yield inconsistent results and to attend insufficiently to the blameworthiness of particular criminal acts. Many states passed rigid sentencing provisions, eliminating much or all parole board discretion and sharply constraining sentencing judges. More recently, sentencing guidelines have been adopted, giving judges greater discretion than they have under the most rigid statutes, but indicating the sorts of factors that lead to a sentence more or less harsh than the average. Even when judges have great sentencing flexibility, marking off classes of more and less serious substantive offenses has some value. But the criminal law's appropriate degree of refinement among types of wrongful behavior depends in part on how much discretion judges have and on how concrete are any guidelines for sentencing. Thus, any systematic and comprehensive appraisal of possible substantive categories needs to be accompanied by a similar appraisal of sentencing provisions.

External Acts as the Basis for Legal Intervention

One way in which law deals with people objectively is by regulating behavior; it does not seek to coerce feelings and attitudes, and it does not investigate feelings and attitudes unless wrongful behavior has occurred. That law concerns external behavior is a basic premise of modern legal systems, though other approaches are possible.

The point of another approach is easy to illustrate with respect to a government trying to achieve religious objectives. Suppose people in a society were almost all agreed on religious beliefs and were united around the premise that correct belief is critical for eternal salvation. Unless the freedom by which people arrived at correct belief was also counted important, the state might try to secure its citizens' spiritual welfare by controlling thoughts. Such a course would not be irrational. Any view of individual freedom that assumes that thoughts and feelings are beyond conscious coercion is, unfortunately, erroneous. A state willing to employ extreme means of compulsory psychological conditioning can certainly affect beliefs and feelings, but it need not go so far. I can remember the McCarthy era in the United States when former communist sympathizers were hounded. At a fairly young age, I developed the sense that any belief in communism as the best system of government was both "bad" and could severely inhibit prospects for a happy and successful life in this country. I am sure that as I grew to maturity, I approached the possible merits and demerits of communism with a less open mind than I considered the soundness of competing positions within the broad spectrum of "acceptable" political views. A religious government might have sporadic televised hearings concerning the views of suspected deviants. Those who admitted to disbelief or doubt about "correct" views might be jailed or dismissed from jobs. The beliefs of these people might not be much altered, but the emerging beliefs of young people would be affected.

If regulation of beliefs could "make sense" for a religious government, so also could it make sense for a secular government willing to take totalitarian control over the lives of its citizens. Such a government wishing to stamp out belief in the superiority of some classes and races over others might employ similar techniques to promote right thinking. Such self-conscious legal coercion to control the thoughts of ordinary adults is antithetical to ideals of liberal democracy.[2]

A government more limited in its ambitions might suppose that a person's thoughts and feelings indicate likely future actions. Why not give people psychological exams that will identify who will probably cause harm in the future, and then subject those people to coerced preventive treatment? The government could disavow any wish to control thoughts and feelings except as necessary to prevent ordinary crimes. Even with this limited ambition, such a system would place tremendous power in the government to decide who was too dangerous. The "science" of predicting behavior is inexact. Many people who would never have committed the crimes the government was trying to prevent would end up receiving coerced treatment. At least in the absence of extreme mental illness, coercing people who have not yet acted in an antisocial way fails to respect notions of freedom of choice and responsibility that are aspects of liberal government.

A modest extension of freedom to believe and feel is the freedom to tell others one's beliefs and feelings. So long as one avoids doing the kind of injury to someone that defamation involves, and avoids encouraging someone else to act in a forbidden way,[3] one can communicate one's own mental states. This is an important part of freedom of speech, and we can regard the simple communication of internal states as beyond the external acts the law may properly try to control.

Another sense in which action can be regarded as external is in affecting others. If I scratch my forehead in private, I am certainly behaving in a sense different from expressing feelings, but my action affects only myself. For the most part the law does not address acts of this sort. Important exceptions involve the use and possession of substances that are deemed harmful and suicide.[4] Prevention of suicide might be justified because of harms to those close to the person who would take his life, but there is also a settled moral conviction that taking one's life is usually a serious wrong. Attempts at suicide are no longer criminal, but encouraging or assisting someone to commit suicide is typically a crime, and public officers will stop suicides by force if they are able. With these and a few other exceptions, our law deals with external acts that involve or affect other people. Overall, then, we can think of the law as dealing *almost* entirely with what is external, in the senses of (1) behavior, rather than pure thoughts and feelings, (2) behavior that goes beyond the expression of internal states, and (3) behavior that involves or affects other people in some fairly direct way.

What about omissions? A failure to act can sometimes be the source of liability, but that liability does not represent control of thoughts, expressions of thoughts, or behavior that does not affect others. What one is liable for is the nonperformance of an external act that would affect others. The law regulates neglect to do what is required on behalf of others.

In contrast with the law, many moral views, religious and nonreligious, emphasize internal states. Having the right feelings and attitudes may be regarded as more important than performing the right acts, and performing the right acts with the right attitudes (loving concern in Christian morality or sense of duty in Kantian morality) may be regarded as better morally than performing the same acts with less worthy attitudes. Further, many people believe that moral training and conscious efforts to adopt a moral perspective should place emphasis on feelings and attitudes. Perhaps feelings and attitudes are the most important influence over time on how people act; feeling loving concern may be a more effective inducement to regarding the needs of others than careful analysis of what others are owed morally. In these important ways, religious and moral perspectives contrast with the law in their greater concern with what is internal and subjective.

Few people in American society would wish the law to alter radically in this respect. If a system implemented by public officials and backed by coercion took internal states and expressions of those states as a major basis for its intervention, the government would be much too intrusive and much too stifling of individual freedom.

The "Pure Harm" Approach to Criminal Law—An Odd and Unappealing Emphasis on One External Element

It has occasionally been suggested that the criminal law's initial focus should be exclusively on whether someone has caused harm, making liability depend on that.[5] Once liability was established, appropriate treatment of the person would be determined. Not only would some external action be a requisite for liability, liability would rest completely on the external fact that one's behavior has caused harm.[6]

The problems with such a regime can be illustrated by the following example:

> James is attending an outdoor barbecue at the farm of a friend, located close to a road on which there is very infrequent traffic. James gets into a heated argument with his wife that makes him angry and embarrassed. With eight people watching, he walks away on the side of the road. Although there has been no traffic passing by the farm in the previous half hour and will be none in the next half hour, at this point Daisy approaches in her automobile, driving a safe 40 miles per hour. Just as Daisy is about to drive by, James throws himself in front of her car. Daisy applies her brakes as quickly as possible, but James suffers serious injuries. All eight witnesses agree that Daisy drove very carefully. All those who know James agree that he gets over his extreme upsets quickly and that had no car come within the next ten minutes he would not have acted as he did.

On these facts, Daisy's action of driving the car was what lawyers call a "but for" cause[7] of James's injuries; had she not been driving her automobile at that place and time James would not have been hurt.[8] Under a system in which causing harm triggers liability, Daisy would be initially liable, despite having done nothing wrong, and being known to have done nothing wrong.[9]

That, of course, does not mean that anything will necessarily be done to Daisy. It may be decided that no form of coerced treatment is appropriate, but how is that determination to be made? One possibility is that at the second stage, the closely examined circumstances of the accident will be determinative. If Daisy acted in an unexceptionable way, no treatment will be imposed. But if this is to be the approach, why have a two-stage process? Why not relieve Daisy of involvement with the criminal process once the police and prosecutors have ascertained that she did nothing wrong?[10]

For the two-stage process to differ significantly from that which presently exists, the bases for evaluation at the second stage must be broadened, which is exactly what the proponents of such a process envision. One possibility is that at this stage Daisy would go through a serious psychological evaluation; if she were deemed a danger to society some form of treatment, with or without mandatory commitment, would be prescribed. A second, somewhat less intrusive, possibility would limit examination to Daisy's external behavior over time; then treatment would depend on her manifested dangerousness.[11] Both these possibilities would shift attention away from Daisy's conduct in the harm-causing incident to an overall evaluation of her propensities.

I have said that the law does not directly regulate thoughts and feelings; that would remain true only in a sense if causing harm led regularly to thorough psychological examinations of people that largely determined how they were to be treated. The fortuitous event in which one was involved *would* lead to one's being treated on the basis of thoughts and feelings not ascertainably connected to one's behavior in the incident. The law would not directly seek to control thoughts and feelings, but it would use thoughts and feelings to decide what treatment was necessary to minimize dangers to other people. If inquiry were limited at stage two to external manifestations of behavior, this particular problem would be avoided, but it would remain true that fortuitous involvement in an incident would produce an overall evaluation of one's life and propensities. This examination would be "objective" in concentrating on external acts, but it would be "subjective" in calling for an extended evaluation of the person. One aspect of law's externality may be that it deals mainly with discrete acts and transactions; it does not attempt to assess people overall. The two-stage harm-based approach to criminal law substantially compromises that ideal. Of course, overall evaluation now happens to a degree at the sentencing stage of some criminal proceedings, but convicted persons are not, like Daisy, the unlucky victims of fortuitous circumstance.

Whatever the view among some behaviorists in branches of the human sciences, the trend in criminal law scholarship is very much against this medical model of a criminal process, which never was supported by more than a tiny minority of people whose main study is law. I shall assume in what follows that for most kinds of legal liability, more will matter than whether one's behavior has been a "but for" cause of damage.[12] I now turn to critical questions about the extent to which objective or subjective standards should control that broader evaluation.

"Reasonable Person" or Subjective Characteristics?

Some of the Issues and General Criteria for Judgment

We are now ready to consider genuinely controversial questions about how objective the law should be. When dealing with people whose behavior causes or threatens harm, how much should the law attend to their actual states of mind and characteristics, how much should it rely on standards drawn from "reasonable persons"?

"Objectivity" in the sense of nonsubjective standards differs from "objectivity" in the sense of external behavior, but they share a hesitancy to make legal results depend on what a particular individual thinks and feels. If every aspect were judged from the standpoint of a reasonable person, legal liability would be determined solely by a person's external movements[13] and their consequences. Any talk of "perception" or "intent" would reduce to asserting what a reasonable person would have perceived or intended in the circumstances. The question of whether an actor's own personal experience and characteristics are to count legally turns out largely to be a question of how far more individualized standards of judgments are to supplement external appearances.

We can distinguish the following factors that might matter for legal liability: factual perceptions, quality of judgment, linguistic understandings, immediate aims, ultimate motivations, and degree of control. I discuss these in turn in this chapter. Any of these factors might be approached from an objective (reasonable person) or subjective perspective, and many intermediate shadings that combine objective and subjective elements are possible. An intelligent critic must look carefully at a precise legal issue and at *what* might be judged objectively or subjectively.

What can one say in general? First, the law should employ criteria for liability that are intrinsically relevant, that relate to the reason for liability. Second, the law commonly should employ criteria that cohere with the best understandings of what exists in the world to be regulated. I do not mean that each legal category should simply replicate differences in the empirical world. Legal rules often draw sharp distinctions when all that life presents is a continuum. But rarely should rules rely on apparently empirical categories that are at odds with informed beliefs about the world.[14] Third, the law should employ criteria that fit with what can be discovered by acceptable methods. If torture and compelled self-incrimination are regarded as unacceptable, it would be mistaken to base legal categorizations on states of mind that can usually be discovered only by these methods. Among possible standards that meet these three threshold criteria, the critical bases for judgment will ordinarily be blameworthiness, deterrence, fairness, appropriate relief, and administrative feasibility.

Factual Perceptions

Criminal liability often depends on the perceived or reasonably perceivable facts.[15] Suppose that Heidi, a hunter, shoots and kills what looks like a deer but turns out to be Joe, who has donned a costume that no one can distinguish from a genuine deer at the distance from which she shoots. If Heidi was certain she was shooting at a deer and had no reason to think otherwise, she will not be liable for any crime. If she somehow knew, or should have known, what Joe was up to, she may be guilty of murder, either "intentionally" killing Joe or acting with extreme recklessness in shooting at him. If Heidi thought, or reasonably would have thought, that her target was *probably* a deer but *might* be Joe, she could be guilty of reckless or negligent homicide. A different problem of perceived and perceivable facts supposes that Heidi shoots and kills Jerry, who is pointing what looks like a gun at Carla and is threatening to shoot Carla. If the gun is real, Heidi's own shooting would be justified[16] and not criminal, but suppose Jerry's "gun" is a fake. Does it matter if Heidi thinks or reasonably thinks the gun was real?

INITIAL COVERAGE

The issue of factual perceptions is most clearly raised when liability is based on taking an unjustifiable risk, and I shall run through some variations on that problem, dealing both with initial liability and with a possible justification. If, when she shoots Joe, Heidi has no idea that she is shooting at a human being instead of a deer, and a reasonable person also would have no idea, then she is essentially like Daisy driving her car, the victim of unfortunate circumstance. She has not committed a crime. But Heidi may be guilty of a crime if she was, or should have been, aware that her target might be a person. Roughly, one can be liable for harmful results if the risk is substantial and unjustifiable and if taking the risk involves a gross departure from how a reasonable person would act.[17] A sport hunter who shoots thinking there is a serious chance that her target is a human being takes a substantial and unjustifiable risk and makes a gross departure from how a reasonable person would act.[18] What conditions should make Heidi punishable or be the basis for distinctions in the seriousness of her offense? If unwise risk taking is ever punished, the clearest case is one in which Heidi is aware of the risk and a reasonable person would also be aware of the risk. What if Heidi's perceptions and those of a reasonable person diverge? Heidi might be aware of the risk—she has a "sixth sense"—although a reasonable person would not be. Establishing her awareness will usually be impossible, so this variation is not of great practical relevance; but if Heidi really does think she may be shooting at a human being, and that can be proven, punishment is appropriate. The important case for consideration is one in which Heidi is not aware of the risk, but a "reasonable person" in Heidi's circumstances would be.[19] Should Heidi be guilty of no crime, of the same crime as if she had been aware of the risk, or of some lesser crime?

Many old cases were not clear whether some actual awareness of risk was a prerequisite for liability for homicide, or at least for reckless homicide. The simple argument for requiring subjective awareness of risk is that crimes involve serious wrongdoing and that a person unaware that he may be causing harm has not done anything morally wrong; therefore, he should not be condemned and punished, even if a serious harm results. The argument for taking the objective view is more complex, emphasizing administrative feasibility and community welfare. Even if the difference between being aware of a risk and not being aware of it is of moral relevance, the attempt of other people to discern what a particular individual thought is very difficult and altogether too complicated for the crude fact-finding methods of criminal trials. Moreover, the criminal law aims to protect the innocent, and deterrence is served by demanding that people measure up to the standards of reasonable people. Therefore, if Heidi has shot in circumstances in which a reasonable person would not have, Heidi should be guilty of the same crime as if she had been aware of the risk.

The intermediate position is straightforward. Because Heidi has acted in a highly dangerous way and caused harm, some punishment is appropriate, but since she is less blameworthy than a similar person aware of the risk, her crime should be less serious. This position probably fits best with how most people feel intuitively; killing someone because one has been careless is a wrong but not as bad a wrong as killing someone in disregard of a conscious risk. The practical implications of this last position may depend on the harm involved. For the most serious harm, death, there may be at least a threefold gradation from negligent to reckless to intentional homicide.[20] For less serious harms, negligent action or even conscious risk taking may not be punished. The modern trend in criminal law is strongly in the direction of treating conscious risk taking as more serious than negligence. Much of the law of torts is quite different. That law concerns itself with who will bear the brunt of a harm. At least if death or direct physical injury is involved, and the choice must be made between the careless actor and the innocent victim, the burden should fall on the careless actor, and that is where the law of torts places it.

Important shades of gray need to be introduced in what I have said thus far. The difference between conscious risk taking and negligence is less in practice than in theory. If subjective risk taking is required for a category of crime, the main evidence for what someone perceived will often be what people in general would have perceived. A jury instructed in terms of subjectively appraised risk may not act too differently from one instructed in terms of objective risk.

Another shade of gray involves preliminary carelessness. The distinction between subjective awareness of risk and failure to be aware calls up visions of one person who perceives something and another who for some inexplicable reason does not. Someone who is driving a car carefully may for one instant fail to see something that he usually would see and that a reasonable person would see. Few people manage to get through life without inadvertent lapses of attention that lead to failures to perceive. Often, however, instances of conscious carelessness accompanied by a vague sense of general risk affect one's ability to perceive particular risks. Suppose that Heidi had not bothered to get the lenses of her glasses changed though she knew she should get a new prescription, or had failed to read a recommended book about hunting safety, or had had a drink to start her morning. She had some notion that a drink, her ignorance, or less-than-ideal glasses could marginally impair her perception, but she did not imagine particular situations or any danger to someone else's life; and at the instant the "deer" appeared, she had no awareness of imperfect perception. As one considers possibilities like these, the distinction between awareness and lack of awareness of risk softens. Forms of carelessness like these may not be sufficient to amount to subjective awareness of a risk on which liability may be imposed,[21] but recognition that particular negligent acts are often the product of self-conscious failures to be careful at some earlier stage strengthens the argument in favor of punishing negligence.[22]

Yet another shade of gray concerns how a "reasonable person" is to be understood when liability rests on negligence. How many of the actor's own characteristics should count? A characterization that is more individualized, more tailored to the actor's own circumstances, is more subjective; a characterization based on people in general is more objective. The appropriate standard certainly includes information acquired by the actor prior to the incident, such as Joe's telling Heidi he plans to roam around in a deer costume. Someone with expert training, such as a doctor, is judged by the perceptions of a reasonable expert, not those of an ordinary person, and distinctive disabilities like blindness are taken into account by the criminal law. On the other hand, the "reasonable person" would not have the actor's moral defects of character (the "reasonable person who is inattentive because he is indifferent") or have engaged in the actor's serious preceding acts of carelessness (the "reasonable person who goes hunting with the wrong eyeglasses"). The harder questions concern more subtle matters of situation, experience, capability, emotional state, and so on.

If criminal liability should depend on moral blameworthiness, perhaps a misperception should be punished only if it really was blameworthy for that individual. In that event, a highly individualized version of the reasonable person might seem desirable, one that took into account all individualizing factors except character defects and preceding carelessness. Then one might speak of "the reasonable driver of ten months' experience, less-than-average intelligence, particular psychological blocks, distracted by three children arguing in the back seat."

Were the standard to be *so* individualized, one might better substitute a formulation regarding failure to perceive that does not involve a "reasonable" construct at all. Liability would simply depend on the actor's failing to respond to a risk that he should have perceived. The theoretical attractiveness of this position is seriously marred by worry about how jurors would determine what is reasonable for people who differ from themselves. The "reasonable person" construct may give the jury more adequate guidance. Someone baffled by the question of just what individual characteristics should be taken into account, and doubtful about how accessible subtle differentiations will be to a jury, might well settle on a reasonable person formulation that leaves some latitude about how objectively or subjectively it is to be taken.

Again, torts is distinctively different from criminal law. The fundamental issues involved in torts are compensation and people's ability to rely on others performing according to standards in the community. For civil recovery in negligence, the argument that the standard of the reasonable person should be mostly objective is more plainly compelling.

POSSIBLE JUSTIFICATIONS

I now shift from initial coverage of a criminal provision to possible justifications for otherwise criminal behavior. Heidi knows she is shooting at Jerry, but she does so to save Carla's life from Jerry's imminent attack with a gun; Jerry's "gun" turns out to be a highly realistic fake. Is Heidi justified? We can imagine at least five possibilities: (1) she is strictly liable, that is, she loses the justification if Jerry was not about to shoot a real gun; (2) her subjective belief exonerates her no matter how unreasonable the belief was; (3) her possible justification depends only on what a person in her place would reasonably have thought; (4) she is justified only if she had an actual belief that the gun was real *and* her belief was reasonable; (5) her justification depends on how her factual perception compares with the standard for factual perceptions for the underlying offense.

We can dispose of the first three alternatives quickly. Strict liability has no place here; if Heidi reasonably thought Jerry was about to shoot Carla, she should not be guilty of murder. On the other hand, Heidi's subjective belief alone should not allow her to get off altogether. Negligent homicide is a crime; if Heidi was negligent in her belief that the gun was real, she is at least liable for negligent homicide. As to the third possibility, if Heidi was sure that Jerry had a toy gun and shot him anyway, she should not escape because a reasonable person would have thought the gun was real.

This leaves us with the last two alternatives. Heidi believed the gun was real; should *any defense* depend on the reasonableness of her belief, or should a defense depend on the elements of the underlying crime? This formulation is a bit abstruse, but a practical application will clarify it. Suppose Heidi's belief is unreasonable. If she loses a defense altogether, she is guilty of murder since she intentionally shot Jerry. If the justification standard fits the elements of the underlying offense, Heidi is not guilty of murder, but she is guilty of negligent homicide. She was sure she had a justification for shooting, but she was carelessly wrong. If she had been hunting and shot Joe believing that he was a deer, she would be guilty only of negligent homicide. Similarly, if she was unreasonably sure that Jerry was a human being whom she should shoot, she would be guilty of negligent homicide and not murder. This last alternative requires subjective belief in relevant facts for a justification; the objective standard of reasonable appraisal comes into play if, and only if, negligence is a basis for liability in the underlying offense.

This approach, adopted by the Model Penal Code and followed by a significant number of states, is set against a lot of history. Under traditional principles, the bases for a justification had to be reasonable or even actually supported by the facts as they turn out.[23] The "reasonableness" approach probably still dominates treatment of claims about justifying facts.

What might be said on behalf of rejecting any claim of justification unless the perception of facts was reasonable? If a mistake is made, an innocent victim bears its brunt, but that does not distinguish justification from the elements of the underlying offense; an innocent victim may be killed if the hunter mistakes a human being for a deer. Among possible arguments for requiring reasonable belief are the following: (1) in many circumstances of possible justification, the actor has done something to bring on the situation; (2) mistakes about justification are likely, especially since a decision must often be made instantaneously; (3) determining someone's actual state of mind when he claims to have perceived extreme circumstances is particularly difficult; (4) some "justifications" are not really justifications but concessions to how most people would react,[24] and these should not be extended further by letting off those whose perceptions are unreasonable.

Insofar as these reasons rely on supposed differences between justifying facts and facts on which basic liability is founded, some systematic empirical study of instances in which mistaken perceptions of both sorts are asserted would be informative. However, imagining empirical results that would warrant the radically different treatment traditionally given the two sorts of factual mistakes is difficult. If actors are sometimes to blame for situations that lead to their claimed justifications, special substantive rules can be developed. If beliefs about justifying facts are especially hard to determine, the burden of proof can be shifted to defendants. If discouraging hasty judgments about justification is important, liability for a crime of negligence should be sufficient.[25] Someone who intentionally shoots with an unreasonable belief in justifying facts should not be treated like someone who knows he lacks any justification.

Two cases of the last decade illustrate how important the degree of individualization is for a standard of reasonable belief, an importance that is, of course, greatest if an honest unreasonable belief provides no defense for even intentional homicide. In one case Jack Abbott, a murderer who had been released from prison after an active campaign on his behalf by Norman Mailer, killed someone with a knife outside a bar after an argument. He claimed that he responded in self-defense to his perception of his victim's movements. Would a characterization of the reasonable person here include Abbott's many years in the violent prison environment, which, it was claimed, led him to interpret movements in this way?[26] In his famous case, Bernhard Goetz was said to fear a serious attack from four youths on a subway, whom he then shot. In this case, would a reasonable person be someone who, like Goetz, had been mugged in the past and who had a psychological make-up like Goetz's?[27] The more individualized the conditions of the reasonable person become, the closer the standard gets to whether this particular person was at fault for not having perceived correctly.

A problem of conceptual terminology accompanies the substantive issue of when a person should be exonerated for acting upon mistakenly believed justifying facts. The problem is both about the most precise terminology and about how a criminal code should be drafted.[28] The obvious competing labels are "justification," a term indicating that action is warranted, and "excuse," a term suggesting that someone who has engaged in unwarranted action is not to blame for it. One possible position is that the term "excuse" is appropriate whenever there is an actual absence of justifying facts. On this view, a person who has acted just as an ideal person would act given available information is only "excused" if the underlying facts turn out to be different from what anyone in the actor's situation could have reasonably supposed. Since the criminal law involves condemnation of individuals and efforts to affect future behavior, it is unfair to label as "excused" rather than "justified" the person who acted ideally, given all available information. Perhaps another phrase that more precisely states the situation, such as "apparently justified" or "justified wrong,"[29] would be desirable, but if one has to choose between "justification" and "excuse," "justification" is far preferable for the person who acts on a reasonable perception. On the other hand, if belief in justifying facts is unreasonable, the more precise designation is "excuse"; from no external perspective has the actor done what he really should have done in the circumstances.

Detached from the provisions of the criminal code, this conceptual problem is straightforward, but the effort to draft statutory provisions complicates it. Suppose a defendant is charged with assault, for which the lowest level of culpability is recklessness. The defendant claims that he believed in facts that would certainly have justified his striking. If culpability for justifications were correlated with culpability for the underlying offense, a jury that believed the defendant would not have to decide whether his perception was reasonable, since negligent striking is not a crime. Perhaps a criminal code should not try carefully to refine categories that will not be employed in actual cases. Dealing with all beliefs in justifying circumstances in broad sections concerned with justifications may thus be defensible.[30]

Quality of Judgment

My second factor, quality of judgment, is not often recognized as distinctive and is a bit hard to explain. Suppose that when Heidi sees Jerry pointing a gun at Carla her perceptions of what may be transpiring and of the likely consequences of intervention are excellent. She has a justification only if her action seems "necessary" to protect Carla. What is *necessary* turns partly on the likelihood that Jerry has a real gun, that he is planning to shoot, and that Heidi could not stop him by other means. This factual assessment is the basis for her decision to shoot, but neither her decision nor an external judgment of necessity is reducible to purely factual components. Suppose Heidi could quantify with exquisite precision. She says: I thought the chance that the gun was real was 55 percent, that if it was real the chance that Jerry would shoot Carla was 60 percent, that if he was planning to shoot, the chance that I could not stop him by yelling at him was 40 percent. Heidi, it turns out, thought there was a 13.2 percent chance that Carla would be shot unless she shot Jerry.

Whether *that likelihood* should be sufficient to shoot Jerry is a normative question, not a factual one.[31] For this question, the criminal law incorporates a normative standard with the term "necessary." The aim is to get people to act in accord with prevailing social values, not their own personal estimates of when harming others is all right. Heidi should not be able to shoot just because she thinks the percentage is high enough, any more than her thinking a risk is reasonable makes it so under a standard of recklessness or negligence. If this analysis is sound, then an objective standard should apply to normative elements of judgments of necessity; for the factual elements concerning likely consequences, whatever degree of subjective and objective components is appropriate for immediate factual perceptions should usually control.[32]

People in emergencies do not think in terms of explicit percentages. What they will say later is something like, "I thought that the gun was probably real and that Jerry would fire it. Shooting seemed the best way to stop him." Ordinary language often mixes the crucial factual and normative elements. From the perspective of neat theory, those applying the law might try to untangle the normative from factual elements, if a partly subjective approach applies to factual elements. But a judge or jury will be hard put to distill Heidi's factual appraisal from her normative one, and it would take an extremely sophisticated understanding to try to accept Heidi's subjective view of the likely consequences while adopting an objective appraisal of the relative values packed into the term "necessary." Imprecision of language combined with the law's relatively crude methods for determining states of mind will lead to some compromise of what might otherwise be a perfect division of subjective and objective appraisal.

Linguistic Understandings

In this section I consider a subject that has less importance for the criminal law than for some other branches of the law: the purport of writings and oral statements with legal significance. I shall concentrate initially on whether contracts and wills are to be given a subjective or objective reading. A subjective approach to linguistic understandings would ask what persons who wrote, subscribed to, or accepted a document's language thought that the document meant. An objective approach would ask how a reasonable person would understand the document. As previously discussed, a reasonable person approach might individualize to some greater or lesser degree by providing sensitivity to context and to certain characteristics of the people involved.

I want first to put aside some complexities which relate to the discussion in Part I. Especially if circumstances have shifted over time since a contract or will was signed, there may have been no subjective understanding of how particular circumstances should be treated. Even as to circumstances envisioned, there may have been no definite understanding about their treatment; the parties may not have focused their attention on a problem or may have implicitly supposed that it remained unresolved. Or the relevant parties may have had different understandings of what the language accomplished. Anyone, such as a judge, who must subsequently interpret a document will to some extent bring his own understanding to bear; he cannot perfectly capture the understandings at the time the document was signed. If a judge attempts to employ the standard of a reasonable reader, he must recognize that there might be a distinction between the reasonable reader's view when the document was issued and a reasonable reader's view when it is interpreted. These are nuances that warrant careful consideration, but I shall move past them to a starker issue.

Judges address most contracts and wills soon enough after their issuance to recapture the original circumstances fairly well, and they can assume that the reading of a reasonable person would not have changed much. Some circumstances actually considered by the people involved may occur in a form not much different from what was imagined. Should the focus of interpretation be the objective significance of the words, that is, what a reasonable person would understand by them, used in context, or should the focus be what the people themselves signified by the words? Suppose *A* and *B* sign a contract and both have the clear sense, revealed to friends, that the particular language means one thing. It turns out that a radically different construction would favor *B* and that a reasonable person would assign that construction rather than the construction originally in the minds (but unspecified in the contract) of both *A* and *B*. If a dispute involves only *A* and *B*, and a judge could be certain of the actual understandings of *A* and *B*, it seems clear that those shared subjective understandings should control, not the "objective" understanding of a reasonable person. It is often said that objective meaning governs the interpretation of contracts, but whether that approach would apply in these circumstances is unclear. The argument for an objective standard even for such situations would have to be: (1) that it is too difficult to ascertain whether an issue in the precise context was really thought about by both people and, if so, how each of them thought about it; (2) that in cases of divided understanding, the understanding of the person who is closer to the reasonable understanding should win; and (3) that to make subjective understandings determinative in the rare cases of shared subjective understandings that deviate from reasonable ones would complicate litigation and produce an unacceptable incentive to lie about what one thought.

For wills, the concerns are a bit different. A substantial purpose of wills is to provide a definite formal statement of a person's intentions, eliminating controversy over what a person close to death really wanted to do with his property. Deciding just what was to count as reliable evidence of a change of heart from the provisions of the will would be extremely difficult, and the incentive to lie would be tremendous if subjective wishes could supplant the provisions of a will. Thus, there are powerful reasons to adhere to wills. On the other hand, since the major purpose of a will is for someone to express his wishes, and others do not justifiably rely on will provisions, which could be changed in any event, construing a will in accord with the writer's wishes makes sense. Still, the difficulty remains of the unreliability of judging what someone "really intended" after that person has died. Letters from him to members of the family, may, for example, not accurately reflect his intentions at the time the will was adopted. If, however, the words are at all vague or ambiguous—for example, a Scotsman with close ties to Scotland and Scottish institutions leaves money to the National Society for the Prevention of Cruelty to Children when there is an institution of that precise name located in London and an institution called the Scottish National Society for the Prevention of Cruelty to Children located in Edinburgh[33]—they should certainly be construed in light of the writer's own background and interests. For contracts as well, some account should be taken of the peculiar background of the parties. But because a will represents only one person, probably some greater bending to the likely subjective wishes of the writer is appropriate.

Similar linguistic understandings can also matter in the criminal law. A written document, to which a person agrees, may indicate how he expects other people to act and may be an undertaking by him to act in a particular way. Sometimes, the expected actions of others (say, whether they will follow prices that one sets) can be a fact relevant to a person's criminal liability. For that purpose, what other people plan to do is treated like other facts. If a person subjectively interprets what others have said to indicate that they will act in a way that would not render his own behavior criminal, he could at most be liable for a crime of negligence. Similarly, if one's own undertaking is to be the basis of liability as an accessory or conspirator, he is not liable for intending to commit a crime if he lacks the subjective intent to commit it, a subject discussed below. In short, a person's understandings of what writings, or oral agreements, signify should be assimilated to his factual perceptions or his intentions.

Understandings of publicly issued authoritative norms are treated differently. A person may be "ignorant" of the law because he is unaware of relevant provisions or because he (or his lawyer) understands a provision in a manner different from its authoritative interpretation. If a person's mistake concerns an independent branch of the law, such as the law of property, his subjective belief that he is authorized to act in a manner that is not actually warranted may excuse. For example, his subjective belief that he owns property will exonerate him from a conviction for theft. If, however, a person is subjectively mistaken about the law of criminal liability, he is guilty. Indeed, even a subjective and reasonable mistake will not excuse. Saying what should count as independent law and what should count as the relevant criminal law is complicated, and the treatment of ignorance of the criminal law is harsh. The logic is that people should learn the criminal law and should not be encouraged to skate too closely to the edges of liability. If a subjective reasonable mistake excused, then a court that decided that a provision meant one thing would also have to decide what other interpretations were reasonable. And could it comfortably say that a lay client had an unreasonable understanding if that understanding had been offered to the client by a lawyer? Were a lawyer's advice to exonerate, by establishing that a client's mistake was reasonable, clever clients might shop around to find lawyers who would give the interpretations with that effect. For most circumstances, the rule that ignorance of the law does not excuse may be appropriate, but the rule can work unfair results. It certainly deserves at least the qualification it has received in some jurisdictions where people can rely on earlier authoritative court decisions or other official statements of what the law provides.

Other central questions about subjective or objective approaches to linguistic understandings concern judicial interpretation of statutes and constitutional provisions, but I leave that vast topic for another place.

Immediate Aims/Intentions

Many crimes, and some torts, are defined in terms of what a person intended. Oliver Wendell Holmes favored a completely objective view of intention for most torts and crimes, taking a different view only about requirements of specific intent. According to a wholly objective view, a person "intends the natural consequences of his act," that is, he is taken to have intended what an ordinary person who performed the same acts would have intended.[34] This approach simplifies fact-finding and may be thought to encourage people to behave according to minimum standards. Under a subjective view, a person intends only what he is actually trying to accomplish. If, to take the facts of a well-known English case,[35] I drive my automobile so that a police officer will be thrown off, I intend to kill or injure him only if that is my actual purpose. This approach better correlates criminal liability with moral blameworthiness. The substantive question for law is whether someone who does not have a subjective intent to cause harm should be treated the same as one who does; the terminological question is whether that person should be spoken of as having "intended" the result. A partially individualized standard is an intermediate possibility, for example, what a blind person or a person of very low intelligence or a Greek woman would intend by such an action.[36] But I shall not discuss this alternative in detail, because it is now widely agreed that crimes, if not torts, of intention do require some subjective intention.

The troublesome issues arise over *how much* one should be taken to have intended if one intends some result related to what has occurred. In expanding what one has intended, the law may adopt a kind of intermediate position between a completely subjective approach and an objective one. At the very least, one is taken to intend what one knows on reflection is indistinguishable in effect from what one actually intends. For example, if one aims to stop an assailant by shooting him, one intends bodily injury at least, even though one does not think about bodily injury at the moment of shooting. Intent is also taken to extend to almost certain consequences. A terrorist who wants to assassinate an ambassador plants a bomb in the ambassador's automobile and explodes the bomb as the car is being driven toward the ambassador's office. Has the terrorist "intended" to kill the driver? If he is virtually certain the driver will die, the terrorist should be treated like someone who aims at the driver's death, although he is indifferent to whether it occurs. Suppose that the ambassador has stayed home ill, and the other person killed by the bomb is a companion sent ahead with documents. As to the companion, it is supposed that if one is aiming to kill one person and ends up killing another instead, he should be treated the same way as if he killed his target. That judgment often used to be put in the form that "'intent' to kill is 'transfered' to the actual victim."

The notion that one intends virtually certain consequences might be extended to highly probable consequences, and perhaps something like this notion has underlain the traditional doctrine that one is guilty of intentional homicide if he intends to do serious bodily harm and death results. Viewed from the subjective perspective, this extension of intent might be regarded more precisely as relying on a combination of intent to achieve one harm and in addition extreme recklessness as to the result of death. Since extreme recklessness (depraved indifference) that leads to death is commonly punishable by the same penalties as intentional homicide, this reformulation would not affect the seriousness of the crime in the ordinary instance. Extreme recklessness toward actual victims is also usually present when persons other than intended victims die.

As they have typically operated, neither the doctrine regarding aim to do serious bodily harm nor transferred intent has been constrained by an extreme recklessness requirement. Even if the actor is such an expert shot that he is sure he can wound rather than kill, or feels certain there is no risk to any but his intended target, he is guilty of intentional homicide if a death he does not wish results. In the case of another person's death, the aim to kill and resulting death of someone seem a sufficient basis for treating the actor like someone who successfully kills his intended victim. The case where only wounding was desired is more difficult; perhaps, then, the actor should be guilty only of assault with a deadly weapon and negligent homicide. On the other hand, the criminal process is not well suited to sift claims that, "I wanted only to wound and I was confident in my ability." It is hardly surprising that these subtle distinctions have not been fully reflected in the legal materials, which have colored an essentially subjective approach with objective criteria of liability. A precise system of labeling could restrict intent to consequences actually aimed at, and some modern codes avoid the conceptual difficulties of a loose notion of "intent" by explicitly imposing liability for death in these settings by particular substantive or causation provisions.

A different problem about subjective intent and objective manifestations is raised by the law of "inchoate" crimes. When can action that is undertaken with a criminal intent be punished if harmful external behavior has yet to occur? This problem is peculiar for the criminal law because other branches of the law do not often concern themselves with planned acts that do not occur. Criminal liability is pushed back from the ultimate harm that is feared by provisions punishing attempts, solicitations, and conspiracies, and by separate provisions forbidding behavior that is preliminary to doing harm, such as possessing illegal weapons or burglar's tools. If the connection is great enough between clearly defined acts that are harmless in themselves and later harmful illegal acts (for example, if seven out of ten privately possessed machine guns are eventually used to commit crimes), few doubt that making the preliminary behavior illegal is appropriate. In instances of solicitation and conspiracy, an actor has engaged in external behavior—speaking or agreeing—that clearly manifests a criminal purpose and precedes harmful behavior.

The most troublesome question about objective and subjective elements concerns simple attempt liability when someone has done some preliminary things, such as rent a car and plan an escape route, which taken by themselves are innocent, with the intent to engage in subsequent acts that will constitute the crime.[37] Some people doubt the appropriateness of liability even when the performed acts together reveal the criminal objective that is being pursued. The concern is that those heading toward crimes might change their minds and should have a chance to do so. A special issue may be thought to be raised when acts that are innocent in themselves, and innocent appearing, are linked with a state of mind to establish a criminal objective. The theoretical argument against liability is that it falls too close to punishing thoughts alone, that instead the law should deal only with noninnocent external manifestations. The contrary view is that a subjective intent to commit a crime plus even "innocent" external acts is enough for punishment. If one accepts punishment for words of solicitation and conspiracy, and one acknowledges that actions lie on a continuum from those that appear to be definitely innocent, to probably innocent, to probably noninnocent, to almost certainly noninnocent, there seems to be no proper objection to punishment if the actor has moved a long way toward committing the crime, if the evidence of criminal purpose is patently clear—for example, a letter to a friend expresses criminal aims, and if establishing liability is not likely to lead to police or prosecutorial abuse in other cases.

Ultimate Motivations

For the most part, the law, or at least the criminal law, disregards an actor's ultimate motivation. It is a traditional saying about the law that it considers intent but not motivation. No clear line exists between the two, and crimes often make relevant hoped-for results and nonimmediate objectives,[38] but the saying about intent and motivation distills two important and general truths. One is that the law generally does not focus on what one hopes to accomplish indirectly and in the long run. If someone assaults a man without legal justification, it will not be relevant that he hopes to discourage the man from seeing his sister and making her unhappy. The other point is that one's general attitudes and perspectives do not matter if one intends a prohibited result. For the basic law of crimes, intentionally killing someone out of motives of love in an effort to relieve suffering may be the same as killing someone in the pursuit of selfish advantage. (As this illustration shows, legal definitions themselves largely determine what aspect of an act counts; a law might authorize relief of suffering, making the intentional causing of death in such efforts unimportant legally.) A feature of law's objectivity is its focus on an event, with a view constrained by legal categories. Ordinarily, the criminal law declines to view situations in their complete contexts.

This picture is softened in various ways. Many considerations that do not find a place in the formal substantive law do figure in sentencing decisions, in prosecutorial decisions to charge lesser offenses or not to charge at all, in jury nullification, and in the exercise of police discretion. As administered, the law is much more individualized and subjective, more attentive to ultimate motivations, than in its definitions of crimes. Further, some substantive doctrines do take a broader account of the situation than ordinary criminal provisions. The balancing of likely harms and benefits that concepts of recklessness and negligence involve permits a fairly wide inquiry into overall objectives. And the general justification and duress defenses consider the broad reasons for actions that violate the standard catalog of crimes. Some particular crimes take into account ulterior objectives, such as whether by publishing information one hopes to aid the enemy. Finally, various excuses from liability based on conscientious objection exonerate those who have particular motives for failing to comply with some laws.

Control

In some instances an actor's complete or partial defense is that his performance of criminal acts was caused by his lack of control over his behavior. Perhaps the most critical issues about "lack of control" concern the insanity defense, but I shall not discuss it. For it, the "control" issue is hard to disentangle from claims of cognitive misperception or failures to understand, and if an explicit "control" criterion is desirable, few doubt that it should be primarily subjective, concentrating on the particular defendant. Thus, I shall discuss the duress defense and the mitigation provided by provocation or emotional distress. These present clearer issues about objective and subjective elements.

According to the duress defense, one is not guilty if one has performed a criminal act under the compulsion of another's threat. Sometimes yielding to a threat is actually a better course of action—one should steal an automobile rather than ignore a credible threat that three innocent people will be killed if one does not. Depending on exactly how the defenses are defined, the duress defense may overlap with the general justification defense. I shall consider only instances when yielding to the threat is not preferable. The defendant then argues: "It would have been better if I had had the courage to resist the threat, but I am not to blame for yielding to it."

Clearly, a subjective yielding to the threat is a *necessary* element of the defense. Someone who is threatened could not rely on the defense[39] if he says to himself: "Well, I've always wanted to commit this assault on an acquaintance; the particular threat of what will happen to me unless I do that does not scare me, but this is a good occasion to commit the crime."

The defense is often conceived as involving an overwhelming of one's reason. The emotional turmoil that accompanies being threatened does distort choice, but emotional upset is not a required aspect of being under duress. One might coolly decide that one is unwilling to risk some harm to those one cares about most even if one realizes that what one does, for example, commit perjury in favor of a murderer, would not be regarded as preferable to resisting the threat and notifying the police.

How much of an objective standard should be imported into the duress defense? It cannot be enough that one has been subject to a threat and has yielded. In that event, someone who simply puts little value on the interests of others would be excused for giving way to a slight threat. A person's choice will be determined by the magnitude of the threat and the power for him of norms not to violate the law and hurt others. A person should not be excused because he cares less than most people about observing legal norms. The power of norms of law-abiding behavior should be judged by an objective standard, probably that of people in general, but conceivably that of some subgroup of the population not categorized by a willingness to break the law.

It is initially tempting to say that the magnitude of the threat ideally should be judged by a subjective standard. I happen to hate hypodermic injections; I would rather have my teeth drilled than have an injection. Many people would prefer to be injected many times over than pay a visit to the dentist. Those various feelings are morally neutral. If I were threatened that I would be held down and given one hundred injections, that would be a "worse" threat for me than for many other people, and it would be a worse threat even if I were capable of coolly considering how unpleasant the experience would be. It would seem that a person who yields should be able to rely on the terror the threat holds for him. But matters are not so simple. Suppose the threat is that I will be disgraced, and I commit a crime that most people would not commit even if threatened with disgrace. I say that I am especially sensitive to my disgrace. Is this like fearing injections or does it just mean I am less willing to sacrifice any selfish interest of my own that most people? If I am just more selfish I should not be excused.[40] In theory, honest responses to a range of hypothetical threats might test this, but a jury in a criminal case will be hard put to figure out if heightened fear or selfishness is operating. Indeed, the jury cannot gauge how much of a reaction is caused by enhanced fear of the threat and how much by comparative willingness to sacrifice the interests of others. Even in theory, these dimensions are hardly distinguishable if the explanation is greater-than-average selfishness. Usually, jurors will have to rely on their sense of when an ordinary person would yield.[41] In practice, then, the law will have to be much rougher than what some nice theoretical distinctions between objective and subjective components might suggest.

One way to ensure that the threat is serious enough is explicitly to limit the defense to specific, very serious threats, such as threats to life, and this was a common approach historically. But such a constraint is too rigid and ungenerous. A sensible approach that lacks this kind of arbitrariness is a formulation that speaks of yielding to a threat that a person of ordinary moral capacities would not have resisted. This is an essentially objective standard but one that leaves jurors free to take account of special features of the actor's situation that do not concern his overall selfishness and other moral strengths or failings. This terminology is preferable to talk of "reasonable people" since such people might be conceived as less subject to emotional stress than most. It is also preferable to talk about people of "ordinary firmness" because the selfish person's willingness to accede to a threat need not be a matter of lack of firmness to resist consequences about which the actor cares.

An alternative approach would be to give the defense to those who cannot be blamed for yielding to a threat. This cast would be more subjective, but would still permit the jury to decide that one could be blamed if one's giving in to the threat was the result of moral failings. If one takes the view, as I do, that yielding to threats is not to be encouraged, one might opt for a stricter, more objective approach that seems ideally suitable to judge the actor who has already yielded.

Provocation or emotional distress is a mitigation; one who kills intentionally in the heat of passion may be liable only for manslaughter. I shall pass over the important point that in such situations a person may strike unthinkingly without subjectively "intending" either death or serious bodily harm and concentrate on the conditions for mitigation from murder to manslaughter.

An argument against any but the narrowest mitigation is that if the defense is too generous, deterrent effect will be sacrificed. Since manslaughter itself is a very serious crime, *and* in instances when the mitigation is claimed, few people achieve any long-term promotion of their interests by killing, successful invocation of the defense cannot much affect *rational deterrence*, though it may influence deep-seated attitudes about the outside range of acceptable reactions for an outraged person.

Much of the discussion of this mitigation has concerned whether it should be limited in very precise ways. In some jurisdictions, for example, the act that stirred the passions had to be a provocation by the victim, the act had to be more than words, and the crime had to follow closely upon the provocation, in the heat of passion. These various limits set out particular external conditions that had to be satisfied for the mitigation to arise. But we can quickly see that they represented, in some sense, an "objective" approach. By taking the most frequent sorts of cases, the things likely to provoke most people, and disqualifying other causes, the limits curtailed claims of special sensitivity. The modern tendency is toward a more extended defense that covers other causes of emotional distress, that does not by fiat exclude words or anything else as a possible source, and that reaches the person who acts after brooding as well as the one who acts immediately. I shall take for brief examination this more generous form of the defense and ask whether it should be understood in subjective or objective form.

As with duress, clearly there is a subjective requisite; a person must have been deeply unsettled emotionally and that must have led to his committing homicide. The issue is how far the defense should also require that some "objective" standard be satisfied. Exactly *what* the objective standard would involve here is itself tricky. Ordinary people do not commit homicide under provocation or emotional distress. Any "ordinary person" standard must refer to circumstances that would cause severe emotional upset and substantial loss of control. An objective standard in these terms would allow the defense only when the triggering event would have such effects on ordinary people. A purely subjective defense would provide the mitigation whenever severe emotional distress caused a lack of control that led to a homicide being committed. The relevant considerations closely resemble those discussed for duress. If the homicide results because one is indifferent to human life on that occasion or because one's general indifference to social norms and the interests of others has led one never to try to develop any self-control, the mitigation should not be available. On the other hand, if one has an especially powerful emotional reaction to the triggering event or one's overall lack of control is something for which one is not responsible (say one is required to take medication that weakens self-control), then granting the defense would seem appropriate though one's reactions do not conform to those of an ordinary person. In this context, it should be relevant if one is a member of some cultural subgroup that treats certain events (say, being spat upon) as much more disturbing than the population at large treats them.

As with many previous illustrations, distinctions in theory outrun the capacities of legal institutions. Special reactions to triggering events are one thing, but how can jurors decide whether an excessive lack of control shows a failure of personal responsibility or not? The best outcome may be to permit the jury to make an overall judgment about the responsibility of the defendant, taking into account the subjective factors that seem relevant. The Model Penal Code talks of a "reasonable explanation or excuse" for the defendant's extreme mental or emotional disturbance.[42] Reasonable explanation here connotes more than a coherent description, such as: "The defendant has always cultivated an attitude of wildness that his extreme anger this time fits perfectly." Rather, the phrase "reasonable explanation or excuse" envisions some moral judgment by the jurors about defendant's culpability. To a limited extent, this means measuring the defendant against other people and introduces a note of objectivity in an approach that is predominantly subjective.

Conclusion

Although I have drawn a few summary conclusions, that has not been the main point of this exercise. Even for narrow aspects of criminal law, we have seen how highly complex are the questions about objective and subjective approaches. If we turned to all of criminal law, to torts, to contracts, to wills, to constitutional law, to corporations, to criminal and civil procedure, complexities and the plausible variations would multiply. Law *is* more objective than religion and morality, but subjective elements are also important. The best mix of elements will vary for different legal rules; it will rest not only on ideal distinctions but also on what people applying the law are able to discern.

7

Fairness in Classification

This chapter explores a different sense in which the law as it affects people might be considered "objective." A legal category may be said to be "objective," rather than arbitrary or unfair. Laws and practices are often regarded as arbitrary or unfair because of the way in which they affect different groups. Of course, every classification treats some groups differently from others: a law against murder treats the group of people who intentionally kill other people worse than the group that does not kill people. But what is objected to as unfair or arbitrary is when the law's unfavorable treatment of a group has no significant relation to a proper purpose of the legal classification. I shall concentrate on laws or practices that treat women or blacks differently from men or whites respectively. I shall ask first whether overt classification in such terms can be defended and then inquire whether laws not drawn in such terms may be condemned because of their differential effects.

Criteria of Race and Gender

Legal classification by race and gender was once deemed acceptable. By now, the attack on explicit use of race and gender has carried the day with few exceptions. The main exception concerns efforts to redress prior discrimination against minority groups and women by affording them some kind of preferential treatment. Such classifications have been the subject of extensive litigation. A few other explicit gender classifications survive, the most notable being in crimes of sexual violence and in the exclusion of women from draft registration and from combat service in the army, navy, and air force, but for the most part explicit legislative classification in terms of race and gender has been eliminated.

I begin with what may seem like a digression: a consideration of noncorrective use of criteria of race and gender by private citizens. I then discuss whether it is appropriate for officers of the law to employ those criteria except for corrective purposes. I briefly treat corrective classifications. Finally, I consider official recognition of the legitimacy of private use of criteria of race and gender.

Private Use

The most troublesome questions about private use of classifications concern actions based on intrinsically relevant and accurate generalizations that result in comparatively unfavorable treatment or low regard for groups that are already disadvantaged.[1] The practical moral question is whether people should feel free to rely on such generalizations. Subsidiary questions of terminology concern labels such as "discrimination," "prejudice," "bias," or "unfairness" for action that is based on the generalizations.

The idea of action based on an intrinsically relevant and accurate generalization needs some explication. Someone might act out of simple hostility or dislike for members of another group. That would not be reliance on a relevant generalization. If, instead, the person attributes to members of the group some negative characteristic that is relevant, reliance on the generalization may still be unwarranted, for one of at least three reasons. The easiest instance is when no basis exists for any generalization on the supposed lines. An employer believes that more Catholics are lazy at work than are members of other religious groups. It turns out that Catholics are as industrious as the rest of the population, and no evidence suggests the contrary; the employer is obviously mistaken to conclude that "Catholics are lazy at work."

The second way in which a generalization can be unwarranted is when a person assumes that all or most members of a group possess a characteristic that is present only in a much smaller percentage of the members. Suppose that a higher percentage of Catholics than non-Catholics were actually lazy at work and that *some* generalization in these terms were therefore accurate; nevertheless, it would be silly to believe that all or most Catholics are lazy or that one particular Catholic applying for work will be lazy if given the job.

The third way in which a generalization can be unwarranted is closely connected to the second. Suppose that there is a factual grounding for the generalization, and that the person relying on the generalization is aware of the relevant proportions—for example, that 15 percent of Catholics are lazy at work and that eight percent of non-Catholics are lazy at work. Still, the generalization is unwarranted in the sense of being unhelpful and illegitimate as a basis for decision if other more dispositive factors are discernible. An applicant's Catholicism would not constitute a sensible reason against hiring her if an initial individualized evaluation were easily feasible or if the job had a high turnover rate—as at McDonald's—and lazy employees could be dismissed with little inconvenience to the firm. Even in the absence of feasible individual evaluation, there might be further subcategorization. If the applicant is an Italian Catholic and studies show that only 6 percent of this smaller group are lazy at work, the employer has no rational basis for hiring an otherwise similar non-Catholic instead.

But let us suppose that the generalization is warranted in the sense that it is accurate, that it bears intrinsically on how one should behave, and that an individualized evaluation is not possible or is not reasonably feasible.

Consider the following example:

> Dressed well, Max, a white American male, is walking down a sidewalk on a city street in the United States. Approaching are three male strangers in their late teens or early twenties, dressed pretty roughly, obviously together, and making some noise. No one else is close by on that side of the street. Max is aware that the probability is very high that he could just walk by and nothing would happen, but he fears that he might be mugged (i.e., force will be used or threatened against him to get his money) or that he will be "asked" for money in circumstances in which he would reasonably fear the use of force if he refuses (to simplify, I shall include this as a kind of mugging, though it falls short of that). Max is also aware that if he crosses the street, he will almost surely avoid that risk, since he is nearly certain these young men will not chase after him. His intuitive decision involves weighing his estimated degree of risk against the inconvenience of crossing the street, perhaps some embarrassment at acting in that way, and perhaps some worry that his avoiding the three approaching youths might hurt or anger them, or somehow wrong them in another respect.

Would it necessarily be wrong for Max to cross the street if all three youths are black but not to do so if all are white, assuming that dress, noise, and so forth, are similar, that the only distinguishing feature in the situation is the race of the three young men? Let us suppose that when economic class is held constant, the evidence suggests that a significantly higher percentage of black youths than white youths uses drugs whose expense necessitates theft or robbery, that a significantly higher percentage of black youths than white youths in Max's city do, in fact, mug pedestrians. I do not know if such a generalization is accurate for some American cities. Even if it appears to be supported by crime statistics, uneven enforcement by the police and courts could be the reason. If such a generalization is accurate, the deep explanation for it may lie in long years of unfair treatment of blacks by whites. But whatever the explanation, if the generalization *is* accurate, the apparent chances of Max being mugged are greater if the approaching youths are black. It is at least possible that the increase in probability is enough to get over the threshold level for crossing the street—say the chances of getting mugged if the approaching youths are black is one in a thousand, if white, one in two thousand. If we assume that the danger of being mugged by approaching strangers could ever be great enough to warrant the minor inconvenience of crossing the street, and we acknowledge that this is not a situation for prior individualized evaluation, it might be rational from a self-interested point of view for someone, white or black, with no negative or hostile feelings toward blacks to cross the street if the approaching youths are black but not if they are white.

Why might it be argued that Max, nevertheless, *should not* self-consciously take race into account? First, not only may the relevant evidence be unreliable, objective bases for judgment may be swamped by images of blacks based on social prejudice. Inappropriate racial attitudes in the society at large may affect what information is made available to us; our own inappropriate racial attitudes may affect what information we retain and what information we forget. And when we need to act, we may be unable to use information accurately, both because human beings are notoriously crude in their probabilistic judgments and because they are even cruder when emotions of fear and prejudice are tapped. We might well recognize that in this society none of us is capable of detached judgments on this subject and we should be extremely suspicious of our "intuitions." Perhaps we all should try to teach ourselves not to act on generalizations when the risk of corrupted or blurred judgment is so great.

A second point is related. If people act on such generalizations, that choice and action may contribute to future habits of making distinctions between whites and blacks when an objective basis is lacking; it may be dangerous for us to indulge ourselves, even if this once we are pretty confident the judgment in isolation makes sense, and we are right about that.

The third point can also be very significant. If Max can *really* cross the street unobserved or can avoid revealing his motive, he need not worry about the effect of his actions on others.[2] But if the reason for the crossing seems apparent, it may reinforce the prejudices of observers. More important, think of the three approaching black youths. The high probability is that they are not muggers. How will they feel if they see a pedestrian avoiding them and they are fairly sure that would not be happening if they were white? Will they react psychologically as if this were just a rational calculation implying nothing about their personal qualities? Occasionally, events have called for moderately strong security measures on the Columbia campus. I know I *feel* that being asked for identification is a kind of personal affront, even when I approve of the security measures, and even when the officer asking for identification is a stranger. I am fairly sure that a black youth who is avoided by a person he will never see again for reasons he cannot determine is going to feel that avoidance as involving a negative reaction toward him. He will feel, moreover, that the negative reaction is based partly on a characteristic he is incapable of altering. I will not try to spell out various effects, but we can imagine how repeated instances of this kind reinforce patterns of prejudice and feelings of inferiority, resentment, and hostility. We *might* conclude that even a pedestrian who is confident that his basis for using the standard is an accurate generalization and who has no opportunity for individualization, would act in a morally preferable way if he declined to employ a racial standard. A sensible concern about mixed judgments and destructive effects should make us troubled about racially based actions in this context.

In common usage and in most systematic approaches to moral evaluation, an act may be morally less preferable than another without being "wrong." Someone might say, "Since Max was genuinely afraid of being mugged, a dangerous, terrifying, and disturbing experience, I really cannot blame him for crossing the street. Doing so was not really *wrong*. But it would have been better if he had chosen not to do it." To conclude that Max's crossing the street would be morally wrong is, thus, a step beyond concluding that it was morally less preferable than the alternative.

In respect to possible wrongness or moral preferability, reliance on gender and age criteria may be interestingly compared with reliance on race. Suppose the three people approaching Max were otherwise the same but were young women of the same age or men over sixty. I assume that overwhelming evidence indicates that smaller percentages of young women and old men commit muggings than the percentage of young men who do so. Few would regard it as wrong for Max to take age and gender into account. Part of the reason may be that young men who are avoided will not be affronted or subject to socially destructive feelings if they understand that women and older men would not be similarly avoided.[3]

It would be convenient if we had clear labels that fit the various moral judgments that might be made about Max's conduct. Unfortunately, the terms "discriminate," "bias," and "prejudice" do not neatly correlate with those judgments. Each has powerful overtones and a highly uncertain range of application. Without trying to elaborate systematic standards for the usage of these terms, I shall mention some of the difficulties and suggest a few guides for clarification. One tangle involves the distinction between the individual actor and the sources on which he relies. Imagine that the statistics about mugging are highly inaccurate, but that Max has no reason to be aware of the inaccuracy. We might be disposed to say that what Max has done is wrong and based on "bias," although Max himself is not subject to blame and has not acted from bias. I am going to cut through these subjective–objective problems by limiting myself to instances when the responsibility for any informational mistakes or failures of moral sensitivity falls on the person making the choice to take race or gender into account.

The word "discriminate" is sometimes used simply to mean "perceive a difference" or "treat differently" ("the director discriminates among her dancers in setting exercises for practice"). There need be no implication that some are treated *less favorably* than others. In most discussions of social issues, however, to say that someone is discriminating is at least to say that he is treating one group worse than another. Still, the term need not entail condemnation ("our law school admissions process discriminates against those with poor college grades"). Use of the term "discriminate" often implies, further, that the basis for differentiation is not closely related to the benefit or burden. Even in this sense, the term is not invariably used to condemn; people who think special benefits for veterans are appropriate may talk of discrimination in favor of veterans. Sometimes condemnation is implied ("That's discrimination!"). If Max takes race, gender, and age (and one might add dress and loudness) into account in deciding to cross the street, he is discriminating on those bases.

Is he discriminating against any group? Being avoided is far from the loss of a clear benefit like a job, but we may think of two strangers passing close to each other on a lonely street as displaying a kind of mutual confidence in each other's civility. People who are avoided are deprived of this minimal, positive transaction. Whether Max's categorization has objective relevance for his act of avoidance will depend on the probabilistic evidence. Whether his reliance on a category is deemed wrong or morally less preferable will depend on a complex value judgment about his moral rights and his interests and those of the three approaching strangers. What should an observer say if he believes Max was warranted in making a judgment based on race? Since the word "discriminate" so easily calls up condemnation, he should either phrase his conclusions without employing that word or should carefully say something explicit like: "Max's avoidance did discriminate against blacks, but his reliance on a racial classification was justified in the circumstances."

Application of the terms "prejudice" and "bias" is perhaps even more complicated. I shall pass over the person who acts out of hatred or from a suspicion that he does not suppose has any objective grounding relevant to his choice. That person certainly acts out of "prejudice" and modern use of the term "bias" covers him as well. Both terms also apply to the person who thinks he has an objective basis but, through his own fault, is suffering a clear misperception about relevant facts. In common dictionary definitions, there is a subtle distinction between prejudice and bias. "Prejudice" involves a judgment or opinion formed before the facts are known or held in disregard of facts;[4] "bias" is a mental leaning or inclination, a propensity that does not leave the mind indifferent.[5] Perhaps "prejudice" suggests a degree of willfulness that need not be present for "bias," but rather than trying to tease out various situations in which one term might apply but not the other, I shall concentrate on two major questions about the term "bias" as it applies to choices based on probabilistic estimates. (Similar questions may be raised about "prejudice.") The first question involves the grounds on which a person may be said to be biased because of the information on which he acts: specifically, when may a failure to acquire further information constitute bias? The second question is whether failures that involve rational choices in light of adequate and accurate information may nevertheless be biased.

Since treatment of the second question illuminates what is at stake in the first, I begin with it. Let us suppose that Max has all the relevant information and assesses it in a detached way. His choice to cross the street based partly on the race of the three approaching youths is, in light of the probabilities, in his rational self-interest. His choice to prefer his own interest would be the same regardless of which particular group might suffer from his action. However, because of the hurt done to the youths, the choice is, overall, less preferable than the alternative and perhaps even wrong. Has Max acted out of "bias" in preferring his own welfare to the general social interest? Some people are inclined to say yes, at least if Max's action is to the detriment of a disadvantaged group. On this view, "bias" becomes a term that sums up the moral judgment either that Max acted "wrongly" or that the alternative action would have been morally preferable.[6]

I believe a narrower usage is preferable. Max has no particular animosity toward blacks; he just prefers minimizing risks to himself when that involves some costs to others. "Bias" has traditionally involved more than general selfishness; it has involved either animosity or some failure of understanding. This can be illustrated by a common circumstance in which the term is used. A law school faculty hires a male applicant in preference to a female. The choice is one that *might* have been made by a group without a preference for males over females, but such choices are also made by groups that unfairly evaluate the abilities of women. The rejected applicant asks, "Do you think the faculty is biased against women?" In this context, she is not asking whether on balance it was socially undesirable or wrong to hire a man, she is asking whether her abilities were unfairly evaluated because she was a woman. If "bias" becomes a general term for undesirable choices in respect to groups, this distinctive meaning would be lost. A related concern is that "bias" has a strong condemnatory tone. To turn all disagreements about acceptable use of categories of race and gender into issues of whether people are "biased" is to inflate rhetoric and obscure various bases of disagreement.

I turn now to the situation in which a person, say an employer, acts on the basis of information that is accurate as far as it goes; he has consciously chosen not to acquire further information that would permit more individualized decisions. If the failure to find out more is without rational foundation, then the employer acts out of "bias" toward those who suffer from the crude categorization he uses. But suppose the employer says, "Getting more information would cost me more than it would gain. My rational self-interest is served by my acting on the crude data that I now have." If the crude information is used for actions that harm disadvantaged groups, there are strong social reasons for employers to get more information, even when that is more costly than their selfish interests warrant.[7] Does the employer's self-conscious choice to prefer self-interest to social interest amount to bias? In one sense, this question is similar to the one just addressed about Max, but the employer's failure goes to the kind of information he has and relies upon. Since bias concerns a mental leaning, and the employer's failure results in a mental leaning he should not have, I believe the term properly applies to this sort of failure. In summary, when a person wrongfully chooses rational self-interest over social interest (and would do the same were other groups involved), "bias" is involved only when the failure reaches to the person's understanding of the relevant facts.

Government Use

The law of child custody in divorce cases has, under the impetus of equal protection decisions on gender classifications, moved to equal treatment of male and female parents. At least, that is the theory. No doubt many judges still end up employing their own senses of gender differences as they dispose of cases, but what they do not say is, "I am awarding you custody of this child because you are a woman." If we can forget about the law for a moment, would it necessarily be wrong for a judge to act on that basis?

Imagine the following case:

> A couple has a twelve-year-old girl and a ten-year-old boy. Both parents have worked for the last eight years and household and child care responsibilities have been about equally divided. The parents have similar jobs. Both have established economically secure living arrangements, and on the basis of character and behavior there is nothing relevant to distinguish them. The judge concludes that looked at as individuals their claim to the children is equally strong.[8] The couple is adamant that it does not want joint custody and that both children should stay together. The judge is aware that whichever parent gets custody will have considerably more substantial family demands on his or her time than have existed when these were shared. The judge has read studies indicating that when a choice must be made between career and family demands, a much higher percentage of women than men will sacrifice career. The studies suggest that the conclusion holds even when such propensities cannot be discerned in advance by any individualized inquiry of which a judge is capable.

Could the judge take the following position? "On everything individual, the parents' claims are equal. I do not know if the usual gender pattern will be followed here, but it is rational to think, despite the lack of existing individualized evidence, that the woman would *probably* devote more energies to the children than would the man, and *probably* the children would benefit from that attention. Therefore, I'll award custody to the woman."

As with the street-crossing example, this seems a rational choice if the objective is to make the decision most likely to serve the interests of the children involved. For reasons just given, I would say the decision is not necessarily "biased." Nevertheless, we can certainly see bases for denying the propriety of such a choice. Again, we have the problem of irrational stereotypes mixing with objective evidence as bases for decision; we have the worry that each party, and the children, will feel that the determining factor is gender; we have a decision that will reinforce patterns of role allocation that may have largely resulted from male domination. *And*, an official of the state is making the decision. The message sent by a custody disposition based on gender is immensely more powerful than the message of a private citizen's crossing the street. Officials have a special responsibility to take into account the social order their decisions will create. There is a strong argument that gender, by itself, should be denied to officials as a basis for decision in a case like this, *even if* using that basis could slightly increase the predicted welfare of children in the individual case.[9]

In the criminal process, judgments may be made that rely in part on race or gender when police decide whether to question people, whether to make a stop and frisk and whether to arrest. When one considers the vastly greater proportion of crimes, especially violent crimes, that men commit, there can be little doubt that gender figures in police decisions to intervene. No doubt, race often figures as well, and when one takes into account the diverse racial compositions of neighborhoods, there will be at least some occasions when race is objectively relevant to whether someone's presence and actions appear suspicious. Nevertheless, the dangers of explicit reliance on racial criteria are serious enough so that police should be encouraged to try to act in a "racially blind" manner,[10] and whatever the police may do on the street, courts should certainly not endorse the idea that racial factors alone are sufficient to bring judgments to interfere over the threshold of probable cause (necessary to arrest) or reasonable suspicion (necessary for a stop and frisk).

Corrective Classifications

By corrective classifications, I mean roughly classifications that reverse prior patterns of discrimination in order to correct their effects. Typically, criteria are used that are not immediately relevant to the underlying reason for choice, but with the aim somehow to make up for the use of similar criteria in the past. For example, being a member of a minority group or a woman is counted positively in a decision who shall be admitted to graduate school or hired for a job.

In some situations, especially educational ones, it can be argued that favoring women and minorities *is* immediately relevant to the reason for choice. For example, members of law school communities often say that a woman is "better qualified" to be a law professor than a man with similar credentials because there are now relatively few female professors, women can learn more effectively if there are more women teaching them, and all students will benefit from hearing women's perspectives that male professors are incapable, or less capable, of conveying. I want to put such "direct qualifications" arguments aside[11] and concentrate on other possible grounds for preference.

The use of criteria of race and gender is unfair when minorities and women are the victims; is the use of such criteria unfair when minorities and women are the beneficiaries? If the entity involved is a government agency, the question of unfairness is also a constitutional question: does the corrective use of these criteria violate equal protection of the laws? During the past decade and a half this issue has been highly controversial, and under the Reagan Administration the position of the Department of Justice[12] shifted from support of corrective classification to sharp opposition. Excluded whites and males claim the use of corrective classifications is unfair; minorities and women who would benefit argue that not correcting the terrible effects of past and continuing discrimination against them would be unfair. The scholarly literature has been enormous. Since I have written at length on the constitutional and moral questions,[13] I shall limit myself here to a brief sketch of the arguments.

The argument against the use of such classifications is straightforward. Deciding on the basis of race and gender is unfair to those who are better qualified (or have waited longer) and lose out, and it sacrifices the wider social interest in having the best qualified people occupy positions.[14] Moreover, the notion that benefits and burdens depend on race and gender, rather than more individual characteristics, is corrosive and destructive, whoever happens to benefit. Therefore, such classifications should never be used, or they should be restricted sharply to situations in which a high percentage of those who benefit were actual victims of prior discrimination by the institution now using race or gender in a corrective way.

In considering the arguments in favor of corrective classification, it is necessary to distinguish some situations and rationales. Suppose all agree that ideally people should be hired without respect to race or gender, but those making individual decisions do not trust themselves, or are not trusted, to decide without cognitive bias. Perhaps male members of a faculty have a strong inclination to believe that women will not be effective classroom teachers. It might make sense to counter this ineradicable bias by establishing a quota of applicants hired who must be women or by roughly assigning some "arbitrary" weight in favor of women applicants. In this instance, the use of a criterion of gender would be to approximate nondiscriminatory hiring as closely as possible in an imperfect world. Were this all that were involved, the argument about justification would largely turn on whether such an extreme measure was really needed to get people to hire in a nondiscriminatory way.

The more controversial issue is whether it is all right to favor people who really are at least marginally less well qualified, in order to make up for something that has happened in the past. Again, it is necessary to draw distinctions. Imagine that at Time 1, *B* has been denied a job (e.g., as a police officer) because he is black. At Time 2, *B* and a better qualified white, *W*, apply for the same job. *B* is given the job because he was the victim of prior discrimination. In this instance, *B* gets the job not because he happens to be black, but because he was unjustly denied it in the past. *W* suffers a certain unfairness—he would have gotten the job at Time 2 if no discrimination had happened at Time 1—but his claim to the job at Time 2 is weaker than *B*'s.[15] Everyone agrees *B* should get the job.

Frequently, an institution will have a hard time identifying exactly who suffered previous discrimination at its hand.[16] Suppose it favors a category of members of minorities or women that overlaps substantially, but not completely, with those who were previous victims. This may be the best it can do to give redress to its own victims. Some people argue that *any* extension of preferred treatment that goes beyond specific identifiable victims of prior discrimination is unacceptable, but when precise identification is difficult, then a program closely, though not exactly, tailored to prior victims is fairer than failing to provide any corrective measure.

The genuine controversial situations are ones in which a large percentage of the beneficiaries are not victims of prior discrimination by the organization involved. Substantial programs in police departments for hiring minorities will, for example, largely benefit younger men and women. If an effort is made to bring minority participation in the force to the level it would have been absent discrimination, older victims of past discrimination will receive no recompense and young members of minorities will be hired in a much greater percentage than they would have been if discrimination had never existed. Some other organizations, such as many northern state universities, may not have engaged in conscious racial discrimination for many decades; the persons they benefit may have suffered gross discrimination from other parts of society, even other parts of the government, but not from the universities themselves. The basic argument that such more generally directed preferences are fair is that when many branches of government have discriminated or allowed discrimination in the past and when pervasive discrimination by members of society continues in the present, it is an inadequate response to limit corrective preferences to the narrow situation when a prior discriminator matches with the people against whom it has discriminated. Apart from fairness in giving the benefit itself, an argument for corrective classification is that increasing the percentage of minorities and women in positions of significance will provide role models and contribute to a sense of opportunity, will partly redress an unjust balance of power among groups in society, and, thus, will in the long run help to destroy stereotypes and reduce unjust discrimination. Corrective classifications in the short run are believed to promote a society in which race and gender make less difference in the long run.

The arguments from fairness and beneficial effect in favor of corrective classifications are powerful enough to rebut the claim that they are necessarily and inevitably unfair. Whether the classifications are actually appropriate and desirable depends on complex factual questions about people's reactions to them, and the disagreement over these factual questions is very sharp. I shall not here try to defend my own view, based on a far-from-systematic appraisal of relevant data, that the likely benefits of such classifications often outweigh the likely harms and that these likely benefits are sufficient to justify them.

The questions about use of corrective classifications by private institutions are analogous to those concerning parts of the government. When it acts alone, a private institution is free of constitutional limits, but statutory bans of discrimination may be relevant. If the government tries to compel corrective classifications, by legislative mandate or conditions attached to grants, constitutional questions do arise.

Official Recognition of Private Judgments

Some of the most troubling questions about use of race and gender as criteria involve the possibility of official recognition of private judgments on those bases. I do not mean here official tolerance of private discrimination, but rather official acceptance of the idea that race or gender could count for a probability that has critical legal significance. I have suggested that the gender or race of approaching persons might matter for whether crossing the street to avoid them was sensible. Suppose that someone in a position like Bernhard Goetz, who shot four black youths on a subway after one youth had asked him for money, actually argued that the gender and race of persons was relevant to his believing that force or deadly force was required in self-defense (or the defense of a third person). He would claim that the persons before him made remarks and physical movements that might or might not have signified the use of force against him if he did not comply with their wishes; the fact that they were black males led him to think that violence against him was more likely, and indeed likely enough to justify his own use of defensive force.[17]

As with my street-crossing example, we can see immediately a sharp difference between gender and race. Very few groups of loud menacing teenage women assault people in subways or on the street. In the absence of an explicit threat or the showing of a weapon by the women, it is hard to imagine circumstances in which an initial use of deadly force against them could be thought reasonable. Now, it might be denied that a judgment *based on gender* would be likely or appropriate. Teenage females are physically less strong than teenage males, and perhaps they would not often act in such a menacing way, so it might be argued there would never really be situations that are comparable apart from gender. I am skeptical. Greater numbers could make up for lesser strength, and a group of young women might act quite menacingly. I believe that most people would assume that young women who acted in a somewhat menacing way would be less likely to carry through with violence than young men who were equally menacing. I think that the implicit reference point for reasonable reactions to menacing males is other menacing males and that the relevance of gender for assessing likely danger in such situations is assumed. (In any event, since most menacing is done by young males, a gender-neutral approach would still yield criteria similar to those for males alone.)

The disturbing factor here is race, and I shall concentrate on that. Plainly white males can be as strong and menacing as black males, but suppose a white man said that he felt particularly threatened because the youths confronting him were black. Part of his argument for self-defense is that the race of his potential attackers helped to make his use of force or deadly force justified.

We can imagine three degrees of recognition by the courts. The first would be judicial acknowledgment that the race of potential attackers would play a role in the determining when measures of self-defense are appropriate. The second would be permitting that issue to be put to the jury. The third would be acceptance of the role of race in affecting subjective beliefs about self-defense.

Judicial endorsement of the race of potential attackers as relevant to self-defense would have much of the negative effect of judicial endorsement of police use of race for stop and frisk or arrest. With one qualification, matters of probability will never be so refined that a court could confidently conclude that the race of attackers is a critical ingredient to make self-defense reasonable. Judicial discussion or decision should omit that element. The qualification concerns violence that itself is predominantly racial. If blacks in a particular white neighborhood have been assaulted and killed by whites, and a black in that neighborhood is menaced by whites, the reasonableness of his reaction will depend partly on the race of his potential attackers.[18] In ordinary mugging contexts, however, judges should not say that possible victims may base their assessments on racial judgments.

If the issue is put to the jury, that body of temporary officials is effectively free to take race into account in determining the reasonableness of self-defense. Since a jury does not publish its own reasons for its decision, the relevance of a racial factor may be buried, and indeed, there may be sharp differences among jurors about its endorsement. Because the jury's reasons are not formally revealed and because it is made up of ordinary citizens, a jury's reliance on that factor represents much less of an official endorsement than judicial reliance. Nonetheless, a conscientious juror might well resist discussion in those terms. In determining what can be *argued* to the jury, a judge should probably forbid lawyers from contending explicitly that the race of potential attackers bears on the reasonableness of self-defense. To permit such argument would be to concede a degree of legitimacy to racial classification that the state should not grant.

Matters are different if what is at issue is the subjective beliefs of the defendant. I suggested in Chapter 6 that for a crime of intention or recklessness, a defendant's subjective belief in facts that would justify his act should be enough to exonerate. If a particular person is terrified by members of a particular race, that could bear on his subjective beliefs, and a lawyer should be able to bring that out to render the claim of subjective belief credible. Here all that the state endorses is the idea that for some people in the society race may be relevant, which is, sadly, an obvious truth.

This conclusion is subject to challenge. The argument against permitting claims and evidence of racially based judgments is roughly this: citizens should be sharply discouraged from making racial judgments; those who make inappropriate racial judgments should not be rewarded by exoneration from crimes of intention and recklessness; and permitting evidence that race has influenced subjective belief will lead jurors to rely on their own prejudices. This argument of considerable force could be mounted as another reason why *all* claims of justification should have to pass a reasonableness threshold to exonerate, but the rather unusual problem of judgments based on race is not a strong enough basis to discard the alternative approach, which is preferable generally, of correlating elements of justification to elements of the underlying offense. A different possibility would be to bar any contention that race has contributed to a subjective belief, while continuing to make subjective belief relevant for crimes of intention and recklessness and allowing other evidence to support a claim that the defendant believed in facts giving rise to a justification. Given the very special harms when defendants assert judgments based on race, this specific exception has much to recommend it, but its preclusion of evidence that might be highly relevant to what someone really believed is probably sufficient to call for its rejection.

Laws That Appear Neutral But Operate to the Disadvantage of a Group

Legal rules that appear objective in the sense of being neutral between relevant groups may operate to the disadvantage of one group. Present disadvantages can be perpetuated by failures of the law to correct past discrimination or to forbid private discrimination, but I want to discuss apparently neutral rules that can operate more directly to disadvantage members of a group, using examples that concern gender. May such laws ever be defended? Are such laws discriminatory?

Suppose in the past, only men were eligible to join the police force. The law is altered to make women eligible, but a height requirement of five feet, ten inches is instituted. A height requirement is not an explicit gender classification, nor does it exclude all women, but it operates to the disadvantage of women. If the requirement was adopted to keep the police force mostly male, or was based on an unfounded male opinion of what it takes to be a police officer, it is plainly unjust. Regardless of its origin, the height requirement is unwarranted if it serves no defensible purpose or a purpose too slight to outweigh the value of equal opportunity. Without doubt, apparently neutral laws may unjustly affect women; without doubt, the law should be scrutinized to identify such instances and reformed to eliminate them.[19]

A word of caution is needed, however. Concluding that the origin of a legal rule lies in male perspectives or that the rule disadvantages women, or both, is not enough. Some rules of this sort may be defended as preferable to alternatives. The traditional rule that an assault victim cannot respond with deadly force unless he or she fears death, serious bodily injury, kidnapping, or rape may be an example. It has been suggested that this rule is based on male experience and works to the disadvantage of women, who are usually weaker than male assailants and unable and unaccustomed to defend themselves effectively with nondeadly force.[20] Certainly this self-defense doctrine is based mainly on male experience; so probably are almost all existing doctrines in criminal law. The rule does seriously disadvantage women; it disadvantages all those who are much weaker and less able to fight than their assailants. Yet for *simple* assault situations, the present rule *in its best form* may be desirable.

Let me clarify. The rule is sometimes put as permitting deadly force only if one *reasonably* fears *immediate* death, serious bodily injury, kidnapping, or rape. This formulation suggests that if someone begins to suffer a pounding with fists that she believes will continue until she is dead an hour from now, she must wait to use a gun, even if *now* may be her only chance to use the gun. This rule would be silly; if a gun is her only way to protect her life, she must be able to use it now. The proper rule requires belief that use of deadly force is immediately necessary,[21] not that the grave harm will occur instantaneously. The best rule does not make reasonableness a condition of using the defense. As I have argued earlier, if someone reacts with deadly force from a genuine but unreasonable fear, she should be liable only for crimes of negligence, and when reasonableness is important it probably should be judged by a fairly individualized standard.

By "simple assault situations," I mean to exclude the "battered wife syndrome." It has been argued that women assaulted by dominating husbands who often use violence are under such extreme emotional pressure that they should be excused for countering with deadly force; it has even been argued that victims of such domination should be privileged, justified, in striking against their aggressors with the only tactics available. I am not here discussing *those* very important and complex issues.[22] I speak only of single assaults by strangers, casual acquaintances, and intimate acquaintances who have not previously dominated their victims. Even in these situations, a woman's past experiences will bear on the reasonableness of her fear of grave harm. The situations I address involve single assaults when the female victim does not think death, serious bodily injury, kidnapping, or rape is likely. A man strikes a woman once or twists her arm behind her back to cause pain, and the woman does not believe things will go further than another blow or two or continued twisting of her arm. Should a woman then be allowed to use deadly force against the man's attack?

Once this question is sharpened, the argument for the existing rule in its best form has considerable strength. One alternative is a new rule permitting deadly force. This *could* be cast explicitly in terms of male assaulters and female victims, but some women are actually stronger than the men who strike them. Some men are attacked by much stronger men and several assailants often gang up on a single victim. A rule that explicitly refers to the gender of attackers and victims might make a symbolic statement against male domination and might very slightly increase the power of women in social relations, but it would have an element of unfairness and would hardly contribute to a social ethos in which gender plays a less significant role than it does now. I thus assume that a new explicit privilege to use deadly force would include all victims who have no fair chance of resisting with ordinary force. Such a rule would greatly increase permitted use of deadly force. Men, by temperament or training, are more likely to use deadly force than women, and an expanded privilege might well end up being relied upon more by males than females. It is, of course, possible that increased defensive rights would curb initial assaults and not produce greater actual *use* of deadly force, but more deadly force would be a serious risk of such a rule.

A much more appealing alternative is a highly individualized standard that would ask if the force used was reasonable in the context. Such a rule is in many ways more sensitive to situations than any rule with sharp categories, but it may provide inadequate guidance about when deadly force is warranted. The present rule in its best form is based largely on male experience and disadvantages women, but it *may* turn out to be the rule that seems best from the perspective of women as well as that of men. At the least, saying that the rule is based on male experience and disadvantages women is not sufficient to condemn the rule.

How the label "discrimination" applies to categorizations that are neutral on their face but have differential effects on important social groups is another troubling terminological inquiry. If the basis for the classification lies in an effort to disadvantage the group, there is no doubt that the classification discriminates. The same is true if the classification is based on unfounded biases against the group that is hurt. At the other end, not every classification that has a differential effect is discriminatory. Almost every legal category will aid or harm a higher proportion of men or women, blacks or whites; such a minimal standard for "discrimination" would deprive the term of significance. When classifications do not explicitly discriminate against a group, are not designed to harm a group, and are actually justified, they should probably not be referred to as discriminating against the group. The hard intermediate situation is when a classification is employed in good faith and accomplishes some legitimate purpose, but its benefits are outweighed by the social harm produced by its differential effects. In the context of fair employment law, the Supreme Court has said that such standards, if not required by business necessity, do discriminate against the groups that are disadvantaged by them.[23] Such a legal conclusion might be warranted on the ground that courts are hard put to discover discriminatory motives and therefore need more objective standards. But using "discriminatory" to mean innocently motivated standards that do not serve substantial employer need is at the edge of what "discrimination" is commonly taken to mean. Interestingly, if this approach makes good sense as a legal approach to a statute that outlaws discrimination, as I think it does, the term in more general discourse is likely to follow the direction taken in the law.

Corrective Efforts

Related questions about achieving rules that are as fair and desirable as possible arise when some reform is undoubtedly needed and the problem is more complex than simple classification in terms of race or gender. There has been wide agreement that change was needed in previous practices of allowing evidence of the prior sexual history of women who claimed they had been raped. Evidence in general of voluntary intercourse with other men is certainly not relevant to whether a woman had intercourse forced upon her on a particular occasion or to whether she has a bad character. Wide admission of such evidence discriminates against women, humiliating actual complainants and invading their privacy, discouraging many women from coming forward, and rendering convictions for rape difficult. If it is said that the same evidentiary practices would be applied for men who assert that sexual relations have been forced upon them, that hardly removes the sting of discrimination. The practices developed with alleged male aggressors and female victims in mind, and an extremely high percentage of sexual assaults are committed by males against females.

How should the practices be reformed? One possibility is judicial scrutiny of common law principles of evidence, bringing admissibility of evidence in rape prosecutions in line with broader standards and a more realistic view of what is genuinely relevant. Another possibility is statutory reform, a course that many states have chosen. One issue in statutory reform is whether presentation of evidence of voluntary intercourse with males other than the defendant should always be foreclosed. The position that prior sexual history is by its nature always intrinsically irrelevant is not plausible. To take an extreme example, imagine a case in which the complainant (victim) bears no signs of violence but claims that she was forced in her apartment to submit to intercourse at knifepoint. The defendant says he was explicitly invited at a named bar to engage in sex with his accuser, that they had consensual sex, and that she became enraged when she learned that his condom had broken and that he had previously used drugs intravenously. The apparent likelihood that he is telling the truth is increased at least *somewhat* if it can be shown that she spends almost every evening at this bar, regularly invites strangers there home for sexual intercourse, and has consensual intercourse with them. No doubt, she was free on this night to refuse to have intercourse, and she may have done so, but her prior behavior would reasonably affect a guess about what probably happened. Even when it has this sort of relevance, such inquiry can be highly embarrassing for the complainant and might discourage some women from proceeding with prosecutions. Evidence of this kind may have a prejudicial effect on the jury and may lead to not guilty verdicts for more actual rapists than not guilty verdicts for those falsely accused of rape. Further, those writing a statute may worry that if any allowance of such evidence is provided, judges will permit evidence of prior sexual history in too many cases warranting exclusion.

If all these premises are accepted, the problem reduces to whether potentially relevant evidence should be excluded because of its highly damaging impact on many victims and its potentially prejudicial effect, as well as because of distrust of trial judges. It is not irrational to argue for the total exclusion of such evidence, but that step is in serious tension with very basic assumptions about our system of criminal justice: namely, that defendants should have wide latitude to introduce matters that reasonably bear on their likely guilt or innocence, and that convicting an innocent person is a much worse wrong than not convicting a guilty person. One might believe that although the evidence can seriously disadvantage women in prosecutions for rape, nevertheless defendants should be allowed to introduce a complainant's prior sexual history in the infrequent cases when that has genuine and substantial relevance.[24]

Conclusion

The discussion in this chapter has suggested the complexity of notions of justified categorization, discrimination, and bias. Sometimes at least, direct private reliance may be warranted according to categories that are generally forbidden to the state. And when rules differentially affect groups in a troubling way, further investigation is required before one sensibly reaches conclusions whether they are, on balance, appropriate.

8

The Generality of Law

A characteristic feature of law is its generality. Legal rules ordinarily are cast in general form, and reasoning within the law is constrained by a principle of generalization, according to which the standards that one applies to a particular case must be applicable to other situations. Part I has examined and rejected the contention that governance by general rules is inevitably a delusion. We have seen how conventions of language and shared social practices permit guidance by abstract standards stated in advance. Chapter 6 considered the relevance of subjective and objective elements. An approach that individualizes the actor's situation and character to a greater degree may be viewed as less objective. Chapter 7 reviewed some of the ways in which general classifications raise issues of fairness among groups.

In this chapter, I concentrate more closely on some important questions about the generality of law. I begin with the reasons for general rules. These reasons turn out to be closely similar to the reasons, touched on in Chapter 5, for having single correct answers to many legal questions. I pause to consider a risk of discrimination that is involved in the use of open-ended references to "reasonable people" or other similar groups. I then explain the idea that principles used in legal reasoning should be general. Finally, I address the claim that the law overall is too abstract in its treatment of persons. This claim is made with special force by some feminist writers who accuse the law of being too masculine. A thoughtful response to this challenge requires attention to the nature of law among social institutions.

Generally Applicable Rules

Part of the ordinary concept of "a law" is that it deals with some general class of situations, treating all instances within the class similarly.[1] The liberal idea of "the rule of law" is that social activities are regulated according to such abstract standards. The application of sanctions depends on how one conforms to rules specified in advance rather than on the *ad hoc* judgment of someone after the event. The opposite of regulation by general rules of law is decision by someone based on circumstances or characteristics that he or she thinks relevant. Modern legal systems include instances of discretionary authority as well as regulation by general laws. As I am using the term "discretion" here, the law allows someone to decide in more than one way.

One may helpfully distinguish unconstrained from guided discretion. Most broadly, the law may authorize one person to decide what is in the welfare of others, constrained only by some extreme outer limits. That is the sort of discretionary authority parents have with respect to minor children. Except perhaps in specialized settings, like mental institutions, public authorities rarely have that kind of discretion with respect to citizens. More commonly, an official deciding about one particular issue is allowed to take into account virtually all of the factors he thinks are relevant to the determination. For example, in deciding whether to refrain from prosecuting people who appear to be clearly guilty of crimes, prosecutors have a discretion that is unconstrained by law.

Discretion is guided when the law contains standards for its exercise. For many decades in this century, enlightened thought about criminal sentencing supported tremendous power for the sentencing judge, acting under vague criteria of welfare for the community and the convicted person. Having examined reports on the background of the offender, the judge would have wide latitude to give probation or a prison term, ranging from, say, one year to fifteen years, for a particular offense. The judge's decision was unreviewable on appeal. Further discretion was granted to the parole board after a sentence had been partially served to decide upon an initial date of release.

The basic arguments for and against lawmaking in terms of general, precisely drawn classes are rather straightforward. General legislation gives clearer guidance about desired behavior than an authorization to some officials to make discretionary decisions. At least if it is consistently enforced, general legislation is fairer in giving notice and more effective in controlling actions of people subject to the law. General legislation also simplifies official decision making by specifying how most cases should come out. On the other hand, such legislation precludes sensitivity to unique circumstances. A discretionary approach permits an appraisal in context of all relevant circumstances and an outcome that is tailored to them. Of course, to say that an outcome is tailored to particular circumstances means that someone must determine this. If different people decide different cases and, as is inevitable, have different views about what matters and how much, a discretionary approach introduces a lack of consistency about essentially similar cases that could be better avoided by application of a general rule.[2] There may be room for arbitrariness and inconsistency in the application of general rules, but it is less than for more discretionary judgments.

The debate concerning sentencing discretion nicely illustrates some of the dilemmas. In the 1970s, highly discretionary sentencing was attacked for being unfair in two senses: inconsistent among like cases and not sufficiently attentive to the blameworthiness of particular criminal acts. Those who supported a "retributive view" of criminal punishment argued for a fairly rigid scale of punishments, under which those who committed similar acts would receive similar punishments. The retributive stance was thought to imply a sharp reduction in discretion. But those who supported substantial discretion said that situations in life were too dissimilar, that any categorizations in substantive law had to be too crude for deciding appropriate punishment. What has resulted in many jurisdictions is modest discretion exercised under fairly strict guidelines and subject to appellate review.

No general and abstract answer exists as to the proper mix of clear general rule and relative discretion. When fair warning and consistency of application are especially important, general rules are preferable; when tailoring to a particular context is of overarching importance, discretion may be desirable despite its drawbacks. Almost all lawyers assume that in a large, modern, complex society of anything like the sort we now have, a decent political order requires large amounts of general rules; the alternative would place too much power in the hands of individual officials and would lend itself to unacceptable arbitrariness and inconsistency.

Three features of law have been thought to make general rules so important. The first is that the authority of legal officials usually does not depend on voluntary acceptance.[3] When legal disputes arise, people find that decisions are to be made about their well-being by individuals or groups they have not chosen. One can draw two contrasts here. If two friends have some personal quarrel, a mutual friend cannot "settle" their argument unless both friends agree. They may agree beforehand that the friend will have this authority or be persuaded, after the friend makes a proposal, that the suggested resolution would be fair. Within an organized club or religious organization, one may find one's interests being dealt with by people one might not choose, but one at least has the freedom to resign. The legal system of a society does not provide this alternative.

The second feature is closely related to the first. The resolution that the legal official comes up with is usually mandatory, and resistance will be backed by the state's organized coercion. The law is partly about forcing people to do things they do not want to do. Disputants do not decide whether they would like to "accept" what an official has done, except in the sense of deciding whether to seek review, and if they fail to comply they will be compelled.

Third, much of the law is "either–or." A crime has been committed or it has not. An official has power to decide or he does not. A witness may properly refuse to testify or he may not. Legalist thinking undoubtedly creeps into ordinary life, but many judgments of other sorts are not of this either-or variety. If one considers whether an act of one person toward another is considerate or fair, one need not be pushed to say yes or no. One can conclude that it was "a little unfair," or, to be more precise, "less than perfectly fair but not seriously unfair."

The mandatory jurisdiction of legal officials, the coercive force of their judgments, and the either-or character of many of those judgments help explain why fair notice and consistency of application matter so much. It is one thing for a friend to offer criticism for an act that violated no preceding standard and that one did not regard as wrong, it is quite another to be put in jail or have one's property taken away on that basis. The reader will undoubtedly have noticed a connection between these three reasons for general legal rules and aspects of the law that distinguish legal interpretation from much other interpretation. The aim to have answers largely determinable in advance is the connecting feature.

Open Standards and Discrimination

An intermediate approach between precise general rules and outright discretion is the use of somewhat open-ended terms that afford the decision maker some latitude to consider various factors, but also constrain choice by implicitly excluding other factors and by indicating how the relevant factors should be considered. Contrasting what he calls "standards" with the opposite pole of formally realizable rules, Duncan Kennedy has written, "The application of a standard requires the judge both to discover the facts of a particular situation and to assess them in terms of the social values embodied in the standard."[4] Recklessness and negligence and the general justification defense are obvious examples of open standards. A general standard is applied, but the force of many relevant factors is not predetermined. (Virtually all legal terms have some openness, but the magnitude of openness in these standards dwarfs that of most legal standards.) The decision maker must exercise judgment about what weight to give competing considerations (e.g., the value of the activity, the magnitude of the harm risked). In contrast with wide sentencing latitude, however, what can be taken into account often is much narrower, typically only factors that are directly relevant to the events in question. And commonly the judgment must be simply for or against liability, although standards controlling comparative negligence and assessment of damages leave some range of options. Open-ended standards can be applied with sensitivity to context, but they present dangers of arbitrariness and inconsistency similar to those involved with the explicit discretionary freedom to choose either way.[5]

A particular problem with categories in statutes and case law that are open is that they may be "filled in" in a discriminatory way. I shall concentrate on the problem of gender. We saw in Chapter 6 that what one reasonably believes can often be crucial to whether one has a justification for using physical force. It is often and accurately said that within the male-dominated legal system categories have commonly been understood from a male perspective. Until very recently this approach was plainly embodied in linguistic terms. The typical standard was a "reasonable man." Of course, the term "man" was meant to refer to "persons" or "adult human beings," but it would be naive to suppose that the masculine phrase did not influence those who discussed or applied the standard to think in terms of males. Even when the crucial vocabulary is made as neutral as it can be,[6] people in the law, mostly men, tend to think in terms of men. A sharp illustration is the definition of punishable "fighting words" as those that would cause an "average addressee" to fight. The idea is that insults and epithets that are dangerously provocative may be punished to prevent violence. What is conjured up is one man employing insults or epithets at another. Since women (and small children insulted by adults) are much less inclined to respond to insults with physical force, it must be doubted whether any spoken words would actually cause the average addressee to fight.[7]

Once the male-oriented sense of many categories is recognized, it behooves those involved in the law to examine assumptions carefully with the experience of women in mind. What further steps should be taken is troublesome. One obvious possibility is to acknowledge that men on the average are different enough from women on the average so that different standards should be employed. Female defendants, for example, might be judged by what the reasonable female would perceive or do. It might even be argued that the social worlds men and women inhabit are so different that no common denominator can be found.

For certain subjects, categorization explicitly in terms of reasonable women may be desirable. If workers are given a right to be free of sexual harassment in the workplace, the standard of what constitutes harassment can be framed in terms of reasonable members of whichever gender is the claimed victim.[8] This will protect women (and men) from what they experience as harassment, instead of perpetuating insensitive perceptions and actions by members of the opposite gender. Since male offenders can be warned to stop rather than dismissed, men will not be penalized immediately for behavior that female victims perceive as harassing but the men perceive as something else.

For most matters, however, the objections to separate standards of behavior for men and women are extremely powerful. In the first place, people deal with each other in many contexts in which essentially similar behavior is expected of men and women who occupy social positions. It would be odd to think of the "reasonable woman" driver, trustee, banker, or doctor as somehow subject to different standards than "reasonable men" in these positions. A second, related problem is that jurors are called on to apply standards of reasonableness. The general assumption is that for ordinary activities like driving a car, jurors can rely on their own experiences; for things like medical practice, they get testimony about professional standards. For driving by female defendants, should male jurors get testimony about reasonable women drivers, or should they defer to female jurors on that subject? In professional cases, would testimony be in terms of the standards of one gender? These approaches would certainly complicate matters. Third, the maintenance of particular standards for each gender would reinforce stereotypes. It might even influence the amount of business members of various professions would get if the standards for one gender were more rigorous than the standards for the other. Fourth, there is a serious issue of fairness. Suppose, as might be the case, that female drivers on the average are more careful than male drivers. Imagine that a woman driving less carefully than the "reasonable woman" but more carefully than the "reasonable man" runs into a bicyclist who has no idea what gender the driver of the car was before the accident. Why should this driver be held liable if a male driver in the exact circumstances would not be held liable, simply because most women happen to be more careful?

Finally, there is the question whether a principle of differentiation in terms of gender could reasonably be contained. If women are to be distinguished from men, why should not other natural or social categorizations be taken into account? Perhaps the reasonable Puerto Rican banker acts differently from the reasonable WASP banker, or the reasonable young banker acts differently from the reasonable old banker. It might be responded that the distinction between males and females is pervasive and affects all of us, all of the time, in ways that these other differences do not. It might also be said that gender consciousness affects us more powerfully than any other consciousness. The first proposition, about pervasiveness, may be true, but the second proposition almost certainly is not, at least when one considers particular subjects. My last real fist fight was in fifth or sixth grade, more than forty years ago, and I do not often see physical fights. If we put aside deep-seated fears of being raped, an average upper middle-class, middle-aged, white woman probably has a perspective about violence that is closer to mine than to the perspective of a young single black woman living in the slums of the Bronx or South Chicago. Perhaps it is unfair to put rape aside,[9] but much violence is plainly not leading toward rape. Female graduates from elite law schools almost certainly practice law more like the male graduates from those schools than like the female night school graduates of the most marginal law schools.

For some subjects, such as tort liability for driving and legal or medical practice, objectively reasonable behavior is the crucial criterion. For these, distinguishing between men and women would be difficult and would constitute a glaring contradiction to the usual aims of law. When a more individualized approach is arguably appropriate because deserved blame is the central consideration, I see no stopping point at gender classification. For the extreme emotional distress mitigation or a claim of justification that serious bodily harm or death appeared likely, considering what is special about someone's experience because she is a woman may well be appropriate, but so also is considering what is special about her experience because she is black or old or a recent immigrant from a country where particular assaultive acts have very different implications. One possibility for such subjects, as Chapter 6 indicates, may be a standard of reasonable behavior that is highly individualized.

Given these difficulties with an explicit distinction between males and females in respect to open standards, the two sensible alternatives are a general standard for everyone or a highly individualized standard. When a general standard is appropriate, as for tort negligence of drivers or doctors, the question arises how to integrate more fully the experience of women.[10] Of course, the practical problem of accomplishing this in a legal culture in which men still dominate is considerable,[11] but I shall concentrate on an interesting theoretical problem. If we consider drivers of automobiles, resolution is relatively simple, one should use all drivers as the standard of what is reasonable. The number of women drivers is roughly equal to men, and women's experience would play as important a role as men's experience. But what of the many positions, such as surgeons, in which men still outnumber women by a huge margin? If reasonable behavior is determined by the present practitioners, the standard will remain predominantly determined by male behavior and will shift in relevant respects only as more women occupy positions. One could imagine the following argument for a different resolution: "Since women were the victims of discrimination in becoming doctors, present medical standards should give disproportionate weight to the standards of women presently in the field." This resolution has some theoretical appeal, but it is too refined for practice. All that is really feasible is trying to ascertain accepted standards by those now practicing.

A related but somewhat different problem arises over the concept of an "average addressee." Under this standard a defendant may be punished if his sharp words would have caused the "average addressee" to fight.[12] "Potential" addressees of words include more females than males, because more females are alive, but suppose it is true that obnoxious words are more often addressed to males than females. Should the standard of the average addressee be so skewed? Probably so.

In this section we have seen that once the gender assumptions in applications of many open legal concepts are recognized and examined, women's experience should count more significantly, but exactly what form a proper corrective should take is sometimes far from simple.

General Principles

Closely related to the idea of general rules is what has often been considered a characteristic feature of legal reasoning: its generality. Roughly the idea is that when judges provide bases for their decision of a case, those bases must cover other circumstances, real or hypothetical, that they would be willing to dispose of in the same way. If, for example, a court is going to decide that a particular Marxist speech is protected by the First Amendment, it needs to provide a principle of the following kind: "Communists should be allowed to preach Marxist doctrine because all people have a right to say what they believe if they do not encourage imminent criminal acts." This principle will function as a genuine basis for decision only if the court believes it should be applied in other circumstances, for example, when a speaker urges that whites are innately superior to members of other races.

In perhaps the most famous and controversial single American legal writing of the last fifty years, Herbert Wechsler asserted that a decision that did not rest on such principles lacked "legal quality," that "[t]he virtue or demerit of a judgment turns entirely on the reasons that support it and their adequacy to maintain any choice of values it decrees . . . ."[13] Critics who challenged Wechsler quarreled with any notion that legal principles could be "neutral" in various senses they thought he intended. They pointed out how genuinely difficult it often is to perceive and formulate defensible principles, particularly if a majority of a court is to agree on an opinion. They argued for judicial latitude to engage occasionally in strategic obscuring of the real principles behind decisions. And they tried to defend *Brown* v. *Board of Education* and other major constitutional decisions on racial classification from Wechsler's worry that the opinions were not defensible in terms of neutral principles and that no other acceptable constitutional principles to support the decisions might be available. The critics did not dispute that the search for principles of at least some generality is a characteristic and desirable aspect of legal reasoning.[14]

If one focuses on the formulated principle that lies directly behind the decision of the case, the quest for general principles of justification is virtually the same as the quest for general rules of judge-made law. As I have treated general rules, they are legal norms that will guide future behavior and determine the possible application of sanctions. In deciding cases under the First Amendment, for example, the Supreme Court establishes various rules to guide future legislation and executive action. If what it says in the Marxist advocacy case is that advocacy of beliefs can be punished only if imminent criminal acts are encouraged (and others believe that the Court has carefully considered that standard and will stick to it), the notion that advocacy of beliefs is protected speech unless imminent criminal acts are encouraged has become a general rule of constitutional law. The concern about general rules focuses on legal standards that guide future action. The concern about general principles of justification focuses on the reasons for the original decision. The announcement of such principles provides some assurance that judges have not reached that decision on an inappropriate basis. If one looks at what might be called the "holding" of the case, and the holding is formulated with some generality, that standard typically functions as an assurance that the decision has not been *ad hoc* and operates as a general rule for the future.

The quest for general principles reaches back beyond "the principle" of the case and thus has much broader application than the idea that "holdings" should be formulated with some generality. A court should be consistent in its interpretive strategy. If it says in one opinion that committee reports carry great weight about what Congress's purposes were in adopting a law, the court implies that in general committee reports should have that kind of weight.

When a court announces principles of interpretation, it is much harder to predict the outcome of future cases than when it announces principles of "holdings" like the principle that ordinary advocacy of beliefs is protected speech. The reasons are not hard to see. A principle of interpretation is at a very high level of abstraction. Even if the court consistently gives great weight to committee reports in determining legislative purposes, it will remain in any future case to interpret the relevant reports to help determine particular legislative purposes, and there will be other relevant indicia of legislative purpose besides committee reports. Further, the weight a report will have will depend partly on the strength and clarity with which it indicates a purpose. No generality can indicate with precision the weight reports will have when the weight in any single case depends partly on how the reports are written.

Another difficulty is that interpretive observations in majority opinions in American appellate courts will have to represent more than one judge. No two judges will have precisely the same interpretive strategy. Judges A and B may give committee reports great weight, but they may count marginally more heavily with A than with B. No generalization could represent with precision the different weight the two judges give to reports, even if a generalization was capable of representing one judge's view precisely.

Yet another problem is endemic given the way opinions are written, in common law countries at least. The arguments in favor of the result are typically overstated and the arguments against the result are understated. Court opinions even in cases the majority judges regard as close are written as if the result is decisively indicated. The inevitable consequence is that the reasons suggesting that result appear weightier than the judges think they are. As long as this style of opinion writing continues, the reader cannot gauge accurately just how much weight any particular argument, such as an argument of purpose from the committee reports, carries. One can hope for relative consistency in judicial statements about interpretive strategy, but, for all these reasons, neither the precision nor the guidance for future cases that one might get from carefully formulated principles of holdings is to be expected.

Is generality in legal reasoning different from generality in all reasoning? To give a reason is to state or imply some general principle. If someone says, "You shouldn't say that because lying is wrong," he means that other lies besides this one are also wrong. Even a person who does not offer a general principle but reaches a decision by totting up factors on each side implies at least three general principles. One is that if all the factors were repeated in precisely the same way in a future situation and no new relevant factors were present, he would decide the same way. Such consistency is a minimal criterion of a "rational" decision. But, so formulated, this principle is of little use, for life never repeats itself exactly. A broader principle of decision is that when similar issues arise, a weighing of relevant factors is the proper way to resolve them. This principle is one of general application, but it gives little guidance as to what the actual outcome of a variant factual situation would have been or will be. Finally, there is an indication which factors are negative and which positive, but this also provides limited guidance about the treatment of other situations.

When standards one accepts do not immediately dictate some outcome, a common method of reaching decisions that is different from "totting up factors" is to try to imagine a more general class of instances and consider how they should be treated. Suppose, for example, a young lawyer who is ill is told by her doctor that if she does not rest herself immediately, she risks serious long-term consequences to her health. She and her senior partner are to consummate an important business transaction the following day, and since she has done the most extensive work on the matter, she knows the client will be less effectively represented if she is absent. Like many young lawyers she is somewhat compulsive about her work and is concerned with her advancement, and like most younger people, finds it hard to take too seriously her own mortality and physical vulnerability. So she is initially inclined to go to the office. But then she reflects on what advice she would give a friend in a similar situation, what she thinks she would expect if she badly needed her personal secretary to do some work and the secretary reported the same risk, what she thinks she would expect of a young lawyer if she were the senior partner. She discovers that in each hypothetical setting, despite the disadvantage to the client, she would advise the ill person to stay home. This leads to deeper examination of her own values, and she finds that she believes that one should not risk serious injury to one's long-term health, unless one's failure to work is likely to risk someone else's life or health. She concludes that her initial inclination to go to work was not really consistent with fundamental principles to which she subscribes. If the lawyer sought to justify her decision to stay home along these lines, she would be able to state a principle of decision of considerable generality and definiteness, one that despite its uncertainty at the edges, would yield clear answers to many related situations.

There is no sharp dichotomy between the approach of totting and balancing factors and the approach of imagining related situations and formulating principles to cover them. They may be employed together: the "principles" approach itself usually reflects and relies on weighing of factors, and the factor-weighing approach will sometimes yield, at least implicitly, principles of clarity and definiteness. Yet there remains a significant difference in method, and it is interesting to inquire why a person would choose to emphasize one method rather than the other if the only concern were to reach the best decision in the particular instance. Two of the crucial variables are the number of importantly relevant factors and one's confidence in one's ability to weigh appropriately.

If there are a great number of important factors to take into account, imagining what are different yet sufficiently similar situations is harder, and so is formulating a principle of decision that does not suffer from acute narrowness (because it replicates the whole congeries of relevant factors) or unhelpful open-endedness. When the crucial factors are few, such as danger to one's health and the importance of one's work, definite principles are easier to conceive.

There is, regrettably, no exact scale for weighing competing considerations as one weighs oranges. An explicit weighing process may itself be something of a corrective to the bias reflected in an intuitive decision, but bias may infect the way in which one weighs as well. Imagining similar settings, especially settings in which one's own position is altered, can be an important further corrective. Thus, the ill lawyer's reflection on other circumstances may more accurately indicate her considered judgment about the values of health and work than her attempt to weigh their importance while focusing only on her own situation.

The effort to conceive similar settings and develop principles is particularly important when people make moral choices. It may be wrong to suppose that the proper moral decision for a person has nothing at all to do with his own special characteristics, but those characteristics are ordinarily much less central for moral choice than they would be for choice of career or spouse or how to spend one's leisure time. The external factors loom larger in comparison with subjective characteristics than for many other decisions people make. This reduces the number of importantly relevant factors and makes it easier to conceive of similar situations involving other people or involving oneself in a different role.

Serious moral choices typically involve some conflict between an action that would serve one's narrow self-interest and an action that would satisfy responsibilities toward others. The dangers of bias are extreme; either we value too highly our own interest or overcompensate and undervalue it. The discipline of imagining similar situations in which we are not involved or play a different role more nearly enables us to place appropriate values on competing considerations.

The search for general principles can also affect our judgment in another way. We may discover that some of our intuitive moral views are not consistent with other intuitive views or with generalized principles to which we subscribe. As we test our intuitive reactions to particular situations against our accepted principles, both may give a little, until we arrive at "reflective equilibrium," in which our sense of right for particular issues matches our principles.

The reasons why attention to related situations and the attempt to formulate general principles can be valuable for making moral and other nonlegal decisions also apply to the legal decisions of a judge. A judge only rarely has a tangible personal stake in the outcome of a case, but biases of all sorts may incline him or her in favor of one party or result rather than another. The discipline of principled decisions can make the judge more disinterested and can signal the reflective evaluation that will more nearly bring congruence of particular outcomes and broad principles.

There are some peculiar features of law and a judge's role that make principles especially important for judges. The main stuff of the law is standards cast in general form—standards found in the Constitution, created by legislatures, or developed in earlier judicial decisions. More amorphous guides to decision, such as criteria of interpretation, are similarly general. One legal ideal is that similar cases should be decided similarly; the outcome of legal disputes should not depend on the personal characteristics of particular litigants or particular judges. There are few, if any, unique situations from a legal perspective. When judges decide a case one way, they do so because they believe there are reasons for the result that would, or at least should, win support among other judges of similar cases if those reasons were understood.

Because of these characteristics of law, a judge naturally compares the result to which he is initially inclined with the outcomes of cases that are clear under existing rules, and he considers what other sorts of cases would be reached by a general principle that would embrace the case at hand. By this process of deliberation, he tests the appropriateness of his initial inclination. Moreover, insofar as decisions of tribunals represent the maturing of collective thought, the technique of posing cases and suggesting principles orally and in draft opinions is a crucial method of communication among judges, one that often precedes final agreement on a result.

The limits of a judge's role provide an additional reason for following the discipline of principles. Legislatures are representative and politically responsible, and the legitimacy of statutes derives largely from these characteristics. Courts are not representative and responsible in the same senses. Their legitimacy lies partly in their ability to justify their conclusions in a reasoned, principled way. For any well-functioning governance, it is as important that decisions seem appropriate as well as that they are appropriate. This is especially true for the courts, which are supposed to dispense evenhanded justice. John Ladd has suggested that an aspect of treating a rational being rationally is to explain "to him through reasons why a decision that adversely affects his interest has been reached."[15] The litigants in legal cases, especially losing ones, have an important stake in reasoned justification. So also do the participants in other branches of government and the community at large.

Generality and A Feminist Critique

One of the most deeply radical critiques of modern law challenges the emphasis on general rules and general principles. One aspect of the challenge is that this emphasis on general principles conceals the extent to which the law favors dominant classes and groups, including men. Robin West says that the "Rule of Law" has failed to recognize values that flow from women's condition.[16] According to Katharine Bartlett, "so called neutral means of deciding cases tend to mask, not eliminate, political and social considerations from legal decisionmaking."[17] Ann Scales argues that the philosophical basis of an approach in which rules transcend results in particular cases is "abstract universality," which "made maleness the norm of what is human, and did so sub rosa, all in the name of neutrality."[18]

The criticism of general principles goes deeper, however, than their tendency to obscure political choices and bias. Reasoning to decision by general abstractions is seen as alienating and less richly human than an alternative approach. A number of male critical legal theorists have made this claim,[19] but I shall focus on the perspectives of some feminist legal scholars.[20]

Their account often draws from Carol Gilligan's influential book *In a Different Voice*, which suggests that there are distinctive masculine and feminine ways of thinking about moral problems. Gilligan contrasts female notions of morality with male notions that turn on abstract rules, principles, and rights.[21] Her study of American women suggests a moral conception in which "the moral problem arises from conflicting responsibilities rather than from competing rights and requires for its resolution a mode of thinking that is contextual and narrative rather than formal and abstract."[22] Gilligan goes on to say that "a morality of rights and non-interference may appear frightening to women in its potential justification of indifference and unconcern."[23] Not all men think in the masculine way and not all women in the feminine way, but the distribution is substantially by gender and may be linked, she says, to typical childhood experiences. She attacks the dominant assumption of writers on moral development that what she identifies as the female approach to morality is a lower stage than thought in terms of abstract rules and principles.[24]

The feminist critique of law I am considering moves from appraisals like Gilligan's to condemnation of the law for failing adequately to take account of the female perspective. Male domination of the culture and legal system have resulted in a law permeated by a "masculine" point of view. Law is seen as particularly masculine among social institutions. Its "objectivity" is condemned, and radical correction is required to implement a more caring approach to human interactions.[25]

To put my comments about law in context, and to avoid misunderstanding as far as I am able, I begin with my own reaction to the thesis about moral perspectives. There is undoubtedly a difference between approaches to morality that emphasize rights, principles, and defined duties and those that emphasize caring concern that is responsive to individualized circumstances. Because of the different variables that characterize the two approaches, any single word labels are misleading, but I shall settle for "principled" and "relational."[26] The difference between "principled" and "relational" approaches is pervasive. People in some societies are more principled than those in others; some groups within a single society are more principled than others. My own experience corresponds with the conclusion that in modern Western societies women more than men exemplify the relational approach. (I am confident that cultural factors have contributed greatly to this difference but am unsure whether, and how much, natural characteristics may also matter.) Ample quotations from philosophers and social psychologists support the idea that abstract thought about moral questions represents a higher stage than relational caring, but it is misleading to suggest that the superiority of abstract thought has enjoyed unchallenged dominance in our cultural history.

Religious perspectives are a vital strand in that history. Christian ethics is often presented as an ideal of loving concern, in which feeling and attitude matter more than intellect, and sensitivity to situations is more important than categorization. This powerful theme in modern Christian writings has roots that go back a long way, to the teachings of Jesus and the letters of St. Paul. The "relational," or what has been called the "feminine," approach to morality sounds a lot closer to this Christian ideal than the principled approach. If we consider the Christian ideal, any notion that in our male-dominated culture the ethics of abstract rights and principles has ever been uniformly considered superior is shown to be mistaken. Well before I read my first piece of feminist writing, Simone de Beauvoir's *The Second Sex*,[27] more than thirty years ago, I regarded my own tendency to intellectualize and categorize personal moral problems as much inferior to the intuitive exemplification of loving concern I found in some others.

Because I expressed these thoughts in a draft before I had any inkling that my wife Sanja was ill, I know they are not a product of the overwhelming sentiments of the time after August 1988, but my personal life since then has profoundly reinforced my feelings. In our life together, I remembered historical and political events; Sanja remembered incidents with colleagues, friends, and family. I remembered the names of professional athletes; she remembered the names of children and their birthdays. She enjoyed talking to people about the details of everyday life, and she would stop for ten or fifteen minutes on a walk to catch up with friends and acquaintances. I mostly avoided "trivial" conversation and headed to destinations with only brief words of greeting along the way. I knew that Sanja's love for those close to her was deep and constant, marvelously supportive, and reciprocated; only after she died did I realize how powerfully her graciousness and concern affected many, many others. She communicated a deep sense of caring, and others responded to her with affection and care. My preoccupation with things that mattered less has made my own life comparatively shallow, and insofar as it has escaped shallowness, the reason is Sanja's transforming love. My experience in living has led me to agree strongly with those who recommend the morality of care and responsibility as equally worthy; indeed, if a sharp division between the principled and relational approaches is to be made, I think that relational morality is superior at the personal level.

The question remains, however, whether the primary principled character of law is itself a basis for condemnation. This question is separate, or at least partly separable, from the desirable character of the political process. What understandings and perspectives should influence the making of laws is a different question from the desirable nature of legal norms and their administration. I am concentrating on the second issue. Even within the law, I do not question that some movement toward more relational approaches is desirable. Resolutions based more on caring concern might be an advance not only in divorce and custody cases but also for some contractual disputes, claims in tort, and other issues. Conciliation and mediation could play a much larger part, and even when decision is by a court between two adversarial parties, some substantive standards could attend more to context and relation.[28] Further, social life would almost certainly be richer if people with civil disputes regarded the law as a painful last resort, trying hard instead to resolve matters in some genuinely consensual way.

Thinking about possible reforms in light of relational understandings is highly valuable, but identifying the law as essentially masculine or principled is not itself a sufficient ground for criticism. As Katharine Bartlett has pointed out, sensitivity to context is in fact an important element of traditional legal reasoning; contextual reasoning typically informs the development of principle rather than lying at the opposite end of some pole.[29] If law is nevertheless more principled than most social institutions and practices, that is not necessarily a defect. I claim, first, that some activities are appropriately more principled than others; second, that in most activities some blend of relational and principled perspectives is appropriate; and third, that in certain very basic features the law needs to be principled.

Suppose six friends in shallow water are trying cooperatively to keep a ball in the air by hitting it to one another. Someone twists an ankle and cries out in pain. The game immediately stops, and attention is directed to the injured player. Suppose in a 200-meter Olympic race, a runner cries out and falls to the ground. The race continues to a conclusion and that runner has lost, even if she would be able to run again in an hour's time. The continuance of the race despite an injury seems harsh, but the alternative presents problems. When winning is regarded as important, a different practice would create an incentive to fake injuries; furthermore, rerunning the race might be unfair to some other participants. The rules for running Olympic races are precise, and physical breakdown during a race is a misfortune that is not reversible. Serious competitive sports are much more rule governed, much less caring, than informal cooperative games. Competitive sports might be much less prominent, and their competitiveness might be softened in various aspects, in a world infused with the relational perspective, but my claim here would not be altered. If the same individuals, men or women, are involved in some competitive games and some cooperative ones, the competitive games are likely to be carried on in a somewhat more principled way.[30]

My second point is that some *aspects* of some activities will be more principled (or "masculine") than others. Consider the process of grading and discussing exams. A student comes to my office puzzled about a grade. In determining the amount of time that I spend, what I discuss, the sort of reassurance I give, I should be highly sensitive to the needs of the individual student.[31] But I am very rigid about changing grades, and I think that rigidity is defensible. I will not change a grade on rereading the paper unless I am persuaded that I could not reasonably have given the grade I did. This means I do not change borderline grades even when my sense at the moment is that a person probably deserves the higher grade. My reasoning is as follows. I have slightly more confidence in my capacity to assess merit and comparative merit when I am doing all the papers together and do not know the authors than when, days or weeks later, I am reading one paper of a disappointed student in my office. I assume I would change the grades of a significant percentage of borderline papers if I read them one more time; it seems unfair to give this chance only to those who happen to come to talk to me. Except in extreme cases, I do not think grades should be altered because of "personal factors," and I find it hard to distinguish any new appraisal of the written exam from my sympathy for the student's disappointment. This is a principled uncaring approach to changing grades that seeks to eliminate relational responses, but perhaps in its indifference to persons the grading of exams is a principled aspect of law teaching. (Interestingly, the absence of clear principles with definite applications makes the giving of grades in essay exams rather contextualized.) Of course, a sensitive affective understanding might lead us to substitute individualized evaluations for exam grades altogether, if our student–faculty ratio permitted. Again, my basic point remains that some aspects of particular activities rightly call for a more principled approach than others.[32]

Is not the same true of the law as compared with many other social institutions? In the close-knit settings of the family or pastoral counseling, there is substantial room for individualization and personalized concern.[33] But the law involves strangers deciding how transactions between two other people, sometimes strangers to each other, will be dealt with. In civil cases, the parties have been free to work things out by themselves, and the law's invocation usually reflects a prior breakdown in communication and trust. Often the law involves strangers deciding between two parties that are hostile toward each other. It is fine to attempt conciliation or mediation, but the law needs to do something if these are unsuccessful.

Features of the law on which I have already dealt are critically important. The authority of legal officials does not depend on voluntary acceptance. Resolution of disputes is often either–or,[34] is mandatory, and is enforced by the state's organized coercion. Many of the shadings of ordinary life and moral judgment are lost. These features of the law help explain why fair notice and consistency of application are so important. As I have said earlier, it is desirable that legal officials be constrained by rules, conform to expectations established in advance, do not act arbitrarily, and lack the power to intrude deeply into the lives of those who come before them. The legal system, as presently conceived, is mainly about corrective justice, and correcting wrongs demands a less sweeping assessment of aspects of an individual's life than many other sorts of evaluations. In a less "masculine" society the legal system might be a less important social institution. This would be a healthy development, more significant but analogous to the decline of serious competitive sports. But unless one accepts an optimistic anarchist view that redeemed human beings under suitable social conditions could do without coercion altogether, one must recognize that no complex society can do wholly without compulsory jurisdiction and organized force to settle disputes and to punish. I shall not argue the point here, but I think there is little evidence that the model of a complex society without some coercive governance is anything other than an incredibly naive and unrealistic ideal. Any decent and fair system for forced settlement and punishment will inevitably, and rightly, employ abstract and impersonal approaches and will be more principled than many other areas of life. To argue, then, that law is peculiarly principled, and therefore peculiarly "masculine," is only a short first step to identifying a range of desirable reforms.

III

Law's Relation to
Broader Sources that
Make It Objective
in Various Respects

9

Law's Relation to Cultural Morality, Economic Efficiency, and Sound Political Morality

This part investigates yet another sense in which law might be said to be objective, its rootedness in broader sources. Part I inquired whether questions of law often have objective, or determinate, answers. My claim that they do rested on the central place that language has in the law, and I developed the connection between legal norms and other prescriptive uses of language. For the most part, I treated the law as a relatively independent enterprise, like a game of basketball or certain narrow aspects of employer–employee relations. However, when I spoke about the general justification defense and other open-ended legal norms, I did rely on the way in which judgments about community morality or sound morality could determine the proper application of legal standards. In Part III, I pick up these threads and consider relations between law and broader sources more systematically, including the effect broader sources may have on the possibility that legal issues on which lawyers disagree have correct, or determinate, answers.

Part II concerned the manner in which law treats people. By employing abstract classifications, downplaying personal characteristics of actors, and attempting to deal with people fairly, the law often embodies "objectiveness" of various kinds. Of course, judgments about appropriate abstraction and impersonality and about fairness involve criteria of moral and political soundness, so the previous three chapters do, in fact, use those criteria. But the standards are mainly employed, at it were, from the outside. I do not concentrate on the intertwining of those standards in the law itself. An important exception is in Chapter 8, where I suggest how generality of principles figures in moral and legal justification. In Part III, I discuss such connections more fully.

What I mean by a broader source is something that reaches beyond the law and that might help determine the content of law. I focus on three broader sources: cultural patterns and beliefs, especially cultural (or social) morality; sound principles of moral and political philosophy; and economic efficiency. When one reflects on the relationships between any of these sources and the law, a number of questions are important.

I shall begin by noting major questions, using cultural morality to illustrate possible connections between law and a broader source. Societies have dominant patterns and norms that are to some degree discoverable apart from what legal rules provide and have a life that is somewhat independent of law.[1] For instance, the practice of unmarried couples living together might be socially accepted, or it might not. Suppose that as far as dominant cultural morality is concerned, this behavior is now regarded as unobjectionable. With examples like this in mind, we could ask: (1) Does the law reflect dominant cultural morality? (2) When a legal standard fails to conform with dominant cultural patterns, does that undermine its legal validity? (3) Do citizens regard a failure to conform as a good reason for disobeying legal standards? (4) Does the law contain specific provisions that require judges or jurors to refer to cultural morality in developing or applying the law? (5) Are standards of conduct drawn from cultural morality used more generally as a basis for judgment in the law? (6) Are modes of reasoning that are aspects of cultural morality used to reach judgments within the law?

Each of these questions is essentially descriptive. However, they are not simply descriptive, in the sense of resting on uncontroversial observations of external facts. Answering them requires interpretation of legal systems and cultures. But the answers do not prescribe what should be, they attempt to say what is.

For each of these descriptive questions there is an analogous normative question. (1) Should the law reflect dominant cultural morality? (2) When a legal norm fails to conform with dominant cultural patterns, should that undermine its legal validity? (3) Should citizens regard a failure to conform as a good reason for disobeying a law? (4) Should the law have specific provisions that require judges or jurors to refer to cultural morality? (5) Should standards of cultural morality more generally be a basis for judgment in the law? (6) Should modes of reasoning that are aspects of cultural morality be used to reach judgments within the law?

There remain another set of questions, which I mention separately because the answers may prove more elusive than for the questions I have just listed. These questions extend Part I's inquiry about the determinacy of law and require intricate conceptual analysis. The descriptive questions are: (7) Does the relationship between law and cultural morality render the law more, or less, determinate than it would be otherwise? (8) What effect would changes in the relationship have on law's determinacy? The normative analogue of these questions is: What relationship between law and cultural morality would yield an appropriate degree of determinacy in law?

Questions parallel to all these may be asked about the relationship between law and sound political morality and the relationship between law and economic efficiency. I shall say more about what I mean by each of these as the discussion proceeds.

In the remainder of this chapter, I address the descriptive and normative questions about law's reflection of these three broader sources, about criteria of legal validity, about reasons for disobedience, and about the use by judges and jurors of standards drawn from the three sources to make judgments within the law. Chapter 10 considers how reasoning within the law relates to broader forms of reasoning. Chapter 11 takes up again the problem of law's determinacy in light of relations between the law and these broader sources.

Law's Reflection of Broader Sources

Does "law" reflect cultural morality, standards of economic efficiency, and principles of sound political morality? When I talk about law here, I refer mainly to substantive legal standards, although I shall comment briefly on legal procedures and institutions. If law reflects some broader source, it may attain a kind of objectivity it might not otherwise have. If, for example, law reflected a correct morality discernable by human reason, it would have the kind of objective status claimed for it by traditional theories of natural law.[2] If law reflected a cultural *volksgeist*, it would be, as Savigny asserted,[3] objectively rooted in a particular culture.

Law and Cultural Morality

Does law within a society reflect dominant cultural norms? In one sense, to ask this question is to answer it. Unless law is imposed from outside by an alien power, a society's law will reflect its patterns of life and morality. We would be astonished if we compared Iranian, Japanese, and American positive law and found no connection between doctrines of law and cultural patterns, including basic moral conceptions. Those who make law try not to stray too far from the community's moral sense, which forms part of their own background. When laws are adopted that are at odds with cultural morality, one of their aims usually is to alter that aspect of cultural morality. Legal procedures and institutions will also correspond to cultural patterns, although usually not in such obvious ways.

For my purposes here, I mean to include under "cultural morality" not only moral norms about personal wrongdoing but also widely shared ideas about appropriate political arrangements, about desirable policies to serve the general welfare, and about social facts.[4]

What I say about law and cultural morality is also largely true about standards of behavior among important subgroups in a society that do not conflict with cultural morality but are too narrow by themselves to count as cultural morality. Accepted standards among members of professions or types of workers are obvious examples. Moreover, law's relation is similar to some aspects of community life that are not directly standards for behavior at all. For example, American constitutional principles of free exercise of religion and separation of church and state might be said to be rooted in our religious pluralism. Religious pluralism is a central aspect of American society that is not itself a matter of cultural morality (though pluralism contributes to a morality of toleration). My conclusions about law and cultural morality represent more general conclusions about how law relates to prevailing social practices and values.

Facile talk about dominant cultural morality can oversimplify the issue, assuming that there is a single and ascertainable cultural morality. Some legal regimes cover people whose outlooks are so varied it is hard to speak of a common culture or "community" at all; shared moral values may be minimal. More important, even within a culture in which many values are shared, sharp division may occur on certain subjects that are important for the law. In the United States in 1991 no single cultural morality exists about the permissibility of abortion. Nevertheless, within the United States, and within the boundaries of most other legal systems, enough shared values are present so that one can talk significantly of a prevailing cultural morality for many major subjects.

The conclusion that law corresponds substantially with cultural morality does not itself tell us what the relationship is between the two. Does cultural morality produce law, does law produce cultural morality, or are both the product of some deeper factor, or factors? One might believe as a matter of general theory that something yet more fundamental produces both cultural morality and law. Marx and Engels insisted that modes of production and relations of production determined class structure and thus largely determined a "superstructure" that included cultural morality and law. Savigny imagined a national spirit, a *volksgeist*, that united a society's historical past with its present culture and institutions. Even if one rejects theories of this sort as incorrect or too vague to be helpful, one may observe that in some societies a common source produces much of cultural morality and law (while perhaps itself being influenced by them). In ancient Israel, Puritan Massachusetts, and some recent Moslem societies, a strong religious vision has been such a source. In every society various features of communal life strongly affect both cultural morality and law, but no single, uniformly controlling factor can be identified, as Marx and Engels supposed. Both cultural morality and law tend to protect and preserve patterns of life and distributions of power. A common source, which may be more or less conscious, is the interests of those who enjoy positions of dominance within the society.

For the narrower relationship between law and cultural morality, law might derive from cultural morality, cultural morality might derive from law, or each might derive in part from the other. In many respects cultural morality seems to have a life of its own, changing, at least initially, in the absence of significant legal support. For example, directly relevant legal change[5] did not produce the growing sexual permissiveness in the United States in the 1960s and 1970s. That development yielded shifts in substantive legal norms and patterns of enforcement. However, the causal relation is not only from cultural morality to law. Legal categories and thought are partly constitutive of culture, and cultural morality is responsive to legal change. Few people now defend the principle that for exactly the same work, women and black men should be paid less than white men, yet forty years ago many citizens accepted that principle. Legal changes, including *Brown* v. *Board of Education*, other important constitutional decisions, and federal legislation, have affected how people view equality. We observe then, patterns of mutual interaction in which cultural morality and law influence each other. Three fruitful insights of critical legal scholars are their emphasis on the interdependence of cultural morality and law, on the tendency of both to make contingent structures and distributions of power seem natural and inevitable, and on human freedom to choose among different possibilities for social life. Conscious choices about legal rules and institutions have a broader effect on cultural patterns.

What kind of objectivity might law derive from substantial correspondence with cultural morality and partial causal dependence on it? Whether the influence of cultural morality on law "just happens" or occurs through conscious decisions of lawmakers to bring law into line with community views, the connection assures that the law is rooted in something broader, that it is not spun out of the web of an autonomous law, is not floating free as the mere fiat of those who happen to make it, and is not simply a series of *ad hoc* compromises emerging from clashes of personal preferences. Of course, insofar as the law generates cultural morality, this correspondence does not show that law *rests* on something beyond itself. And for many comparatively technical decisions about substantive law and legal institutions, cultural morality may have only remote bearing, except in its endorsement of policies of efficient administration, predictability, and so on.

Even when cultural morality substantially determines the content of law, the resulting objectivity of law is only of a particular kind. Cultural moralities vary significantly. Is there any assurance that a dominant cultural morality is appropriate? If one believes that fairly concrete universal standards of moral judgment should be used to measure social practices, then some cultural moralities will appear more acceptable than others. In that event, the conclusion that the law of a society fits with its cultural morality is no guarantee that the law is right or good from the standpoint of correct moral and political standards. Even if the law of Nazi Germany did fit with the cultural norms of German society during the 1930s and early 1940s, that did not make the law objectively good from some yet broader perspective.

Could one plausibly claim that the cultural morality of any society is proper for that society, and that, therefore, law that corresponds with the cultural morality is also proper? Understood in one way, such a claim is empty and confusing; understood in another way it is inaccurate. Suppose someone who says that a cultural morality is "proper" for a society means that no external standards of "proper" exist, that one cultural morality is as good as another and, therefore, what any society considers proper is proper. This approach gives up any idea of objective moral standards and any external perspective[6] from which to evaluate a society's morality. If such a person says that law is objective because it conforms with dominant cultural morality, he asserts nothing more than law's rootedness in broader social patterns; any reference to "proper" is meaningless and confusing.

A meaningful claim that a cultural morality is "proper" presupposes some standards for what is proper.[7] For example, taking human happiness as the crucial evaluative criterion, one might say that a cultural morality conducive to happiness depends on political history, geography, economic capacity, education, theological belief, and so on. Under the broad standard of happiness, very different cultural moralities might be suited for different societies.[8] If different cultural moralities are appropriate for different societies, laws conforming with appropriate aspects of cultural morality are objectively well suited in their appropriateness.

If external standards of propriety are applied, they will almost certainly suggest that some aspects of cultural morality are not well suited for the societies in which they exist. We know that individuals have many beliefs, attitudes, and practices that are destructive and self-defeating in terms of the individuals' own or desirable objectives. Cultural morality can be similar, failing whatever objective standards of desirability exist. A common reason, of course, is that parts of the morality will benefit some members of society, usually the powerful, at an unacceptable expense to other members. Obviously if law fits with these undesirable aspects of cultural morality, that fit does not show conformity with any objective standard of goodness or rightness.

I turn briefly to the normative question whether it is desirable for the law to correspond with dominant cultural morality. The general answer is yes. Discrepancies between law and dominant cultural morality are sources of tension and resentment, and they threaten the effective functioning of legal norms. Law in conflict with community morality produces dislocations and instability and tends to defeat expectations. This is not to say that law should enforce all that community morality requires. Some matters are best left to informal social relations. Some conscious choices that law should deviate from existing community standards are also called for, especially when existing standards are believed to offend higher moral principles. If strands of cultural morality can be identified that operate peculiarly to the harm of disadvantaged groups in society, some form of opposition within the law may be appropriate. Nevertheless, fit with community standards is ordinarily one measure of wise law.

This conclusion that law desirably fits with cultural morality is not self-evident, even for aspects of cultural morality that are acceptable. It might be argued that human beings so easily "reify" patterns of life that only a high level of instability and internal conflict can maximize human freedom.[9] On this view, severe tension between law and cultural morality might be welcomed as a positive good. I shall not try to respond to this argument in depth, saying only that being dragged in different directions does not usually enhance people's freedom in a significant sense. Human beings need some basic security and stability. Freedom is enhanced if the law leaves many choices unrestricted, but law should not often forbid behavior that cultural morality either requires or treats as a fundamental subject of free choice.

Law and Economic Efficiency

Much writing about law over the last two decades has emphasized the possibility that law may contribute to economic efficiency. If law, or certain aspects of law, can be understood as contributing to efficiency, then law can be rooted in helping to achieve this social goal. Economic efficiency may be regarded as an aspect of cultural morality or cultural norms, as a rationally effective means to achieve cultural values,[10] as an aspect of sound moral and political philosophy that includes effective means to achieve genuine values or personal preferences, or as grounded in all these ways. I treat it separately because it is now so central a concept in much contemporary discourse about law.

Economic efficiency concerns the production and allocation of goods. I shall concentrate on allocative efficiency. Economists agree that Pareto optimality is one measure of efficiency. If someone is made what he or she regards as better off, and no one is made worse off, the situation is Pareto superior to that which has preceded it. In an absolutely free market with perfect information and no transactions costs, trades would occur until a Pareto optimal situation was achieved. No situation would be Pareto superior to the one that exists, because no mutually advantageous exchanges would remain to be made. This does not mean that every Pareto optimal situation is preferable to every situation that is not Pareto optimal. If one person has all the goods, that will be Pareto optimal, since further trades cannot leave him as well off as he now is; any exchanges could only worsen his position. More equal distributions that are not Pareto optimal may be preferable. Nevertheless, it is true that for every distribution that is not Pareto optimal, there exists a preferable (more efficient) Pareto superior situation.

Another standard of efficiency, the Kaldor-Hicks, or wealth,[11] standard is more controversial, though commonly employed by writers on law and economics. It posits that a second situation is superior to a first if some are placed in a better position and transfer payments *could* leave everyone in at least as good a position. According to this standard, a gain in efficiency can occur even though some *are* left in a worse position. If a bicycle that is worth $50 to me is allocated to someone who values it

$100, a gain in efficiency has occurred. If I am left $50 poorer, the new situation is not Pareto superior to the old one. Nevertheless, since a transfer payment of between $50 and $100 from the other person to me *would* have left us both in a better position than the original position, the new situation is more Kaldor-Hicks efficient than the old one. In a sense, the society now has $50 more of wealth (the extra value of the bicycle to the person who has gotten it) than it did before.

The ways in which law can contribute to economic efficiency are essentially twofold. First, legal rules can create conditions in which a market that is comparatively free and uncostly can operate. Rules to enforce contracts and rules against monopolies are designed to assure a free market; rules against theft make it worthwhile to trade in the market. Second, for subjects as to which a free market could not operate effectively, or for which other values are thought to outweigh the possible benefits of such a market, legal rules can be employed to try to replicate the hypothetical results of such a market.

If economic productivity and welfare are taken explicitly or implicitly as significant objectives, we would expect to find many legal rules designed to contribute to economic efficiency. That is true to a degree even in centrally organized economies. In those economies, genuinely free markets may be rejected as unjust or inhumane in various respects, but centralized decisions about what products to make and what to charge for them will give at least some effect to the perceived preferences of members of society.

It has sometimes been claimed that common law rules tend toward being efficient.[12] Part of the argument is that judges may take efficiency as an objective and work reflectively toward efficient resolutions. But since even in many areas of private law judges patently have not focused their attention on what rules would be efficient, a more complex explanation has plainly been needed. Some added features of this explanation are (1) that parties will "bargain around" inefficient rules, reducing their significance, (2) that patterns of litigation will produce disproportionate challenges to inefficient rules, and (3) that concepts of reasonableness and other aspects of cultural morality and professional practice will implicitly reflect notions of efficiency. The argument that each area of private common law moves toward rules that are efficient has always seemed strained to all but the most zealous advocates of the thesis that efficiency *should* dominate common law adjudication. Even those who claim that the common law works toward efficient results do not suppose that legislation systematically does so. Much of legislation is based on interest group pressure that frequently is at odds with efficient outcomes. Legal norms may be partly reflective of ideas of efficient outcomes, but they are also affected by much else.

Should economic efficiency be an aim or the governing aim of the law? If we focus on Pareto optimality, it is clear that it should be at least *an aim* of the law. It is desirable to make people better off when that is possible without harming others. At least so far, no one has devised a substitute for free economic markets that is nearly as effective in satisfying people's preferences. The combined experience of communist countries strongly suggests that central organized direction cannot replicate the free trades that allow people to move to Pareto superior positions. Plainly, Pareto optimality cannot be the *aim* of the law. Sometimes a less efficient result is to be preferred to one that is Pareto superior. In cases of justified paternalism, law prevents what is perceived as a desirable trade by both participants for the sake of at least one of them. Parties to the transaction may not perceive, or act in accord with, their own best interests. Laws against purchases of heroin and against prostitution are commonly defended in this way. Moreover, permitting the buying and selling of something, such as sex, may have pervasive and potentially harmful effects on how that thing is considered by people in the culture generally.[13] Once such indirect effects are taken into account, one can rarely, if ever, be confident that no person will suffer from a willing exchange or from the law's approval of willing exchanges. Finally, and of greatest importance, most legal rules directly make some people better off at the expense of others. Standards of Pareto optimality and Pareto superiority cannot guide us as to when that is justified.

The wealth standard is potentially much more useful, in the sense that it might serve as a more general guide to desirable law, but it is also deservedly much more controversial. The wealth standard measures the value of a good for a person by what the person is willing to pay for it, and treats a gain in general wealth (as in the bicycle example) as a gain in efficiency. One problem is that when all the intricacies are analyzed, it is often very hard to say which of the alternative rules will be most wealth enhancing for society. A more radical difficulty is that distributive considerations, and moral rights and expectations, may indicate that a result that enhances wealth, and is therefore efficient under the wealth standard, is not always desirable. Remember, that standard is cast in terms of whether compensation *could* make both sides better off. If the compensation is not in fact forthcoming, it may be unfair that the particular person who would pay less for a good does not get *either* the good or some compensation for not having it. Such unfairness may be likely if the deprived person is poor and cares a great deal about something, for example, the apartment he rents, that he could not afford on the free market. The wealth standard takes as a given the existing distribution of wealth. According to it, those willing to pay more for something value it more, but those willing to pay more do not always care more.

Consider, for example, whether the law should abate a loud noise made by a factory that disturbs a neighboring community of poor people. The factory would rather pay $1,000,000 a year than spend money to reduce the noise or move elsewhere; the present 20,000 residents would rather get $800,000 a year than have the noise stopped. It would, at least in the short run, be *Pareto* efficient for the factory to pay the residents between $800,000 and $1,000,000 per year and continue to make the noise. But the law may lack the means to dictate this solution; it may be too difficult to administer. Among other problems, how could a legal officer get honest enough answers from residents placing different values on stopping the noise to assure that *every* resident feels better off without exceeding the amount the factory will pay? Once the scheme of payment is envisioned, individual residents have a tremendous incentive to lie about their own points of trade-off, to say they require more money than they do to be "paid off" for tolerating the noise. These are familiar problems with arranging "market transactions" in such settings, or in even being sure what "the market" would yield.

But imagine that one is confident that allowing the noise to continue would be efficient in the sense of wealth enhancing, that overall the monetary value to the factory of making the noise is more than the monetary value to the residents of stopping it. Should the noise be allowed, though no payments, in fact, will be made? This might seem especially unfair if the factory started the noise long after the community was in place, but I want to pass over that concern. There is another serious problem of unfairness. Suppose that any middle-class or rich community of 20,000 would require much more than $1,000,000 yearly to accept continuance of the noise. The poor community dislikes the noise just as much but its residents are desperate, lacking adequate food and clothing. They would accept an average of $4,000 per person only because they value the money so highly. (This shows how this measure of efficiency accepts the given distribution of wealth.) If the residents are not in fact going to be paid, it is unfair that the noise continue next to the poor community though it would have to stop were the nearby community middle class or rich.[14]

This example illustrates the obvious truth that "wealth maximization," insofar as it is a comprehensible concept,[15] is not a "good in itself." It can be desirable only if connected to human satisfactions, protection of rights, or the promotion of virtues. Any argument that wealth maximization is the proper objective of a political system is demonstrably fallacious,[16] though I shall not attempt the demonstration here.

A somewhat more modest claim is that decisions about "rights" and fair distribution are proper matters for legislatures, but that courts developing the common law should always aim for efficient wealth-maximizing outcomes. It has yet to be satisfactorily explained why these other considerations are beyond the boundaries of the common law; if one thinks of our factory example as raising a problem of common law nuisance, with a court having to decide if the noise will be stopped or be allowed to continue, one can see why courts should consider fair distribution.

What we are left with as plausible is the still more modest claim that wealth maximization is *an* appropriate aim of many legal rules. Willingness to pay is often a fair gauge of satisfaction, and losses on some occasions may be offset by gains on another. When neither free markets nor forced transfer payments are practically feasible, arranging things so the usual outcome will be that those who place a higher monetary value on goods get them is sensible.

Sound Political Morality

What conformity of law with sound political morality means and what it would entail is a bit more complicated than the matters discussed thus far. The basic idea is that there are correct judgments of moral and political philosophy, that insofar as law conforms with these it is objectively sound. The relevant descriptive claim about law's relation to these judgments is that its conformance with them makes law objective in this sense; the normative claim is that law should be objective in this way. The classic notion of natural law, that human law is in some sense derivable from a higher moral law, combines these descriptive and normative dimensions.

The main difficulty in treating this subject concerns the strongly held and sharply differing positions over what kind of objectivity may be claimed for moral and political judgments. The controversy is over both (1) what sort of objectivity *is* being claimed by people who make judgments and (2) what sort of objectivity *can rightly* be claimed. For this problem, which lies at the center of moral philosophy, I shall have to content myself with some clarifications, a sketchy categorization, and my own nonexpert views. These will allow the reader to understand what follows and to substitute his or her own competing positions where they differ.

I begin with three obvious points. First, conformity with "correct" political morality can confer on law only the objectivity inherent in political morality itself. If there is no objective basis for moral and political judgment, then conformity with some set of moral and political judgments could show how the law is placed in some broader context, but would not establish law's objectivity in a significant sense. The second point, already made in discussion of cultural morality, is that "correct" or "sound" must be taken here to mean something more than what dominant cultural standards happen to be. If one says there are no measures other than dominant cultural ones of the society whose law is being examined (or of the society doing the examining, if those are different), then one's claim that law has the objectivity of corresponding with a broader source amounts only to the claim that law corresponds with dominant social morality. Third, the beginning of this chapter and the rest of the book are replete with judgments about political morality. I have suggested, for example, that lawmakers should concern themselves with distributive considerations, that in general, law should not be contrary to cultural morality, that fair notice of prohibited behavior is important for the criminal law. An inquiry about the objectivity of judgments of political morality includes an inquiry about the status of such judgments.

An extreme skeptic may think no standard exists for correct moral and political judgments. He may nevertheless make judgments, but these will, in his reflective view, represent only his own individual preferences or feelings or those he shares with some larger group. Conformity of the law with such judgments would confer on the law only the "objectivity" of agreeing with him and people of like opinion.

For law to achieve a kind of objectivity in conforming with judgments of political morality, there needs to be at least some standard of correctness, or some status for judgments, that the extreme skeptic denies. I shall here disregard the question of status except insofar as it bears on standards of judgment. Suppose someone says that true morality is what conforms with the will of God. On this view, true morality has a status that transcends the social life of human beings. However, unless this perspective also affords human beings help in deciding what is morally right, it does not affect moral judgment. My concern is with possible standards of judgment.

I shall consider four broad possibilities: (1) A judgment is required by basic requisites of simple rationality (a contrary judgment would reflect a demonstrable failure to think clearly). (2) A judgment is not required by simple rationality but is required by a richer notion of reason (a contrary judgment would fail to be reasonable). (3) A judgment, although not accepted by all reasonable people, is supported by a balance of relevant reasons, and those relevant reasons are ones that all reasonable persons can assess. (4) A correct judgment is indicated in part by reliance on standards, such as religious revelation, that in some sense are not available for everyone. At least for the first three categories, we must further distinguish judgments that hold for all societies and those that may lack universal validity but follow from certain fundamental choices of social organization, such as liberal democracy. Rather than trying to explain these categories further now, I shall proceed with some illustrations. My own belief is that various judgments of political morality can be correct in each of these ways, though for some judgments I am far from confident in just which categories they fall.

Simple Rationality

What H. L. A. Hart has called "minimum content natural law" exemplifies judgments that are required by simple rationality.[17] Hart does not claim that survival is a true human good, but he notes that virtually all human beings wish to survive, that our institutions presuppose the aim of survival, and that our language assumes survival as a good. Taking survival as a starting point, he indicates what sorts of norms will be necessary in society if the aim of survival is to be furthered. The basic analysis is in terms of means–end rationality. If the objective of survival is sought, certain kinds of standards are required in morality and in law as a necessary means. Given a world of limited resources and human characteristics of vulnerability, approximate equality (Hart means here approximate equality of capacity, not moral equality), limited altruism, and limited understanding and strength of will, people can survive only if there are rules protecting their physical bodies and their property, requiring the keeping of promises, and providing some sanctions against those who violate the rules. If Hart's descriptive sociology is correct, these features of human social life will always be present, and every society advanced enough to have a separable law will exhibit the norms he supposes in both its morality and law.

Hart emphasizes that the benefits of the restraints do not, to qualify here, need to be extended to all those within a society or even a majority. Conceivably a minority that protects itself will use force, or extreme persuasion, to set up a regime in which many people are treated like draft animals for the welfare of the privileged minority. If Hart is correct about what survival requires, and I think he is, one cannot imagine any political morality in which survival is a significant value that will not include this minimum regulation. It follows then that there will be *some* commonality between any plausible claims about sound political morality and every cultural morality and legal system. It would be strongly irrational not to have rules protecting survival within the law, if survival is valued. Since every law will have such rules, any law will possess a kind of objectivity in reflecting certain basic features of sound political morality.

One must be extremely careful at this point not to suppose that more has been established than has. This metaphysically modest means–end account provides no basis for saying that the law is objectively good in a way that transcends historical and existing human preferences, or for saying that one legal system conforms more with sound political morality than another, or now conforms better or worse than it once did. Hart does not claim that survival is better than individual or corporate suicide. He has no answer to the person who says we should all try to die as quickly as possible. Many who read Hart's passages for the first time mistakenly suppose that we can at least say that a legal system is better *from this perspective* if it serves the aim of survival more effectively and provides its protections more generally. But Hart claims nothing about how survival rates against other values. As long as a society counts survival for something, it may rate promotion of the true faith, or courage, much higher. Barring a situation in which survival is badly served, and no other competing value is served better than it would be if survival were better served, "minimum content natural law" does not offer a basis to say that a legal system is corresponding with sound morality to a greater or lesser degree. The same point is true about the extension of protection. Recall, Hart's characteristic of approximate equality is descriptive; it does not foreclose an attitude of moral superiority, or indeed simple tyranny without any claim of moral justification. If one group manages to subject another to the worst forms of slavery, or even sends them to death camps, saying, "You may be physically our equal but we are the master race," this does not offend minimum content natural law. As long as a legal system manages to protect some portion of the population, this account alone does not show the system is worse than one with more extensive protection.

If we limited ourselves to nearly universally shared values and asked what sorts of norms were necessary to serve those values for at least part of the population, we could include some values other than survival: bodily integrity (not losing limbs), physical health (independent of its connection to survival), minimum psychological security, minimum happiness. Including these values might give some further guidance about appropriate norms. But reference to them would not establish that any of these valued states are *really* worth having, it would not settle questions of trade-offs against other valued states, and it would not show that the ambit of protection should be extended.

BASIC REASONABLENESS

For ordinary human thought, the step is short from saying that survival, health, happiness, and so on, are almost universally valued to concluding that they really are valuable. Philosophically, this step from "is" (survival is widely valued and can be protected in this way) to "ought" (survival ought to be protected and therefore ought to be protected in this way) may be troublesome, but practically we have little difficulty accepting that survival (under ordinary conditions) is objectively preferable to death, that health is preferable to illness, that happiness is preferable to unhappiness. The traditional natural law position, drawing heavily from Aristotle and Aquinas, takes just this step. Our understanding of human life enables us to say what is good for human beings and roughly what moral norms and legal norms are conducive to good.[18] Saying that death is preferable to life, illness to health, may not offend simple rationality, but it is deeply unreasonable.

Unfortunately, concluding that certain values are objectively rooted in the human condition and human reason, and that these values warrant protection, does not alone carry us very far. Without some ordering of values and without principles defining which people are entitled to protection, the catalogue of "correct" answers to questions of political morality will be very limited. A reasonable understanding of the human condition does, I believe, tell us *something* about the ordering of values in a good life. Pursuing aesthetic values at the expense of *every* human affection is, for example, undesirable. But many variations in emphasis among people of different historical epochs and social orders and among different individuals in the same society will be reasonable. What may be more troublesome for individuals who must resolve how to live is that reasoned understanding can leave open many alternative choices for each of us.

The problem of choice for law (and for standards of cultural morality) differs from that facing individuals in their own lives. The problem of choice for law is how much to guide or compel individual decisions and how much to leave to the discretion of individuals.[19] Should the law force ordinary adults to pursue aesthetic values rather than increasing their knowledge of science, or vice versa? Most people would comfortably answer that such choice is best left to individuals once they reach maturity. Should laws push people toward caring for and identifying with fellow citizens and toward actively participating in the political process, or should they leave these matters to individual inclination as well? That is a matter of disagreement. If one approves of a government that leaves a wide range of choice to individuals about how to live, the problem of ordering values becomes less serious for political morality than personal morality. Part of the foundation of liberal government is extensive liberty of choice for citizens. But the fundamental choice to have liberal government is not one that reason plainly requires.

Whether the law says much or little about ordering values for individual lives, it must determine who is to be protected, in what respects, and to what degree. Some people now assume that a basic premise of human equality can be derived rationally, that it is somehow inherently self-contradictory to deny that people are equal. That view is mistaken.[20] It is not irrational to say that people with superior qualities deserve superior consideration or even that among people who have similar qualities, a number have been singled out for special consideration by God. Does a somewhat richer conception of reason yield a premise of equality? It is *unreasonable* to believe that human beings of ordinary capacities deserve *no* consideration, and slavery and similar practices can be ruled out as deeply unreasonable.[21] Perhaps it is also unreasonable to deny that human beings of ordinary capacities deserve equal consideration, in some sense, by their governments.[22] Certainly the argument in favor of equality is backed by powerful reasons; it is now widely regarded as compelling, even if a reasonable person could reject it.

Some notion of equality is part of the groundwork of democracy. John Rawls, for example, talks about "a system of fair social cooperation between free and equal persons" as the basic premise of liberal democracy.[23] Modern theories that correct political institutions and norms are those that no person could reasonably reject,[24] or that would be adopted by people in hypothetical conditions of ignorance,[25] or that would emerge from unrestrained dialogue[26] are all elaborations on the theme that equality is central. These theories provide some reasoned bases for conclusions about what sorts of laws would be appropriate, although one may debate which theory provides a superior account of equality and precisely what institutions each would yield. Once we accept some basic assumption about human equality, much about an acceptable moral and legal order follows.

A BALANCE OF RELEVANT REASONS

Some people believe that all political questions can be settled on a reasoned basis. Many questions will be difficult, and disagreement will persist about better answers, but according to some balance of reasoned argument, certain answers will be better than others. Certain substantive outcomes will be better than alternatives or certain procedures and institutions will be the appropriate method of compromising competing preferences. On this view, any law can be measured against a sound political morality whose tenets are accessible to a common reason, and a judgment can be rendered on whether the law is appropriate.

The less modest version of this position is that basic choices among forms of government and social life *and* more particular decisions are subject to reasoned determination. On this version, a choice to have one kind of law rather than another is subject to a reasoned judgment of correctness "all the way down." A more modest version does not claim that reasoned evaluation can settle all disagreements over basic forms of government. There may, for example, be no reasoned basis for deciding between a religious republic and liberal democracy in a society in which almost all members adhere to a particular religious faith. Once a basic form of government is chosen, at least a form in which reasoned evaluation has a prominent place, particular decisions will be subject to reasoned determination. Thus, political questions within a liberal democracy will have correct answers determined by a balance of reasoned arguments that draw from liberal democratic premises.

My own position is more complicated.[27] I do agree that an answer can be correct in the sense of being determined by a balance of relevant reasons even when competing positions are not unreasonable. I think there are correct answers in this sense to some choices among basic forms of government and to some decisions within basic forms of government.

But I do not think all issues of political morality are subject to resolution in this manner. That is, I think substantial gaps remain. There are some subjects of political morality as to which reasons of a sort all can assess, or even such reasons considered within the parameters of shared premises of liberal democracies, are inconclusive. Among these subjects are the protection that should be accorded higher animals and fetuses and the extent to which wealth should be redistributed to the poor.

One possible outcome of this limited skepticism could be a view that within the range for which common reason is inconclusive, no correct answer exists. That is not my own view.

CRITERIA THAT IN SOME SENSE ARE NOT AVAILABLE
TO EVERYONE

Perhaps there are (sound) standards of judgment for correctness that in some sense are not available to everyone. The standards might be ones on which outsiders cannot be expected to base assessments, they might even be incomprehensible to outsiders. Very briefly, I believe there are moral and political answers that are correct in the sense of better fitting with God's plan for human welfare. Common reason plays an important part in religious belief, but it cannot settle which religious perspectives are correct.[28] Some people will be fortunate enough to reach a religious understanding that approaches truth more nearly than other understandings. Religious insight helps guide political and moral judgment and those with more nearly true religious insights will have an extra source to help them toward moral and political truth. This does not mean religious insight will yield easily discoverable answers to questions on which common reason is inconclusive. Some think religious truth does provide simple, ready answers, but I do not. But my own views do exemplify the more general possibility of sound criteria of correctness that are neither purely subjective nor wholly culture dependent, but which reach beyond what common reason can discover.

DESCRIPTIVE AND NORMATIVE PERSPECTIVES

In considering claims that law conforms with sound political morality, we can see that aspects of the law might conform with political morality that is sound in each of these various senses. The "objectivity" that conformity with sound political morality will confer on the law will depend on the "objectivity" that the relevant principle of political morality enjoys. As a descriptive matter, we can say, beginning with Hart and proceeding to less modest claims about the content of correct morality and politics, that the law of any society will enjoy *some* conformity with sound political morality. The degree of conformity among legal systems will vary and will vary even among legal systems within a general class, like liberal democracies.

Normatively, when sound principles of political morality are identifiable, or are identifiable on the basis of reasoned argument, it is apparent that the law should correspond with them insofar as that is possible. This conclusion is subject only to some caveats. There should be some hesitancy to override deeply rooted contrary cultural morality, and the transition from present principles and practices to more ideal ones should not be too abrupt. More significant, there is room for argument whether it is even the business of some lawmakers to ascertain sound political morality as opposed to cultural morality. It may be claimed that judges, for example, have a responsibility to enforce the morality of the community, not to make independent judgments about moral questions.[29]

Whether in a pluralist liberal democracy citizens and officials should seek conformance of the law with sound political morality that is discoverable only on the basis of religious perspectives is a tremendously complex subject I shall not address here.[30] I shall, however, claim in Chapter 11 that the content of existing law in a secular polity like the United States should not be regarded as determined by such perspectives.

The preceding discussion has indulged many omissions and oversimplifications. I shall mention a few. I have not distinguished between whether a correct answer is *actually* ascertainable or is ascertainable only in theory. One might believe there is a sound principle based on the best reasoned arguments without thinking that real human beings are capable of identifying it with any confidence. A related point is that I have not distinguished between the best human beings can do at a particular time and the best they might ever be able to do. People have limited experience and information. A principle that genuinely has the better of the available understanding at a certain stage of history may be seen in later centuries to be flawed. One might say that the principle in its time really *was* soundest or that it was not soundest but that it was the best according to existing human understanding. I have suggested but not emphasized that many moral principles of considerable generality may be soundest for some societies and not others. In a close-knit tribe of Eskimos eking out a survival existence, full principles of abstract political rights may not be sound, even if they are sound for members of advanced democracies.

Determinations of Invalidity Based upon Incompatibility

What is the legal significance if otherwise authoritative legal rules or doctrines are contrary to standards supplied by one of these three broader sources? We can imagine cultures in which judges or other legal officials might treat such legal rules and doctrines as invalid. A rule enacted by a legislature might be considered not genuine law if it were contrary to patterns of cultural morality or aims of efficiency. As far as I am aware, neither of these standards, *in and of itself*, has ever been regarded as a basis in common law systems for formal invalidation of constitutional, statutory, or administrative provisions.

Something that resembles, but is not quite, invalidation on grounds of these broader standards can happen with respect to customary law and common law. Customary law depends on existing customary practice. What has once been a rule of customary law can cease to be so if customary morality or practice alters radically. The civil law doctrine of desuetude, which treats a statutory rule that has lain unenforced for many years as no longer in effect, has a somewhat similar import. Such rules typically no longer correspond with community practices, and the gap between present practice and attitudes and the old rule may be one criterion for judging if the rule has lapsed.

With respect to common law doctrines, analysis is a bit more complicated. Courts that announce common law doctrines often consider which approaches will conform with customary morality and will be efficient. As Melvin Eisenberg has argued persuasively,[31] the scope these doctrines are given in subsequent cases and their continuing force often depends on judgments about customary morality and efficiency. A doctrine that is found wanting will lose force and eventually be overruled or abandoned by some less straightforward technique.

At stages in the history of England and the United States, the use of sound political morality to invalidate statutory rules has been a serious issue. Laws that violated natural law and natural rights were occasionally considered invalid for that reason alone. Those times have passed.

For the present, the genuine issues about legislated provisions concern the extent to which cultural morality, efficiency, and sound political morality are used to *interpret* or *apply* legislation and constitutional clauses, as well as to guide enforcement. Legislation that is interpreted or applied may be something like the general justification defense, which "trumps" liability under ordinary criminal provisions. Constitutional clauses, like the due process clauses of the federal constitution, will be restraints on government power under which some lower legal norms are struck down. In either event, the broader source, through a statutory or constitutional filter, would effectively be used to invalidate aspects or applications of positive law.

Which of our three broader sources are used in this way? Within the United States, an administrative action taken under a statutory standard that incorporates economic criteria might be invalidated if it fails to promote efficiency. Apart from this, standards of interpretation used to invalidate rarely, if ever, employ unvarnished standards of efficiency.[32]

Laws that are perceived to violate various moral rights or require immoral actions may be rejected in whole or in their applications to particular circumstances. When courts make such judgments, drawing distinctions between their own perceptions of true principles of political morality and standards of cultural morality usually will be hard. Courts often draw both from some analysis of what is *really* fair or just and from community standards on those questions. A well-known due process test, for example, has sometimes been put as what is of "the very essence of a scheme of ordered liberty,"[33] an apparently universalistic inquiry; what is close to the same test has been cast more recently in terms of the traditions of the English-speaking peoples,[34] a (broad) community-oriented approach. Further, since virtually all important cultural values will find their place in the positive law itself,[35] distinguishing between values that may somehow be drawn from that law and those drawn from broader sources is very difficult—a topic to which I shall return. Nonetheless, mainly through the medium of constitutional interpretation of open-ended clauses, both basic cultural values and perceptions of true moral and political principles come into play as sources for invalidating particular positive legal standards or cancelling their application.

Our legal system presents countless occasions on which various officials must decide whether to enforce particular laws; the system also requires decisions about how to allocate resources for enforcement. These decisions are strongly influenced by judgments of whether legal norms offend cultural morality, violate sound principles of political morality, or are inefficient. Since a failure to enforce does not (except, possibly, if continuous over a long time) affect the formal validity of a legal norm, these decisions do not invalidate legal rules, but they can render the rules of little or no effect, a kind of "invalidation in practice."

I now address the normative questions. Should judgments of conformity underlie decisions to treat positive legal norms or their applications as invalid? I assume that judgments about cultural morality should figure in judicial review of customary law, and that judgments about that, about efficiency, and about sound political morality properly help determine the scope and continuing force of common law doctrines. (I return to this topic later in this chapter and in Chapter 11.) Such judgments also appropriately bear on enforcement. If extensive formal regulation and limited resources require decisions about what norms to enforce, judgments that particular norms are contrary to cultural morality, violate sound political morality, or are inefficient are all criteria for deciding that enforcement would be undesirable or at least less desirable than the enforcement of other norms. Without developing this subject further,[36] I shall focus on declarations of formal invalidity or nonapplication of statutory rules.

The classic natural law tradition posits that an immoral law is not "really" a law in some sense, and a lot of ink in legal philosophy has been spilled over this question. Insofar as the question is a practical one about official authority, it mainly concerns whether judges will have the power to declare immoral laws invalid. As I have said, judges in common law jurisdictions do not have this power in its simple form. In the United States, however, judges do have a fairly flexible power to interpret ordinary and constitutional norms in light of moral and political values. One lesson of the deliberations of the Senate Judiciary Committee on the Supreme Court nomination of Robert Bork, which preceded the rejection of his nomination, is that the practice of invalidating legislation on the basis of open-ended norms had wider public approval than many critics of the Court previously believed. In a society in which there is considerable disagreement about fundamental values *and* some distrust of the judiciary, introducing these broad criteria of legal validity through open constitutional clauses is preferable to granting judges a wide-ranging authority to invalidate whatever is immoral. There may be a place for scholarly rhetoric that immoral laws not invalidated or likely to be invalidated by courts are "not really laws" in the sense of failing to conform with the true purposes of law. But apart from some relevant constitutional norm, judges should not declare statutes to be "not laws." Exactly how wide judicial latitude to develop open-ended norms should be is a controversial question that goes to the heart of debates over constitutional adjudication. I favor a fairly generous latitude, but I shall not defend that position here. Cultural morality as well as judgments about sound political morality should figure in applications of open constitutional norms.

Nonconformity of the Law with Broader Sources and Noncompliance by Citizens

Citizens may consider compliance with rules from a prudential perspective, what is in their own long-term interest, or from a moral perspective, what should they do overall. No doubt some people judge that a rule that is highly inefficient or offensive to a community or morality is less likely to be enforced. This would provide a prudential reason not to comply. Some branches of law, notably remedies for breach of contract, virtually encourage prudential noncompliance with some civil duties when that will serve one's economic interests. One is supposed to pay damages for an economic breach of contract, but one need not perform the original duty.

What of the moral responsibility to obey? Failure of the law to conform to cultural morality or sound principles of political morality is regarded by many people as relevant. Some may also find a moral justification for noncompliance in the economic inefficiency of a rule. A person who imagines that one's moral duty, derived from God or from an extremely powerful social contract, is always to obey the law may think no failure of conformity to these broader sources can eliminate a moral duty to obey, but few modern Americans take that strict view about the vast number of legal standards to which they are subject. For them, a grossly unwarranted law may not deserve compliance. And even those who believe in a moral duty to obey all laws probably think the duty is more powerful when law is morally sound than when it is objectionable.

I shall be very brief about the normative questions because I have explored them in depth elsewhere.[37] If law violates sound moral and political standards, fails to conform with cultural morality, or is inefficient, that can be relevant to whether a person should, morally, comply with the law. Subtle judgments are required to decide, however, whether compliance with law on a particular occasion is a moral duty or is morally preferable. Often these judgments are highly complex; no simple correlation exists between the failure of a law to conform with a broader source and justified disobedience.

Specific Provisions That Require Reference to Broader Sources

Are there provisions within the law that require those interpreting or applying the law to refer to any of the three broader sources I have discussed? We could imagine a legal system that worked roughly in the following way: Legislators, consciously or not, would make sure that the law corresponds largely with cultural morality, sound principles of political morality, and aims of economic efficiency (an important subcategory of cultural morality and sound political morality). Those who interpret the law would look only to the law for their guidance and would not need to pay attention to broader sources. On the other hand, we can imagine a system in which the law adjusts to the guidance of these broader sources in part by incorporating within itself standards of reference to the sources. At least upon surface examination, our system is of the second kind.

Our law contains some legal standards that require judges or jurors, in part at least, to refer outward from legal rules and doctrines and the meaning of the language in which they are cast, to broader sources as bases for decision. Open-ended constitutional clauses of the kind I have mentioned are examples. The "cruel and unusual punishment" clause requires that judges decide what punishments are "cruel," an inquiry that requires references to basic community standards[38] or true moral principles, or a combination of the two. Many statutory regulations of economic matters are written, or have been interpreted, to call on judges to make judgments about economic efficiency; antitrust laws are a notable example. Standards that embody the duties of trustees require courts to determine what are traditional and accepted standards within the society for acting in certain roles. Ordinary standards of reasonable behavior in criminal law and tort law may be the most pervasive instances of evaluation by some mix of cultural standards and sound standards of political morality, importantly including economic efficiency. A common formulation of nuisance law asks whether the gravity of the harm outweighs the utility of the actor's conduct,[39] and we have seen in Chapter 4 that the general justification defense also requires a broad weighing of harms and benefits.

Sometimes the standards are mostly for genuine case-by-case application. When the standard concerns the reasonable behavior of ordinary citizens, leaving the decision to a jury is especially appropriate. In that event, a decision does not lead to a formulated standard for future cases. Alternatively, general standards are the groundwork for more precise standards that themselves operate as applicable rules in subsequent cases. Constitutional clauses are usually applied in the latter way. If the Supreme Court says that involuntary denaturalization is cruel and unusual punishment,[40] that rule becomes part of the modern fabric of the constitutional clause. In the application of many open-ended standards, some combination of these approaches occurs. Judges decide that certain things are reasonable or unreasonable, but leave a wide range in the middle for jury assessment.

I have said initially that *upon surface examination* our system includes references to broader sources, in order not to prejudge the following question: are these really references to broader sources or are they references to values as they are already reflected in the law? Roughly, the latter idea would be this. The law itself has all sorts of rules, doctrines, principles, and practices that reflect orderings of values. Not surprisingly, the correspondence is great between these orderings and what an examination of cultural morality, economic efficiency, and sound principles of political morality would indicate. What those interpreting or applying the law do is to make a judgment about orderings already within the law; they do not refer directly to the broader sources.

For practical purposes, it may not make a great deal of difference whether those who interpret and apply law understand themselves to draw exclusively from legal materials or to rely directly on broader sources, but as Chapter 11 will develop, the issue has considerable theoretical significance. After providing an illustrative case and making an initial clarification or qualification, I will defend the proposition that decision often involves direct reference to the broader sources.

In the poignant case of *Repouille* v. *United States*,[41] Learned Hand's opinion described the legal issue in this way:

> The District Attorney, on behalf of the Immigration and Naturalization Service, has appealed from an order, naturalizing Repouille. The objection is that he did not show himself to have been a person of "good moral character" for the five years which preceded the filing of his petition. The facts were as follows. The petition was filed on September 22, 1944, and on October 12, 1939, he had deliberately put to death his son, a boy of thirteen, by means of chloroform. His reason for this tragic deed was that the child had "suffered from birth from a brain injury which destined him to be an idiot and a physical monstrosity malformed in all four limbs. The child was blind, mute, and deformed. He had to be fed; the movements of his bladder and bowels were involuntary, and his entire life was spent in a small crib." Repouille had four other children at the time towards whom he has always been a dutiful and responsible parent; it may be assumed that his act was to help him in their nurture, which was being compromised by the burden imposed upon him in the care of the fifth. The family was altogether dependent upon his industry for its support. He was indicted for manslaughter in the first degree; but the jury brought in a verdict of manslaughter in the second degree with a recommendation of the "utmost clemency;" and the judge placed him on probation.

The opinion assumed that whether Repouille had a "good moral character" depended on whether his act of homicide was morally reprehensible. How should a court answer that question? We can imagine its drawing a conclusion from legal materials, or measuring the conduct against prevailing cultural morality, or trying to decide for itself if the conduct was seriously immoral, or perhaps employing some bizarre test of economic efficiency.

The court said that accepted moral conventions determined "good moral character"; Judge Jerome Frank dissented on the ground that the correct statutory test was the "attitude of our ethical leaders." Neither opinion treated existing legal norms as mainly determinative of whether Repouille's killing of his son was consistent with having a good moral character.

The fact that broader sources can be relevant does not mean that a discernible ordering of values within the law is irrelevant. The law provides substantial evidence about cultural morality and may guide a judge's thought about sound political morality. But even apart from its evidentiary significance, any ordering that the law indicates is likely to matter for how an open-ended reference within the law would be interpreted or applied. My claim is only that cultural morality, economic efficiency, and sound principles of political morality also count directly, that how judges and jurors fill in open-ended norms of the sort I have mentioned is not just a question of trying to discern how the law treats relevant values.

This point is most obvious when one considers questions put to juries, such as whether behavior is reasonable. In some criminal and tort cases, there may be no important dispute about what actually occurred, or even about a defendant's state of mind and prior background. Yet the jury must determine if the defendant acted reasonably (or, in criminal law, acted in gross disregard of what a reasonable person would do). These so-called mixed questions of law and fact require the applications of a legal standard to a particular state of facts. Since normative evaluation is central, these questions are sharply distinct from ordinary factual ones, such as: was the defendant ten miles away when the crime occurred? For purposes of our inquiry, the questions count as legal ones, and indeed, in some cases the judge may decide that action is reasonable or unreasonable as a matter of law. When the jury is called upon to apply a standard of reasonable behavior, a juror's reference must be to what he or she perceives to be correct standards or perceives to be cultural or professional standards, or to some mix of these standards. Jurors are not legal experts, and they are certainly not attuned to the subtle ways in which the law weighs certain values.

The jury must make a similar assessment when it considers the competing claims of value for the general justification defense, deciding if the harm a defendant avoided is greater than that the law seeks to prevent. In some jurisdictions this "weighing of values" for that defense is done by juries; in other jurisdictions it is done by judges. No one has suggested that the nature of the inquiry turns radically on who makes it. If the jury's assessment is not controlled by values somehow discerned from the law, neither is the judge's. Many other standards applied by judges, such as "cruel and unusual punishment," cannot reasonably be understood as dependent wholly on what one could discern from the corpus of law itself, even if that corpus is taken to include the various principles and theories that help explain it. Thus I conclude that, not only upon a surface look but also upon deeper examination, our law contains standards that require judges and juries to refer to broader sources to interpret and apply the law.

Are these sorts of references desirable? The first two parts of the book establish that general language is capable of giving direction in many instances and that the ability of people to rely on general language in the law to plan their activities is an important feature of legal systems. Often, the kind of guidance that can be given by such language is greater than can be accorded by open reference to correct moral and political standards, or economic efficiency, or cultural morality. For many circumstances, people need that greater guidance, and for those circumstances, the law requires something more precise than an open-ended reference to broader sources.

However, strong reasons sometimes support providing such references. First, it may be very difficult for the law to provide the required amount of detail. The precise responsibilities of drivers, doctors, trustees, or bankers cannot all be spelled out in advance. A closely related reason is that the relevant variables in situations may be so complex that even detailed general language could not capture them all. Here lies much of the impetus behind standards of reasonable behavior in tort and criminal law. Finally, there is the problem of changing social conditions and values. Precise language adopted now may not be adequate for the future. A list of all punishments deemed impermissibly "cruel" in 1789, for example, would not provide for new punishments that might be conceived.

For these reasons, providing language that gives some general guidance is often appropriate, leaving up to someone else decisions about the status of particular actions or practices. A legislature's referring explicitly to cultural morality, correct standards of political morality, or economic efficiency is not common, and what is relevant for courts, and administrative agencies, to consider may be significantly constrained by the language that is adopted. Nevertheless, the implicit invitations to make judgments in something like those terms, often involving some mix of perceived cultural morality and sound morality, are a healthy part of our law.

The Broader Sources as More General Bases for Legal Interpretation and Application

Are standards drawn from cultural morality, sound political morality, and economic efficiency bases for decision in legal cases even when no particular legal standard requires judgment in those terms? Conformance with identifiable community standards and with true principles of morality and justice are taken as desirable attributes for legal norms; in questions of interpretation and application of statutory and constitutional norms, arguments that one outcome would contravene cultural moral standards or sound political morality are generally regarded as appropriate. For many aspects of interpretation of legislated norms, arguments in terms of efficient outcomes would be regarded as appropriate. Such arguments also figure, as I have mentioned, in the development and abandonment of common law doctrines. Thus, for our legal system, arguments based on these broader sources are considered widely appropriate.

With respect to this more general use of broader sources, the same theoretical question arises that I considered with respect to narrower standards: are judicial inquiries possibly limited to values as discerned from legal sources? When arguments about injustice or inefficiency or cultural morality are made in respect to legal issues more generally, it is usually hard to distinguish whether reliance is placed on the broader values reflected by the law or on the broader sources themselves. Judicial opinions are likely to be unrevealing, in part, because judges will not aim to expose a difference between what they draw from the law and what they draw from elsewhere. Nevertheless, we do see cases where the direct influence of the broader sources is clear. In *Home Building & Loan Ass'n* v. *Blaisdell*,[42] for example, the Supreme Court considered whether very strict state restrictions on the right to foreclose mortgages violated the clause of the Constitution that says no state shall pass any "Law impairing the Obligation of Contracts."[43] Although these seemed the very sorts of restrictions on property and contract rights that worried those who wrote the clause, the Court said there was no impairment. Of course, its result was supported by statutory laws protecting debtors, but that kind of legal support should not count for very much when what is being interpreted is a clause meant to protect against popular legislative erosion of property interests. The overriding impetus to the decision appears to be that, given the terrible economic conditions of the depression, the state's restrictions were just and were supported by a broad community sense. Although it may not be easy to prove, there is little serious doubt that when direct legal sources do not resolve a case, courts are influenced by these broader sources.

Since it is generally desirable that law conform with sound moral and political standards, cultural morality, and, at least in some domains, economic efficiency, arguments in these terms are appropriate for difficult cases, even lacking a legal standard that refers to broader sources. It is arguable that judges who lack plain authorization to refer to these sources should limit themselves to values as they are presently reflected in the law, or to values as they are presently reflected in the law and in the culture. However, for reasons already suggested and ones that will emerge more fully in the next two chapters, either limitation would amount to an undesirable constraint on the judicial role.

10

Objectivity in Legal Reasoning

This chapter is about reasoning within the law, reasoning employed to interpret and apply law. One critical question is how far such reasoning is objective in the sense of having interpersonal validity. A closely related question is how reasoning within the law relates to other forms of reasoning. The latter question is an extension of last chapter's inquiry about legal decision and broader sources. I conclude that reasoning within the law is not simply a subcategory of any other form of reasoning. It combines different kinds of reasoning. No particular feature of reasoning within law is distinctively and uniquely "legal," but the context of legal decision colors the force of reasons that matter. Legal reasoning has substantial interpersonal validity, but reasonable people can disagree about the precise force of reasons and, in close cases, about whether the reasons on one side are more forceful than the reasons on the other. Much can be said about legal reasoning, but in this chapter, I say only enough to support these conclusions. Even in what I do say, I sometimes settle for assertion and explication rather than sustained argument. I am aware that in many respects all I accomplish in the chapter is the statement of plausible accounts, not a convincing showing that opposing perspectives are mistaken.

Reasoning Within the Law and Legal Reasoning

"Reasoning within the law" is all reasoning that is relevant to reaching decisions about what the law provides. By "legal reasoning," I mean, more narrowly, whatever reasoning within the law is not reducible to other forms of reasoning. (By using that phrase, I do not mean to prejudge whether there is any such thing as distinctively "legal reasoning"—by no means a simple question.) Except when an answer seems obvious, judges on appellate courts usually defend conclusions with opinions that engage in reasoning. Part of our tradition is that appropriate reasons for decision should generally be ones that properly appear in opinions. For the reasoning to matter, it should bear on the result that is reached. It should be relied upon and not be used as a manipulative tool to support results reached on other bases. This does not mean a judge's first sense of the right result must come from working through the reasons; it is enough that a result reached intuitively is subjected to the scrutiny of reasons to see if it stands up. But reliance on reasoning does mean that if the reasons lined up very differently, the decision might well come out the other way. A judge must remain open to the possibility of rejecting a conclusion that is not supported by relevant reasons.

The earlier chapters establish that much reasoning within the law is not distinctively legal. Part of deciding what the law contains is assigning normative language its undisputed meaning in clear applications, the sort of exercise discussed in the first five chapters. Even when meaning is not initially clear, some steps employed to determine it do not involve anything distinctly legal. If a court relies upon a dictionary to determine the meaning of an unusual nontechnical word, its reasoning "that the word probably has a meaning assigned to it in authoritative dictionaries" is not legal reasoning; it is general reasoning about the meaning of language people use in social context.

I need to be careful here. I certainly do not want to suggest that meaning can be understood apart from context. Embodiment of the word in a legal rule is part of the relevant social context. That could influence the legal meaning to be assigned, that is, distinct features of the law or legal reasoning might lead one away from a meaning one might assign in another context. The law and any distinctive legal reasoning lie in the background of all steps of reasoning to decision, even in "easy" cases, since they largely determine what steps are appropriate. Legal reasons may lie below the surface even when stated reasons do not seem distinctly legal. All I am asserting is that there are *steps* in the reasoning of many legal cases that involve ordinary ways to determine the meaning of authoritative language; a nonlawyer who speaks the language can perform these about as capably as a lawyer.

The previous chapter has already indicated, although not quite in those terms, that other kinds of reasoning, not distinctively legal, are relevant to decisions about the law. In that chapter, I inquired mainly about the correspondence between deciding legal cases and standards of behavior drawn from three broader sources, cultural morality (expansively understood), economic efficiency, and sound principles of political and moral philosophy. Thus, a court might ask whether the homicide committed by Repouille violated cultural morality or sound morality, or it might ask whether allowing harsh terms of credit for poor urban buyers is efficient. Here I focus not on standards of behavior, but forms moral reasoning that are aspects of broader sources of evaluation.

With respect to efficiency, it is hard even to conceptualize a line between a form of reasoning and substantive standards. To decide if a rule or practice is efficient in a particular sense is to engage in the form of reasoning that determines what is efficient. This involves the abstract and hypothetical reasoning in which economists engage; it also involves assessment of actual preferences and behavior, and perhaps of what behavior would occur in circumstances that will not be realized. To treat efficiency as legally relevant is to commit oneself to a rational methodology for determining what is efficient. Of course, a court might take an economist's word on these things rather than go through the analysis itself, but it would still be adopting the principle that this kind or kinds of reasoning count in reaching a legal decision.

How forms of reasoning relate to substantive standards is similar, although more complicated, for sound political morality. Recall that what I am including as sound political morality involves criteria of judgment that transcend particular cultures and are universally valid (in some sense) or derive from some basic form of political society, such as liberal democracy. To say that judges try to rely on such criteria is not, of course, to prove that such criteria exist, but I have indicated both how judges might refer to them and that my own belief is that they do exist. How would a court decide that a punishment was "really" cruel and, therefore, unconstitutional? Judges might suppose that correct standards of political and moral philosophy are intuitively obvious; then they could state the standards without exhibiting any process of reasoning. If they believed they should arrive at standards mainly by employing authoritative scripture, they might consult a religious text and whatever modes of reasoning were regarded as appropriate for interpreting the text. In modern liberal democracies, judges are unlikely to believe either of these approaches is warranted. They will think that sound standards of moral and political philosophy embody coherent principles and that some process of reasoning is available to deal with disputes. They may think that one can *reason from* empirical truths and some basic moral standards (thought to be universally true or fundamental to a kind of political culture, as equality is fundamental to democracy) to help derive more particular moral conclusions. They may think basic moral standards link together so the validity of one claimed standard can be tested by its coherence with other, accepted, standards. In any event, if they regard sound judgments of political morality as relevant, they are committing themselves to forms of reasoning by which such judgments are reached. These all are aspects of reasoning within the law. Since part of any moral or political judgment relevant for a legal decision involves the place and nature of law, these judgments will be colored by their legal context, but much of the reasoning is of a sort in which nonlawyers are as competent as lawyers.

Whether a commitment to cultural morality as a source of legal decision is tied to forms of reasoning is less obvious. In a limited sense, the answer is clear. Cultural morality must be ascertained. To give weight to cultural morality requires using means to determine what norms of cultural morality are, and I have argued in Chapter 9 that this often requires more than divining the subtle weight of various legal materials. Moreover, as I shall develop more fully in the next chapter, cultural morality requires "construction." Someone must make a choice about what is to count as "cultural morality," and two people in complete agreement on the sociological and psychological facts might disagree about that. At a minimum, a judge would have to use the forms of reasoning necessary to determine what makes up cultural morality and what cultural norms are.

The harder question is whether there is also a commitment to forms of reasoning within cultural morality. One might imagine cultural morality as constituted by various substantive judgments and practices beyond which a judge need not go. Perhaps these judgments and practices lack a reasoned connection, perhaps any such connection is too hard to discover, or perhaps it is simply not a judge's business to worry about that. The judge simply asks how the community regards something, as the court asked about Repouille's killing of his son. But such a vision would be a gross oversimplification of community norms and practices. Ways of thinking about and resolving problems are an aspect of cultural norms. *One* reason why any particular version of efficiency has the status it does is because that method of resolving problems has a certain amount of cultural support. Within the culture there may be ways of resolving conflicts, and some cultural values, such as individual autonomy, may relate closely to how one reasons about some moral and political problems. A skeptic who doubts that values and concepts of reason can transcend cultures may believe that all our methods of reasoning are simply reflections of cultural evaluation and practice. But even one who is not skeptical in this way must acknowledge that the threads of cultural forms of reasoning are intertwined with substantive standards of cultural morality. Usually courts will not pause to examine whether forms of reasoning do or do not have transcultural validity; they will simply employ those forms of reasoning that seem within our culture at least to be intrinsically appropriate.

I have said that reasoning within the law includes much reasoning that is not distinctively legal. I have mentioned reasoning endorsed by culture, reasoning appropriate to determine sound political morality, reasoning about the ordinary meaning of language, and economic reasoning. One may add reasoning appropriate for the social sciences, including history, political science, sociology, and psychology. Although the legal context affects the import of much of this reasoning, critical aspects of reasoning within law can often be carried out as effectively by nonlawyers as lawyers.

Autonomy and Objectivity

The preceding section shows that reasoning relevant to reaching legal decisions, in its entirety, is not fully autonomous. Some elements of reasoning within the law are forms of reasoning common to nonlegal inquiries. In this section, I inquire whether some or all of the reasoning in law is autonomous in any sense. First, however, I want to connect this problem with the broader concerns about objectivity.

A judge's reliance on a form of reasoning is itself not enough to establish that the reasoning is objective. The reasons offered must be something other than an expression of the particular judge's feelings and attitudes. For one weak sense of objectivity, the reasons in law must have some interpersonal validity. Another weak sense might be that reasoning in law is rooted in something outside itself. For a much stronger sense, there might be a best or correct form of reasoning that would yield distinctive right answers to legal problems.

If all reasoning in law were a branch of some broader kind of reasoning, such as moral reasoning, that could contribute to the rootedness of law in something larger. If, further, that broader reasoning had a strongly interpersonal character and yielded definite answers to hard questions, then identifying legal reasoning as a branch of it could provide reassurance about the interpersonal force of legal reasoning and the determinateness of answers to legal problems. We can see these possibilities most clearly in the idea that common law reasoning should somehow reduce to reasoning about economic efficiency. If that were *all* there were to common law reasoning, that branch of legal reasoning would have all the objectivity of a combination of economic analysis and techniques of discovering facts needed to apply economic analysis.

Insofar as reasoning in law is *autonomous*, it cannot draw objectivity from being a subcategory of a broader form of reasoning. Yet that *might* prove an advantage in terms of possessing certain kinds of objectivity. Suppose that moral reasoning turns out to be largely subjective, involving rationalization of personal feelings and attitudes and having little interpersonal quality. Were some reasoning in law to be a distinctive form of reasoning, it could turn out to be more solid, more strongly interpersonal than moral reasoning. In that event, identifying reasoning in law as autonomous might allow more encouragement about the possibility of definite answers to legal questions than would be true if legal reasoning were one limb of an infected tree of moral reasoning.

Whether there is indeed something called legal reasoning that is autonomous has been a confusing subject because subtle nuances of difference are packed under the heavy rhetoric of "autonomous or not."[1] To consider if there is a distinctive legal reasoning that is, in a significant sense, autonomous, we must ask wherein its autonomous character might lie. One possibility concerns the place of authoritative materials in the law. Like moral reasoning and prudential reasoning about how to achieve given objectives, reasoning within the law is practical reasoning about what should be done. But reasoning within the law is largely about the meaning of authoritative materials and their implications for practical issues that arise in social life. This aspect does distinguish law from techniques of determining efficient outcomes and from typical modern secular thought about moral and political philosophy, which does not rely on previously made and recorded normative decisions. It also distinguishes law from ways of ascertaining cultural morality,[2] mainly sociological and psychological inquiries.

As a species of practical reasoning that gives great significance to preexisting standards that are authoritative, however, reasoning in law is hardly unique. Such reasoning is involved when children, or baby-sitters, try to follow the directives of parents, when subordinates attempt to carry out their bosses' instructions, when players try to conform with the rules of games, when members follow and apply the rules of academic faculties or social clubs, when religious people seek to act on an understanding of the textually revealed will of God. Among the institutions that affect us, only the state, apart from religious organizations and the family, has pervasive effects on the lives of its members. The state is unique in its employment of organized coercive force. The specific materials that form the base point of reasoning in law in any society are also unique. They are not the same materials used for reasoning in other respects, and they have a complexity not found in other authoritative standards. Since the nature of the state and the materials of the law are special, it would be surprising if a refined balance of reasons in the law would be exactly the same as for other endeavors. If one thinks of reasoning from authoritative legal materials as involving a distinctive *legal reasoning*, the distinctiveness does not lie in the basic process of reasoning from authority, but in something more complex.

Other grounds for the distinctiveness of legal reasoning might lie in particular techniques of analysis or in important principles that guide the reasoning process. Perhaps legal reasoning is distinctive in its reliance on analogy or in more specific starting points, such as "penal statutes should be strictly construed." I may start with the observation that despite its occasional complexity, legal reasoning is largely explicable to nonlawyers. In some branches of science, in higher mathematics, and in more abstract forms of economics, to name a few, aspects of reasoning may be simply beyond the grasp of someone unfamiliar with the discipline. Parts of the law have technical lawyers' terms that a layperson does not know, and the interrelation of relevant provisions, say in the Internal Revenue Code, may be so complicated a nonexpert could not retain all the crucial steps. Further, a nonlawyer may not grasp exactly why some arguments are stronger or weaker than competing arguments. Certainly laypersons often get bored long before they understand the heart of the reasoning. Yet, when I think of major decisions in fields I know something about, constitutional law, criminal law, torts, and contracts, I cannot recall one whose underlying basic arguments would be incomprehensible to a person of ordinary intelligence and a high school education. The major reasons in law are not distinctive to law. I cannot think of a characteristically *legal* reason that does not have a familiar analogue in common experience and judgment. Let me illustrate briefly with five major sorts of guides for legal reasoning.

(1) Statutes, and other legal documents should be construed in light of their purposes; particular language should be construed in terms of the provisions as a whole. This is exactly how people ordinarily interpret the directives of superiors. Business subordinates and baby-sitters are not supposed to take a remark out of context, and they interpret their responsibilities in light of general objectives. A baby-sitter told to "make sure Susie gets to the beach" does not take five-year-old Susie to the beach if a driving rainstorm follows upon her parents' departure.

(2) Judicial opinions should rest on generalizable principles and rea-

sons. In Chapter 8, I discussed the idea that reasons given for a particular decision and legal principles developed in opinions should be ones that would have force for the judges in other cases. This generality is a corollary of the proposition that the *reasons* in an opinion should actually be relied on. As contrasted with simple intuitions, it is part of the character of a reason or a principle that it has some general force. Although legal reasoning may involve more specificity about possible future applications, the notion of general force for reasons is an aspect of rational thought about moral choice and indeed of rational thought in general.

(3) Legal reasoning is (often) by analogy. Analogical argument has an important place in the law. One begins with a practice that is clearly legal or clearly illegal and reasons by analogy to determine the status of a practice whose legality is disputed. Lawyers frequently have more confidence in the closeness of an analogy than in some generally stated proposition of law, and analogy has been thought to be at the heart of common law method.[3] If reasoning by analogy enjoys a central place in the law, it is hardly a method distinctive to law. When people face everyday moral problems or try to decide whether a foreign war would be justified, they frequently reason by analogy. They compare the problem before them with actual or hypothetical problems for which they think the answers are clear: "Is possible engagement in the Persian Gulf more like the (justified) Korean War or the (unjustified) Vietnam War?" Another point that is illustrated by this example is that reasoning by analogy is not sharply divided from reasoning in terms of general propositions. The manner in which one decides whether an analogy is close or distant is by addressing the respective facts in terms of general propositions of relevance: "The analogy to the Korean War is closer because response to an unwarranted invasion is involved." Many of the general propositions that are relevant for comparing analogies in law are, as Melvin Eisenberg has suggested, drawn from ordinary concepts of morality and sound policy.[4] Thus, not only in the technique of reasoning by analogy but also in the propositions that go into analogical comparison, law is not sharply distinct from broader forms of reasoning.

(4) Precedents should be followed and used as analogies. In its formal doctrine of precedent the common law may distinguish itself from other institutions, but in all walks of life we acknowledge the force of prior decisions. Once a problem has been carefully thought through, a sensible person does not expend equal energy when the problem arises again. Further, in all areas of life, we reason from decisions made in one situation to decisions in other situations that bear some similarity. But it

might rightly be said that the doctrine of precedent goes further; it gives positive *normative* force to the existence of the earlier decision. Even this narrow idea is familiar. Once a privilege is extended to one child in a family, or to a member of a larger group, others take that as itself an important argument for being given the same privilege; those who have granted the initial privilege perceive this argument to have force, even if they now think that the initial decision was mistaken.

(5) Penal statutes should be strictly construed. This sounds like a more technical legal doctrine related to the fearsome power of the criminal law. But suppose a father before going out says to his daughter, "Remember, go to bed at 11:00 o'clock when the movie is over. If you don't, you'll lose your allowance for a week." When he arrives home at 11:45 and she is still up, he says, "I told you to go to bed at 11:00." She responds, "You said I could stay up until the end of the movie, and tonight was a three hour movie." He meant the 11:00 hour to be the crucial part of the message, and he suspects his daughter understood that. Nonetheless, he will hesitate to punish on the basis of an unclear directive. The same is true of superiors at work who act fairly. There is a widespread attitude that unless behavior of a subordinate was obviously bad given the values of the institution, he should not be punished unless he has disregarded clear directions.

I suggested earlier in this chapter that the relevance within the law of standards drawn from broader sources incorporates the modes of reasoning characteristic of those sources. For example, moral reasoning is necessary to determine what moral standards are and how, from a moral point of view, they might apply to particular situations. What we now see is that even when judges are not self-consciously looking to broader sources but are doing legal reasoning, their basic premises and the forms of reasoning in which they engage connect closely to prudential and moral reasoning and to general reasoning about the implications of authoritative materials. Often it will be impossible to say where "legal reasoning" begins and reasoning from broader sources ends. Many arguments of fairness, for instance, may occupy some blurry domain in which legal ideas are not differentiated from moral and political ones.

Law has no distinctive forms of reason; legal reasoning is not autonomous in any simple sense. Yet the ability to reason effectively within an advanced legal system requires training and practice, acquired in professional school and in work under experienced practitioners. Legal reasoning is not mastered by learning a list of abstract propositions. Like other practical callings in life, it is learned mainly by doing.

If legal reasoning is not very different from other forms of reasoning, why is experience engaging in it so important for being a competent practitioner? Any "autonomy" of legal reasoning rests on the distinctive mix of relevant reasons within the law. The mix derives from the special functions of law, the richness and complexity of legal materials, the institutions that make legal decisions, the coercive force of legal judgments, and other aspects of legal systems that I have discussed.[5] There are at least three ways in which the mix of reasons is distinct. First, the *blend* of reasoning from authoritative sources with threads of other kinds of reasoning is not exactly replicated elsewhere. What are the implications of a precedent? When is a precedent so close that it cannot be fairly distinguished and so unfortunate in its effect that it should be overruled? The character of law affects how questions like those are addressed. The second way in which the mix of reasons is distinct is in how the broader reasons combine. The respective places of sociological inquiry and moral analysis are not quite the same for reasoning within the law as for reasoning toward other social decisions. Finally, reasons that look very similar may have a different weight within and without the law. Autonomy of individual choice is a reason not to put too much personal pressure on someone for whom one cares, when one thinks that person is not living well; it is also a reason not to interpret a criminal statute to forbid a significant choice about lifestyle that does not impinge directly on others. Exactly how much force the claim of individual autonomy will have depends not only on specific legal materials but also on the difference between legal constraint and personal pressure.

As we have seen, distinctive legal reasoning is not a subcategory of any other single kind of reasoning; nor is it any neat, easily explicable, combination of various forms of reasoning. Using the arresting image of a building, Charles Fried suggests that what is distinctively legal determines details at the bottom twenty feet, while grand structure is determined by moral and political philosophy.[6] In terms of reasoning within the law, the break is not sharp; the more distinctively legal mixes with the more directly moral and political at the bottom as well as at the top. It is true that in matters of detail at the bottom, the other forms of reasoning are least competent to indicate results, but their significance is not exhausted before the last twenty feet.

Objectivity and Interpersonal Force

I now return to the fundamental problem of how far legal reasoning has interpersonal force about what matters and about the weight of what matters. I have claimed in much of the book that the import of the general language of authoritative norms as it applies to standard cases has a kind of objective, interpersonal validity. In the simplest case, the natural language of a statute is construed in application to mean what all the relevant people think that it means. Within a culture at a certain time, one can speak of language objectively meaning one thing and not another, and within certain systems participants may be normatively constrained to assign language this objective meaning. That shared understanding largely determines the meaning assigned to language is a universal phenomenon and derives from the nature of language. The difficulties about objectivity arise when understandings are not shared, or when the shared understandings that do exist do not cover the situation at hand, or when the problem for decision does not turn on assigning particular language some meaning. Do forms of reasoning within the law for these more complex circumstances also have an objective, interpersonal quality?

I begin with another illustration. In connection with the hypothetical problem about dog-leashing in Part I, I considered proposed readings that would entirely defeat the aim of the rule because they would create impossible administrative burdens. Within any system in which authoritative weight is given to the political choices of a group, the prudential argument that a particular interpretation would effectively undercut a choice of the group would count as an argument against that interpretation. The power legislatures have relative to courts is a cultural phenomenon, but rough agreement on their respective roles is very wide.

Many other sorts of arguments have some clear force within the legal system: arguments based on authoritative materials, on values embodied in the system, on consistency, on the appropriate roles of different actors within the system. If I am right that broader sources figure in the ways I have suggested in legal decisions, arguments from those domains are of some force as well, at least some of the time. A powerful argument that one rule is more efficient than another will carry weight when efficiency matters, and an argument based on community standards will carry weight when community standards matter. Basic standards of practical reason and more distinctly legal arguments always have some weight.

Lawyers agree on which arguments have some force much more easily than they agree on how much force arguments have and on what the summing of arguments on each side amounts to. If the law, or the law in combination with general norms of practical reason and broader sources, somehow indicates the precise power of each relevant argument, this precise power is certainly not something actual human beings can determine and agree upon. Reasoning in law does not, like reasoning from geometric axioms, yield demonstrably true conclusions.

This problem produces great skepticism in some observers: if the force of arguments is hard to state and controversial, then in any case of reasonable arguments on both sides, presentation of the arguments for the winning side amounts to little more than a cover for the private preferences of judges. Before we let the difficulty of determining and stating the force of arguments lead us to extreme skepticism, we need to recognize the universality of this difficulty. Suppose I am making a self-interested decision about where to begin teaching law, free both of authoritative norms and of relevant moral obligation. In comparing two offers, I know that the following reasons all matter: (1) what I will teach; (2) the intellectual stimulation of colleagues and students; (3) the congeniality of the law school environment; (4) support services and opportunity for research; (5) the pleasantness of the community; and (6) salary. Arguments based on these factors have force. But I would have a hard time saying how much force each has for me. Certainly any general designation of force would be impossible. Comparative differences in salary could be very important if the lower salary required a substantial sacrifice in living standards, but in a higher range a difference of even $10,000 a year might seem relatively unimportant. Similar things might be said about faculty congeniality. I might hate sharp conflicts, but not much care if the environment was one of benign indifference or close positive relations. Even if all I am asked to do is to indicate the various forces in this context, I may have a hard time. I can assess the total outlook and make a decision, but I may have difficulty saying what mattered most and how much. Yet in this circumstance, no one should quickly leap to the conclusion that the reasons that I offer as relevant are really covers for a decision I reach on other grounds (although such conscious or unconscious rationalization is possible). Nor would acquaintances throw up their hands and conclude that *nothing* could be said about the comparative force of reasons for me.

Similar difficulties surround the effort to assess the force of various legal arguments in context. Even a single person has a hard time describing the power he or she assigns to reasons, and of course, the power one person assigns will be understood to depend partly on the power assigned by others (since those participating in the law should accord normative significance to shared understandings). As I have noted, language in majority opinions must adequately capture the views of judges who in fact assign somewhat different force to particular arguments. And opinions aim to persuade; our tradition of opinion writing is to overstate the combined power of the arguments found jointly sufficient to produce the result and to understate the combined weight of the contrary arguments.

The force of reasons within the law is not completely subjective; many arguments are widely acknowledged not to be too powerful, others to have great force. Nevertheless, there are no formulas for proper assignments of force and there are divergent evaluations. Within a substantial range, the only conceivable sense of fully objective degrees of force would be those assigned by some correct, but humanly unattainable, standard of assessment. This possibility will occupy us in the next chapter.

I want to touch on a related problem, the use of explicit balancing tests in constitutional law and elsewhere. A balancing test involves a weighing of all relevant factors on each side. It may be said that only an explicit balancing test can be objective because only it assigns weight to all that really counts. It may be claimed, to the contrary, that balancing is inevitably subjective. What I have said thus far largely resolves these questions. There are modes of reasoning, most notably the construction of language, that do not employ explicit balancing. Even when some value development is involved in reasoning to decision, the reference may be to how a present practice relates to some underlying value, such as the wrongness of compelled self-incrimination. A court may not consider all that could be said for and against the debated practice. When balancing takes place for some cases, it may occur only at the edges of defining and applying relevant concepts, with most cases left to resolution by an application of controlling concepts. Explicit balancing is not the only legitimate or objective form of reasoning in law, and often other modes of reasoning will be preferable.

A harder question is posed by the worry that far from being objective, balancing is actually highly subjective. Although there may be important variations in the burden a party must bear (a "rational basis" test is quite different from a "compelling interest" test), balancing involves looking at reasons with no preassigned weight. No doubt, balances are sometimes just covers for results reached on other grounds, but the two more fundamental concerns are (1) that the way the interests to be balanced are formulated is extremely arbitrary, and (2) that no basis exists to weigh the competing interests objectively. On the first point, it is true that courts are often overtly or unconsciously manipulative in the manner in which they characterize interests to be balanced. However, if, as Roscoe Pound suggested long ago, interests are put at the same level in terms of generalized social interests and phrased in a fair way, the interests to be balanced can be formulated in a reasonably objective way.[7] The problem of the weighing process is more elusive. Legal values, practical reason, and broader sources may dictate weight to some degree, but for reasons already explored they will not indicate precise weights in any straightforward sense. The way interests are balanced will often appear to be naked or arbitrary. But it would be a mistake to conclude that all that is involved is the subjective sense of weight of individual judges. Conscientious judges are trying to assess weight in accord with basic premises of the legal system and culture, and in accord with reason. Even when they succeed, expressing what they have done will be very hard. Sometimes, no doubt, little more occurs than the particular subjective weighing of individual judges, but even when something more interpersonal occurs, verbal statements depicting methods of balancing are not come by easily.

This chapter has treated reasoning in the law. It and Chapter 9 establish the context from which I take a deeper look at the problem of determinacy of legal answers in the final chapter.

11

Correct Answers to
Legal Questions

This final chapter revisits the subject of the first part of the book, discussing the possibility of determinate, correct answers to legal questions. Part I treated as correct an answer on which virtually all lawyers and others familiar with the law would agree, and against which there was no powerful normative argument consonant with the legal system. Subsequent chapters have developed the nature of legal standards and of legal reasoning, and how these relate within the law to broader standards and forms of reasoning. These chapters have provided a fuller picture of what lawyers consider when they seek to answer legal questions, and they begin to suggest the many respects in which the views of lawyers diverge about the answers to hard legal questions. These chapters did not, however, weaken the fundamental conclusions of Part I: namely, that for many legal questions a single answer is agreed upon by lawyers and that for other legal questions such agreement is lacking. According to the perspective of Part I, we can say that many legal questions have determinate answers and others do not.

In the course of that part, I left open whether answers to legal questions might be correct in some different way that would reduce or eliminate the range of indeterminacy. That is this chapter's topic, one requiring the richer view of legal standards and reasoning presented in the last three chapters. If more legal questions have correct answers than Part I argues, the law is more objective than it contends. If every legal question has a correct answer, the law is fully objective in the sense of having determinate answers. This chapter inquires (1) whether, under defensible standards of correct answers, such answers exist for every legal question or for more legal questions than Part I indicates; (2) whether these standards of correct answers are distinctive to the law or more general; and (3) whether one can believe in correct answers for the law without also believing in correct answers to questions of sound political morality? The extreme version of the claim that correct answers exist is that every, or virtually every, legal question has a correct answer. Much of this chapter is devoted to the plausibility of that claim, which I reject. But I also consider, and defend, the more modest claim that many more questions than Part I suggests have determinate answers.

Standards of Correct Answers

What does a standard have to be like to determine correct legal answers? Standards of legal correctness must be accessible to human beings; they cannot rest on some truth that is wholly undiscoverable by human beings.[1] Since legal analysis involves ascertaining the meaning of linguistic directives and engaging in forms of practical reason, absolute demonstration in the manner of a geometric proof or scientific experiment is out of the question.

The answer to a legal question must *in some sense* be provided by the law. This is an obvious but important point. A common view of the judicial function, associated with Cardozo[2] and H. L. A. Hart[3] among others, is that the law provides answers to many cases, but that in some difficult cases judges must act like legislators and create new law among "the gaps." Suppose that a theorist combined this view of the law and judges with the belief that sound political and moral philosophy supports one ideal outcome to every problem that faces a legislature. Maximum happiness utilitarianism is a philosophy with this import; according to it, the best piece of legislation (or decision not to legislate) is that which best promotes happiness. Existing law, or "the law," does not provide an answer to what the legislature should do, even if there is a correct answer, under utilitarianism (or some other philosophy), to the choice it faces. Legal questions judges consider concern the existing law. If judges sometimes really act like legislators, and should act like legislators, the final determination how to decide in those instances is not determined by the law, even if "the science of legislation" contains a correct answer.

The most promising avenues for correct answers to legal questions are in terms of the answers supported by the best reasons or the answers an ideal judge would reach. Since an ideal judge would be able, as an ordinary judge is not, to assess all the arguments in the best way, these two approaches come close to collapsing into each other, and I shall treat them as identical. The idea is that every legal question having a correct answer has a single answer supported by the best reasons. This answer is also the answer an ideal judge would reach. Actual lawyers and judges may disagree about what the answer is, but judges strive to find such an answer, and the answer does exist.

Before proceeding further to see whether criteria for correct answers can be reduced to something more specific, I pause to consider briefly some complexities in the concept of best reasons and an ideal judge, as well as how judicial psychology bears on the possibility of correct answers.

To decide exactly what the "best reasons" might mean, one must address the problem of historical stages of understanding and the problem of perfect as opposed to real judges. The first point is easiest. Suppose a particular legal standard requires a sound moral judgment, so that the legal question turns on resolution of a complex issue of morality. One need not believe in a simple version of "moral progress" to suppose that the moral understanding of the most sensitive people may increase as the deposit of human experience and perspectives increases. Perhaps the reasons for one moral position would seem stronger to the most intelligent, thoughtful, fair, and caring people of this culture, but arguments for a contrary view might seem stronger to such people five hundred years from now. Some arguments might be novel, other arguments made at both times might seem then to have more weight. From what standpoint are the "best reasons" to be judged? Are some cultural limitations in capabilities to understand to be built into the criterion of "best reasons," even if a real judge considering sound morality should be as "farseeing" as is humanly possible?

A related problem infects the use of an ideal judge as a standard. If the "ideal judge" is perfect and has superhuman capacities of cognition, synthesis, and appraisal, it is possible that an ideal judge would find a position stronger that the best judges, and even the best judges imaginable with actual human capabilities, would find weaker. It is doubtful that we should identify a correct legal result with what a perfect judge would decide if the crucial basis for that judge's determination is somehow not accessible to the best imaginable human judges, who would decide to the contrary. If we were asked what *factual judgment* was "best" at a particular time, would we not focus on information that could actually be processed by *real* human beings with existing informational techniques, not on what a superhuman being could have done with every scrap of information available to any person? May not something similar be true in the realm of reason in law and political morality? Perhaps the "ideal judge" should be conceived as someone with the maximum human capacities constrained by historical limitations on understanding.

Neither the criterion of "best reasons" nor the criterion of "what an ideal judge would decide" is free of important ambiguities and difficulties. Conceivably, what might be a correct answer under one construction of best reasons or an ideal judge might be incorrect under another construction. Of course, actual judges and their critics can only act within their own limitations; for them these subtleties about a "correct answer" thesis will not matter. I shall assume in what follows that "best reasons" are to be conceived in terms of understandings of which people are then capable and that the ideal judge is not superhuman, but the most competent human being imaginable. The analysis that follows would not be altered in crucial ways, however, by a different construction of these concepts.

The idea that a legal question has a correct answer and that judges seek to find that answer is opposed to an account that includes the notion that judges are legislating outcomes. Insofar as disagreement between the two accounts concerns the psychology of judges, I believe the "correct answer" account is accurate for nearly all questions. Judges see their task as searching for a correct answer, and they do not commonly perceive the law as "running out" (or leaving room for a legislative choice) in respect to hard questions. I think some judges sometimes do conceive of their role in particular cases as "legislating" the best result for the future, but I suppose these instances are now fairly atypical. Shifting conceptions of the judicial role could increase or decrease these instances in the future. In any event, it is not judicial psychology for its own sake that I am examining. Judges who believe they are "discovering" the law may be deluding themselves; there may be no law to be discovered. Understanding judicial psychology may shed insight on other questions, but the question on which I concentrate is whether it is true from some critical perspective that the law yields a correct answer to every question, or to many more questions than Part I asserts.[4]

I have so far concluded that it makes sense to speak of a correct answer as one that would be indicated by the "best reasons" and reached by an "ideal judge," even if able lawyers now disagree about the answer that judges should reach. The soundness of this conceptual approach receives some support from the fact that judges deal with most legal questions as if there is a correct answer to be discovered, but a judicial psychology of discovery does not prove that discovery is a reality.

One possible way of deciding what answer is better is to see what the dominant opinion in the interpretive legal community accepts as the better answer or recommends as means for determining the better answer. Could reference to dominant opinion by itself yield a satisfactory approach to discovering the "best reasons"?

I urged in Part I that meeting expectations is a strong aspect of legal interpretation, that legal officials should not range *too* far from what other relevant officials have decided and are deciding. Indeed, one of the reasons why I claimed that judges are bound to apply the language of legal rules had to do with this point. Part of my full position is that present assumptions within the interpretive legal community matter a great deal, and they matter for some reasons that do not apply to the interpretive communities of literary critics, anthropologists, or theologians. However, dominant opinion is not by itself a sufficient determinant of "best reasons."

On many precise legal questions, few within the community may have views. When views exist but are divided, there is no neutral way to determine dominance; for example, what is the relevant weight of opinion of a state judge, a prominent lawyer, a leading scholar, the Attorney General of the United States? Certainly the test could not be a hypothetical public opinion poll of every lawyer, or every lawyer and every citizen who thinks about legal interpretation.

More important, no one believes that for every issue, judges should follow ascertainable dominant opinion, either as to results or interpretive strategies. On some fairly technical matters, judges or scholars who delve into them may emerge with a more considered perspective than those whose opinions are based on less knowledge. A judge should not reach a result just because it accords with the dominant view. Proper interpretive strategies remain a subject of intense controversy. Among the legal elite, shifts in emphasis depend partly on who is appointing judges and on which intellectual trends have been in fashion from the time new judges were in law school up to the present. On some questions, dominant opinion in the legal community may reflect the particular interests of lawyers or the "establishment" in opposition to the interests of a broader public.[5] Judges sensitive enough to recognize this divergence should not assume that their responsibility is to reinforce privileges of members of the profession and others in society who are already powerful.

Present dominant interpretive practices, even when they are properly employed, often do no more than mark out a range of possible options for how a norm is to be understood. This means, as I have said in Part I, that they will yield an answer to some legal questions but not to others. For the others, they will not determine answers but they will constrain the process of justification. This constraint is what Owen Fiss stresses in his challenge to "nihilists." But the "objectivity" for which he contends falls far short of the objectivity of correct answers.[6] It may turn out that dominant views in the interpretive community upon which judges properly rely will yield some correct answers that are not accepted by virtually all lawyers. Such reliance may reduce the range of indeterminacy beyond what Part I suggests, but substantial indeterminacy will remain.

Correct Answers from the Legal Materials?

In this section, I consider whether best reasons leading to a correct answer come from within or from outside the law. I address this question mainly in respect to this extreme thesis that every legal question has a correct answer, but I also attend to the more modest thesis that many legal questions on which reasonable lawyers disagree have correct answers. The extreme thesis about correct answers within the law is that every legal question can be resolved correctly on the basis of values as they are reflected in the law, without any admixture of reference to broader sources. The notion would be that when more immediate criteria, like the language of an authoritative statute, leave matters in doubt, one choice will cohere better with all the legal materials than any other. That choice is correct.[7] I have mentioned this approach in Chapters 9 and 10, but here I explore its implications more systematically.

I need first to deflect potential confusion about the idea that all relevant values are reflected in the law. It definitely does not mean that the values that are "legal values" have no other status in the culture. Such a position would be absurd, as the previous chapters indicate. Religious liberty, equal treatment of equals, and fair warning of punishable behavior are legal values, but they are also values of cultural morality in the United States and sound political morality, at least in liberal democracies. Rather, the idea of values within the law is this: that from the law itself one can derive a subtly distinctive specification, ordering, and weighing of relevant values, and it is this specification, ordering, and weighing on which judges do and should rely when they interpret the law. A superbly intelligent and capable judge would start with the structures of our government, our legal institutions, and our substantive and procedural norms of law. With these he could do the ideal job of assessing values within the law. Such a judge would have to comprehend and develop a coherent system of moral and political philosophy, and apply its principles, but he would apply his extraordinary powers of cognition and apprehension to the legal materials, free of debatable prejudgments of his own about sound positions in moral and political philosophy. The correct value assessment would then be drawn from the law itself, not from the judge. What the ideal judge would manage to do self-consciously is what actual judges *try* to do in a more intuitive way.

On this view, the law would be self-contained, significantly autonomous. More important, this view holds out the promise that legal questions may have objectively correct answers even if analogous normative questions outside the law do not have such answers. Many people are skeptical that all, or even most, questions of political morality, including accommodations of competing claims of human welfare, have correct answers. The law deals with questions of political morality, and it resolves many competing claims of welfare by making trade-offs among them. If the law is a self-contained system that yields its own ordering and weighing of values, and the legal materials bear sufficiently on all questions that could arise, one could speak of correct answers to all legal questions as those that would perfectly reflect everything to be found in the law. One could believe, it appears, in objectively correct answers to questions within the system, based on the best reasons within the law, even if one were otherwise skeptical. Since all actual human beings fall far short of the ideal judge (even my sense of the ideal judge), many answers would, of course, be hard to determine or controversial. No actual judge would always be right, and observers often would be unsure whether a judge was right on a particular occasion. Nevertheless, the claim that every legal question has a correct answer might seem more modest philosophically than a claim that questions of political morality have correct answers. Perhaps, therefore, even skeptics about objective answers to interpersonal comparisons of welfare and to other problems of political morality might be persuaded to the thesis of one right answer to all legal questions.

The idea of the law as a self-contained system does roughly conceptualize much legal thought and reasoning, explaining how legal materials are used in legal arguments and also explaining how legal questions may have correct answers when the pure moral or political analogues to those questions are highly controversial. Part of the claim that many legal questions have correct answers based on "best reasons" rests on the ways in which values can be drawn from legal materials and legal institutions. Radical skeptics often point out how the legal system embraces contrary values,[8] yet reasoned analysis of the law often suggests circumstances in which one value is to be given primacy.[9]

The law's own reflection of values does help support the thesis that correct answers exist to *some* problems about which reasonable lawyers disagree. Any supposition that *all* legal questions can be resolved in this manner, however, is impossible to sustain. I shall discuss four difficulties: standards that refer to broader sources outside the law, techniques of legislative interpretation, premises on which values reflected in the law are developed to determine "mistakes," and the nature of much ordinary reasoning within the law.

Chapters 9 and 10 concluded that some standards in the law direct attention to broader sources and that the application of those standards often requires reasoning appropriate to the broader sources. These conclusions undermine any idea of the law as completely self-contained. Whether a broader source is *the main* or *a significant* basis for a decision, the answers to some questions involving reference to the broader source depend on the answer provided by that source. For those questions, a correct answer exists only if the broader source yields a correct answer.[10] This reality undermines not only any claim that the law is wholly self-contained but also the philosophical modesty of a thesis that every case has a correct answer. The law sometimes requires value assessments that do not depend wholly on the legal materials; a single correct answer may depend on there being a single correct answer to the broader issue that is put. As Chapter 9 develops, mixed questions of law and fact count as interpretations or applications of legal norms. Thus, if a nuisance standard requires a weighing of the value of carrying on an offensive activity against the value of stopping the activity,[11] the case will have a single correct answer only if there is a determinate answer to that comparison of value. The thesis that there is *always* a correct answer can be supported only if the broader sources to which the law refers always have correct answers.

The second general difficulty with the idea of a self-contained law providing correct answers to all questions is close to the one just discussed. It is widely agreed that part of the business of legislatures is to resolve competing claims of welfare. Under even a modestly purposive view of statutory interpretation, courts will have to interpret and apply statutory language that is distinctly unrevealing.[12] When other interpretive indicia are inconclusive, courts will be left to decide what, within the broad legislative parameters, would be the best resolution of particular competing claims. Again, it is hard to see how the crucial legal question that will emerge can always be settled without judicial resolution of competing claims of welfare.

The third general difficulty about correct answers under a self-contained law is even broader in its scope. The law cannot itself produce a systematic ordering of relevant values. No law will be completely coherent in its treatment of values; there will be tensions and inconsistencies. An ideal judge would have to choose between conflicting principles, discarding some as "mistakes." Some of these problems could be resolved by the sheer bulk of the materials on one side, but matters would not always be that simple. The strong consensus now is that an ideal judge would not be able to resolve all such questions by starting *neutrally* from the legal materials, that is, he could not resolve the questions solely on the basis of the overall "fit" of competing answers with the materials. He would instead have to introduce some independent normative moral and political views.

The delicate relation of "fit" to independent moral and political views is illuminated by the developing theory of Ronald Dworkin, the leading proponent of "one right answer." Early on, he made clear that he did not think "fit" could do the job alone.[13] He spoke of a number of theories of a given legal system, all of which might "fit adequately," with the choice between them determined by a judgment of moral and political philosophy.[14] In the more fully elaborated theory of *Law's Empire*,[15] Dworkin relates legal interpretation to other interpretation and stresses the extent to which those interpreting the law will bring their own best judgments about political morality to bear on the legal materials they interpret. Each interpreter seeks to give the best interpretation of the materials; this effort will combine many perspectives, which are analyzed with great sophistication by Dworkin. Fit and independent judgments of moral and political philosophy will be relevant, and an interpretation that fits less well may be chosen if it is strongly preferable on other grounds.

Finally, one way of understanding reasoning within the law is that it pervasively involves reference to broader sources. In his careful analysis of common law reasoning, Melvin Eisenberg suggests that analogies are chosen, legal principles are read expansively or narrowly, and decisions to overrule are made in light of moral norms and policies accepted in the society.[16] These norms and policies are only partly revealed in existing legal materials. On this account, reference to the broader source of cultural morality[17] is part of the fabric of ordinary legal reasoning, and the outcome of many cases will turn on its content.

All four difficulties with the idea of a self-contained law invariably yielding correct answers lead in a similar direction. In making many legal decisions, judges need to rely upon broader sources; the law, taken by itself and somehow neutrally understood, cannot provide a correct answer to those cases. The prospect of any correct answer at all depends on there being a correct answer within the broader source.

Correct Answers from the Broader Sources?

The extreme thesis that every legal question has a correct answer could be maintained if a correct answer always lies in every relevant broader source. One conceivable possibility is that all appropriate reliances on broader sources really are judgments based on cultural morality, that determining standards of cultural morality is a psychological and socio-logical—a factual—inquiry, and that such factual inquiries about domi-nant attitudes have determinate answers. Put so simply, this approach cannot be the basis for a correct answer to every case. However it is constructed, dominant cultural morality will not have an opinion on every subject. Opinions will be too evenly split or too few people will have opinions. An even more important difficulty is that cultural moral-ity cannot be neutrally constructed by judges. In the *Repouille* case, discussed in Chapters 9 and 10, Judge Frank in dissent argued that the opinions of ethical leaders should be the standard.[18] Whose cultural morality should count for the death penalty? In public opinion polls most people support the penalty, but suppose it turned out that most people who are personally acquainted with its operation, most people who have thought hard about the issue, and most "experts" in relevant fields think the death penalty is morally unacceptable? Does dominant cultural morality support the death penalty, reject it, or fail to yield a judgment? More abstractly, how large must a dissenting group be before one con-cludes that there is no cultural morality on an issue? Do all opinions count the same, or is more weight to be given to those whom a practice touches closely, those who feel more intensely, those who have thought more about the issue? How much does actual behavior matter as com-pared with professed belief? Do views in the near historical past matter only as evidence of present views, or do they have a weight of their own? Determining cultural morality is *not only* discovering the facts; two observers with perfect knowledge about behavior and people's actual and professed beliefs might disagree about whether, *overall*, the community accepts or rejects a practice. For cases in which dominant cultural moral-ity is central and is doubtful, a prior normative decision must be made about how that morality should be understood. Since it seems unlikely that the law itself will fully answer this question, some judgment of sound political morality is needed. Thus, a correct answer to these cases will depend on there being a correct answer of sound political morality.

There remains the greatest difficulty of all for the thesis that all references outside of law are to cultural standards and that these yield correct answers. It is implausible to suppose that the best construction of every "referring out" standard is exclusively in terms of present or continuing cultural morality. Certainly the intent of those who framed all the relevant standards, legislators, drafters of constitutions, and judges, was not this, and it is hard to think of a good reason for construing all the standards in this way.

In a theory that is both more limited and more complex than the simple version I have just discussed, Melvin Eisenberg claims that heavy reliance on cultural morality in common law adjudication is consistent with a view that every common law case has a correct answer. Eisenberg's theory is limited to common law decision; he does not claim that values relevant to constitutional and statutory cases are inevitably drawn from cultural morality. With respect to common law cases, Eisenberg challenges not only straightforward claims by myself and others that judges sometimes properly rely on their own judgments about what is morally right,[19] but also Dworkin's rich theory about how independent moral and political judgments figure in legal interpretation.[20] Eisenberg says that because courts are institutions to which people go to have existing standards applied, because courts are not politically representative in the manner of legislatures, and because legal decisions apply retroactively, judges should decide on the basis of standards that exist within the community. The moral norms and policies to which courts look should be those of the community.[21]

Whether Eisenberg is right to recommend such heavy reliance on community views is a complicated topic, and not one I shall address in depth here. Nor shall I even attempt to summarize the full content of his thoughtful theory. What I shall do is sketch a few of his assertions and claim that they indicate a need for reliance, which he does not recognize, on independent judgments of moral and political philosophy. Eisenberg says that when norms of social morality collide, or when there is substantial support for and opposition to a moral norm that underlies an established rule, "the preferred solution would usually be to maintain the rule."[22] How is a court to decide when social support for a norm is great enough to generate a collision with another norm, or to counteract cultural opposition to the norm? Courts must determine how much support is enough support;[23] it is hard to see how either the law or existing cultural norms will answer that question. Judges will need to make judgments of political morality about how much support should really be enough for courts to rely on. Eisenberg suggests that a court may give more weight to a norm that is waxing than to one that is waning,[24] but exactly how much should the weight be adjusted when a norm seems to be growing stronger or weaker?[25] Again, it is hard to see how a judgment of political morality can be avoided. According to Eisenberg, common law adjudication should be guided by models of congruence with the appropriate weight for culturally accepted social propositions, consistency within the body of law, and stability of doctrine.[26] For some legal issues, these ideals will be in competition with one another, as when existing doctrine is in tension with present cultural norms, and a judgment of political morality is appropriate to determine how much priority to give to each. Another point, drawn from something implicit in Eisenberg's mention of consistency within the law, is that constitutional and statutory standards influence common law decision. In an instance where correct application of a constitutional standard affects the best common law outcome, and the constitutional standard calls for a moral judgment not drawn exclusively from the community, the best common law decision may depend on that judgment. These brief remarks are hardly adequate to show that Eisenberg must concede the relevance of independent judgments of political morality for common law adjudication, but I do not see how he can avoid doing so. The necessity of such judgments for the construction of cultural morality, which proved such a difficulty for a simple claim that cultural morality is the only broader source that matters, seems to infect Eisenberg's more elaborate and nuanced theory as well.

Any supposition that all references to broader sources are to economic efficiency and that questions of efficiency have correct answers similarly fails. The construction of appropriate concepts of efficiency, and particularly the relevance of the wealth, or Kaldor-Hicks, standard, is controversial. So also is the precise place that judgments of efficiency should play. As I have argued, it is not plausible to think the more efficient result is necessarily the best from the standpoint of sound political morality. Thus moral and political judgments, made independently or drawn from cultural morality, are required to determine when efficiency matters and how much and what concept of efficiency is appropriate for the situation.

If neither efficiency nor dominant cultural morality can be conceived as a sole source that will yield correct answers to all legal questions that invoke broader sources, the two in combination also cannot perform that task. Judgments of sound political morality are required to construct the appropriate concepts of cultural morality and efficiency and to determine in context how much priority each has. And some standards, such as the provision on cruel and unusual punishment, seem to call for something beyond judgments about cultural morality and efficiency. They seem to call more directly for judgments of political morality. This does not mean that all, or any, legal references are "simply" to questions of sound political morality. Suppose, for example, the possible cruelty of imprisonment as a form of punishment is raised. Even if convinced that highly preferable, more moral, alternatives exist, a Supreme Court justice should not wholly disregard community practices and sentiment. He should not hold that imprisonment per se is "cruel and unusual" in this society at this time, given the law's overwhelming use of that penalty and the support for it in cultural morality. When standards in the law explicitly or implicitly direct the judge to broader sources, usually more than one source will matter, and the proper mix will depend on the issue. Since the judgment about mix is itself largely one of political morality, guided only to a limited degree by the legal materials, we are thrown back to the question whether there are correct judgments of moral and political philosophy. In light of all the standards of the law that call for judgments from broader sources, a thesis that there is a correct answer to every legal question could be plausibly maintained only if questions about sound political morality have correct answers. If they do not, or if sometimes they do not, the thesis that there is one right answer to all legal cases will collapse.

I shall reserve for the moment general approaches to that broad problem because I want to mention at the outset the particular difficulty of weighing competing claims of welfare.[27] I have argued with respect to the noisy factory disturbing a poor neighborhood that a nuisance standard requiring comparison of the value of the activity against the harm that it causes should not be reduced to some efficiency calculation of monetary value. The nuisance standard, and many other standards requiring reasonable behavior, may require interpersonal comparisons of welfare. Economists have been skeptical of the possibility of making interpersonal calculations of utility; such calculations lend themselves to no scientific measure because one person cannot know what another is experiencing. Since legal standards that appear to call for such comparisons are not all reducible to judgments of economic efficiency or cultural morality, the prospect of correct answers sometimes will rest on there being correct answers to interpersonal comparisons of welfare.

One might try to avoid this conclusion by contending that *somehow* the crucial questions the law puts are qualitatively different from resolving competing claims of welfare. No doubt what is involved is often constrained in some way and is not a pure question of interpersonal utilities.[28] But once the reference to interpersonal welfare is acknowledged, it is hard to see just how the critical legal questions could be qualitatively different, so they would yield correct answers even if the underlying competing claims of welfare have no correct resolutions. It would be heroic to assume that the law just could not contain standards requiring judgments of interpersonal welfare, when many statutory directions to administrative agencies seem to embody such standards and when people in ordinary life make interpersonal comparisons of welfare with considerable confidence.[29] I conclude that for some questions, the thesis that the law yields a correct answer does depend on a belief that there is a correct resolution of competing welfare claims.

Whether questions of sound political morality, including interpersonal comparisons of welfare, have correct answers is very important to whether many legal questions have correct answers. If many questions of political morality have correct answers, the range of correct answers in the law will be greater than it would otherwise be. If all questions, or all relevant questions, of political morality have correct answers, the thesis that all legal questions have correct answers remains plausible. It is time now to address the fundamental problem of correct answers to issues of political morality. My treatment is brief and sketchy; drawing from Chapter 9, I suggest some major possibilities and problems. I indicate my own views, but I do not purport to provide systematic answers to questions about knowledge and moral truth that divide modern philosophers.

I indicated in Chapter 9 that some positions about political morality could be irrational, and I discussed Hart's "minimum content" natural law as an example of what is rationally required. The demands of simple rationality will not be of much use for resolving the issues of political morality that face courts, and the limited substance of minimum content natural law illustrates why. As Hart says, given certain virtually universal values, such as the desirability of survival, and certain basic human characteristics, it would be strongly irrational for a society's law not to include protection of persons, property, and promises. Unfortunately, this minimum content natural law is compatible with too wide a variation in norms to assist judges. As I mentioned in Chapter 9, minimum content natural law does not tell us which people in society should enjoy these protections, or how much one value should be respected in comparison with others. Nor does it require a particular kind of property for those whose property is protected; communal rather than private property is sufficient.[30]

In Chapter 9, I suggested that some possible answers that are not strongly irrational may nevertheless be deeply unreasonable, or (though not deeply unreasonable) contrary to a balance of reasons, or not in accord with criteria of soundness that are (in a sense) available only to some citizens. In this chapter I have suggested that a decision in law is correct if it is supported by a balance of reasons and would be reached by an ideal judge. If we focus on legal questions whose answer turns on a sound judgment of political morality, we can conclude that the legal question will have a correct answer if a balance of ordinary reasons supports a particular answer to the relevant question of political morality. I shall return shortly to that subject, but first I want to inquire about the status of judgments based on criteria of soundness that are not available to everyone.

I shall concentrate on the idea that correct answers to moral and political questions are somehow connected to God's loving will that human beings flourish and to God's perfect understanding of what is needed to promote that. This is not the place to address the obstacles to belief in such a God, or to argue that if there is such a God, morality may properly be conceived as the effort to conform with God's understanding and will. I shall say only that I believe in such a God, and I believe further that if God knows what is best for us, and wants that for us, it is reasonable for us to try to act in that way. How might such belief, accepted by many people in this society, connect to the problem of correct answers that concerns us here?

It matters greatly whether, and how, human beings can discover what is right and good. I mentioned the conceivable possibility in Chapter 9 that aspects of how we should live might not be accessible to human beings to any degree. Suppose some forms of life or acts were "good" from God's standpoint but wholly undiscoverable by human beings. For purposes of human judgment, this goodness, as I suggested earlier, would be irrelevant. Since legal questions concern human judgment. a "correct answer" to a legal question cannot rest on standards wholly beyond human understanding. Suppose, instead, that God's understanding is accessible only to a relatively small minority whom God happens to have chosen, and no one, not even the members of the minority, is in a position to know who makes up that group. Again the standard of correctness is unavailable practically for our society and should not be viewed as a criterion of legal correctness. Most religious believers in our society think that God's truth is much more widely available, but it is at best grasped only partially by human beings. Adherence to religious communities and personal experience and inspiration are thought to constitute major sources of insight. These sources, to oversimplify, are not subject to interpersonal validation by those who have not had the experiences and are outside the religious communities. If this perspective is correct, that is, if truths about moral and political life that connect to religious truths are ones to which human beings have access, it makes sense to say that answers that actually conform with that truth are correct. This conclusion holds however uncertainly we may grasp the truths and however greatly they may be distorted through the lens of our own self-centeredness and fallibility. It is in this sense that I believe all questions of moral and political philosophy do have "correct answers."

Does it follow from this view that all *legal questions* that turn on questions of moral and political philosophy also have correct answers? It does not follow. Imagine that there is a moral question, say the moral acceptability of factory farming of pigs, as to which shared or generally available standards of reason are inconclusive. The moral question has a correct answer only in light of sources of understanding that are connected to what we may roughly call theological truth. These sources are not subject to interpersonal reason and validation by persons who do not accept the theological premises. The central issue is whether reasons based on these sources count for a "balance of reasons" that constitutes a correct answer in law.

We must look to the underlying principles of our legal system. Given principles of religious liberty and separation of church and state that guide us, a reason that rests on a theological truth that is not generally accepted should not count as a reason for what the existing law provides. In other words, if we ask whether there is a correct answer to a legal question based on a balance of reasons, we need to limit ourselves to arguments and reasons that do not rest directly on unshared theological claims.[31] Much more might be said about this, but I proceed to consider the possibility that there are correct answers in the sense of answers supported by a balance of reasons that do not involve theological presuppositions.[32] These are answers that would be reached by an ideal judge not relying on any essentially theological arguments.

To consider what a balance of reasons may resolve, we may start with the idea of traditional natural law, that reasonable reflection on human life in society will reveal what is a good life for human beings and what a good society is like. Although this approach may well establish some conclusions—that people need psychological security, that love is better than hate, that friendship is good, that knowledge is preferable to ignorance—people can reasonably disagree about what is good for themselves and for societies in general. Plainly different cultures have significantly different notions of how important various values are and of how people should live with respect to each other. Furthermore, although the point is often overemphasized by calling ordinary tensions and conflicts among values "contradictions,"[33] there are variant ideas about desirable lives and social orders within any particular modern society.

The skeptical view that there are no "objective" criteria for choosing between radically different forms of lives and societies competes with the view that some forms of life and society actually promote a greater flourishing than others, and that human reason is capable of ascertaining these forms. The latter position need not deny that what is the best life may vary for individuals within any society, or that what is the best law and morality may vary to some extent depending on cultural factors and stages of economic development. Nevertheless, even with this kind of partly variable content, the natural law position claims that better and worse are accessible to human understanding according to reasoned interpersonal evaluation.

The coverage of "best reasons" in the sense of reasoned interpersonal evaluation increases if one takes into account deontological arguments that do not depend on controversial concepts of the good and if one uses basic premises about the particular type of society in which one lives. Suppose one thinks that it is unreasonable to deny that all human beings should receive equal consideration. Some practices, such as slavery and racially segregated education at the behest of the dominant race, may be subject to condemnation on that basis. Various values, such as liberty of speech that attacks existing social arrangements, may be fundamental for liberal democracy, even if they could reasonably be rejected under other reasonable social orders.

How often will a balance of reasons yield correct answers to legal questions when reasonable lawyers disagree about the answers? This is a tremendously difficult topic about which people have widely divergent responses. My aim, as it has been in much of this chapter, is to sketch major positions and my own view without attempting systematic development. I concentrate on answers within our own legal system, where courts are guided by rich authoritative materials, complex institutions of governance, and broad premises of liberal democracy, as well as whatever reasons are available for people in general.

We may imagine a particular legal question that raises issues of cultural morality or sound political morality or both and does not have an answer on which virtually all reasonable lawyers agree. Recently in the news is the question whether under federal statutory law[34] and the Constitution[35] money may be used for university scholarships limited to minority students.[36] The Supreme Court precedents do not yield a clear answer to the question, and if they did, many people believe the Supreme Court should shift direction and come down much more solidly for or against "affirmative action" in the form of preferential treatment than it has so far. Most discussions of the question, at least most that go beyond narrow reliance on precedents, invoke broad concepts of equality and corrective and distributive justice, and talk about the effects of such selectivity. Reasonable people disagree about what justice requires and allows, about what the present dominant effects of minority preferences are, and about what the long-term dominant effects will be. Reasonable lawyers disagree sharply about the question whether such scholarships should be held to be permissible. In light of this disagreement, can we sensibly believe that a correct answer exists?

The skeptic says no. People disagree because reason does not resolve the issue. What divides people is preference, status, prejudice, and cultural experience. For such sharply disputed issues, there is no balance of reasons. The proponent of "one right answer" argues, to the contrary, that a balance of reasons often coexists with disagreement. Consider that at some stage in human development, it was reasonable for even the most enlightened persons to think that the earth's shape was more like a flat board than a sphere. *Now*, all reasonable people exposed to relevant evidence think it is highly probable the earth is roughly a sphere. During some period, it must have been true that a balance of reasons supported the sphere view, but many reasonable people thought the contrary. Of course, the shape of the earth is a matter of fact, whereas the permissibility of selective minority scholarships is a normative question, but our experience in dealing with normative questions also suggests that a "balance of reasons" may yield an answer. We approach questions in law and political morality on that supposition; even when an answer is difficult and we are uncertain what it is, we feel we are searching for a correct answer, not just expressing a preference or displaying a prejudice. The "one right answer" theorist moves from the contention that a "balance of reasons" *often* inclines one way or the other, despite uncertainty and disagreement, to the conclusion that it *invariably*, or almost invariably does. Issues on which disagreement is great or most people are highly uncertain are merely instances in which our perceptions are cloudy or the balance happens to be extremely close. These *may* be instances in which our own reasoning does not yield a confident result, but they hardly indicate an absence of a balance of reasons one way or the other.

The skeptic is likely to respond that our experience is full of delusion and rationalization, that we fool ourselves into thinking we are right, or probably right, or uncertain about what is right, when all we have is a preference, or prejudice, or class interest. Some skeptics say that normative questions are distinct in this respect from factual ones; others have a skeptical view about truth and knowledge as they relate to facts.

At the level at which I have put this disagreement, it is apparent that reason provides no conclusive proof. Reason cannot prove that a correct answer exists when intelligent people who listen to all the available reasons disagree. The skeptic has an explanation of why people often *feel* reason will resolve things, so that piece of experience is hardly decisive. On the other hand, since the "one right answer" view is compatible with broad disagreement and uncertainty, and with great difficulty in ascertaining the balance of reasons, the fact of disagreement among reasonable people over an answer does not show that "reason has run out" like water from a glass that has emptied. Neither side has a "knockdown" argument against the other.

It is sometimes claimed that if we recognize that all understanding is intertwined with language and culture, this division between the skeptic and the right answer theorist is revealed to be misconceived. But that seems incorrect. Even if all understanding is within the "language game" of a particular culture, some propositions can be stated (i.e., "viewed from space, the earth has the shape of a checkerboard") that are false in a more general way. The possibility remains that *in some broader way*, normative propositions could also be correct or incorrect. If I am wrong about this, it remains true that *within the culture* some questions will be ones of correctness, some questions ones of preference. Dispute can take place over which sorts of questions very difficult legal questions are. A shift to the perspective that all understanding is culture bound alters the shape of the division between a skeptic and a right answer theorist, but it does not eliminate the division.

Another approach might be to say that, like all other questions, this "right answer" question comes down to what works best. That is, the "correct" answer to the general question is what will best promote human welfare. If people will be better off thinking in terms of one right answer, then there *is* one right answer in the only sense that matters. However, the relevant standard of human welfare cannot fairly be taken as independent. The "right answer" theorist may say that people's *rights* should be protected and that this means discerning a balance of reasons within the law; the skeptic may reject this approach. The issue of defining the *relevant welfare* is thus not separate from whether a correct answer exists. In any event, the pragmatic approach is not especially useful if we lack compelling information about whether it promotes human welfare to treat difficult legal and moral questions as if they have correct answers.

I have concentrated on the two extremes. Many people's intermediate sense is that even difficult legal and moral questions often have correct answers, in the sense of answers that a balance of relevant reasons favors, but that such questions sometimes do not have correct answers. That is my view about reasons relevant for legal decision. I do believe, contrary to the more extreme skeptics, that one can often speak of reasoned non-theological argument as stronger for one position than another, even when reasonable lawyers disagree. To this extent, I think a criterion of "best reasons" does indicate that there are correct answers to many legal questions on which lawyers disagree. However, as I claim at length in another book,[37] when *all* nontheological criteria of reasoned interpersonal evaluation are employed, they are radically inconclusive about many important questions, including the consideration human beings should give to higher animals, the status of the fetus at five months after conception, and the extent to which the poor should be assisted if the institutions for assistance will reduce average welfare. I believe that often in respect to matters within the law *and* questions of political morality, including some interpersonal comparisons of welfare, there is no legally relevant "balance of reasons" in favor of one side. For these legal problems, I would say no "correct answer" exists, in the sense that matters for a law whose content is not dependent on the resolution of disputed theological questions.

Enlightening Dialogue over Right Answers?

The complexities I have examined indicate how far our theoretical understanding must move from an appealing self-contained legal system that provides a unique ordering and weighing of values. How does *any* plausible account compare with the apparently straightforward idea that the law provides objectively correct answers to legal questions? Imagine that Faith, who has just lost a case 5–4 before the Supreme Court, manages in a bar to buttonhole Justice Diepe, the writer of the Court's opinion, who is feeling in an expansive mood to discuss jurisprudence.

FAITH: Justice, I was a little disappointed to have lost my case and am very interested to know why. My lawyer said I should win, and that seemed right to me.
JUSTICE DIEPE: Well, I'm sorry that the law was against you. We were just applying the law impersonally and objectively.

FAITH: But the vote was 5–4 and you reversed the court below. What's more, my lawyer says that if Justice Strong had not retired and been replaced by Justice Strange, the case would have come out the other way. How can you be sure the law was against me before you declared the law to my detriment?

JUSTICE DIEPE: You have made an excellent point. In this life, little is certain, and I have to confess to you that although my opinion tried hard to make your position look absurd, the case was pretty close. To be a bit more precise, the best judgment of myself and my colleagues was that the law was against you.

FAITH: Justice, I am really impressed by your modesty and open-mindedness, and I buy what you say. Sometimes I have to make decisions that I am not certain about, too. But, if you don't mind, I'd like to know just what it means to say "the law was against me." Do you mean the legal materials, that's what my lawyer referred to, were stronger on the other side?

JUSTICE DIEPE: That is the judgment in many cases, but to be honest, not in your case. I thought the legal materials slightly favored you, but the position was much less appealing from the moral point of view.

FAITH: Are you saying that "the law was against me" even though the "legal materials," what my lawyer also called "fit arguments," were slightly in my favor?

JUSTICE DIEPE: In a word, yes.

FAITH: Well, how do you know my arguments were so much worse morally? Do you mean that this was your best guess about existing community morality, or some objective moral realm that is rationally determinable by real people, or something like that?

JUSTICE DIEPE: I'd be less than candid if I claimed that. I went by the moral ideas that seem right to me, but I am frankly perplexed by their status. Perhaps there is some sense in which there is a right moral answer to this question in terms of the arguments that would be more compelling to some ideal person, sometime, but I'm not confident about that. I am not sure how far moral judgments can be measured by standards accessible to human understanding of a reasoned kind.

FAITH: So, "the law" here comes down to the attempt of five justices to apply the moral understandings that seem best to them.

JUSTICE DIEPE: Yes, that's right. Say, I'd love to talk to you about literary and biblical interpretation, about Gadamer and Habermas, and Fiss and Unger and Dworkin? Can you stay a little longer, say three more hours?

FAITH: I'm afraid not, Justice. This is about all I can take for one evening, along with my four scotches. But I've got to say I am not all that reassured about the objectivity of law and "correct legal answers."

JUSTICE DIEPE: I'm sorry. Life is not reassuring. We do the best we can.

When Ronald Dworkin originally was writing, there seemed a sharp distinction between his idea of judges discovering answers in hard cases and H. L. A. Hart's notion of interstitial legislation. But that distinction seems largely to have evaporated. Dworkin's insights about the mental processes of judges, what they are trying to do, have really not changed much, and his idea that judges are trying to discover the right answers under the law, just as literary critics are seeking to give the best interpretations they can, remains sound. But it is highly doubtful whether his present views suggest that there is always a correct answer under the law in any sense ordinary people would recognize. Perhaps, to encourage faith in law, there is a positive value in public ignorance about what a thesis of correct answers entails. If not, extensive educative efforts are needed to make the public more aware of the scope of a sensible thesis that difficult legal questions that divide reasonable lawyers always have correct answers.

Interpretive Theory and Practice and the Boundaries of Interpretation

In this final section, I consider a question about the relation between theories of interpretation and interpretive practices, and I comment briefly on the conceptually troubling boundary between interpretation and disregard or subversion.

Focusing mainly on literary criticism but supposing that his insight has relevance for other forms of interpretation, Stanley Fish has suggested that one's view of what it means to interpret will not affect one's practice of interpretation.[38] This suggestion has some plausibility for many human endeavors, and it may be largely true for literary criticism. We learn by practice and seeing others perform. Subsequent philosophizing may not much affect practice, if it affects it at all. (I am inclined to think that philosophizing taken seriously is bound to have at least a *slight* effect on practice.)

If Fish's insight has a general plausibility, its accuracy does not follow for every form of interpretation and theorizing about it. A reservation is clearly appropriate for religious interpretation. Imagine that Joanne learned to interpret the Bible in study sessions in which some sophisticated theologians participated but in which theories of interpretation were not explicitly discussed. Later Joanne faced strongly competing positions about whether the Bible is the infallible word of God or not, whether it contains definite propositions about how to live or is basically an unfolding story of encounters with God that reveal God's nature, whether any prior authoritative interpreters have rendered interpretations that have a status as high as the Bible itself, whether God now contravenes or has in the past contravened ordinary natural processes. It would be astonishing should Joanne's interpretive efforts plunge forward unaffected by how she answered these questions, once she recognized them. Her answers would have an important bearing on how she would "interpret" the Ten Commandments, the Genesis account (or accounts) of creation, the "virgin birth," the raising of Lazarus, the stories of the empty tomb and what follows, and the concept of a trinitarian God as found in scripture.

A similar point applies about theories of legal interpretation, although the illustrations are less striking. Because of settled government structures, because of the authority of courts, and perhaps partly because of the mundane subjects of law and legal interpretation, legal interpretation in a particular system has a larger core of settled practice than modern theological interpretation. Still, seriously competing views about much of legal interpretation have a distinct bearing on practice. One pervasive issue is how far the judgments of the past should rule the present: how far should modern interpreters be guided by the apparent import of such past judgments rather than the needs of the present as modern interpreters conceive them? For legal interpretation, this is *not just* a dispute over how far past rules and intentions *can* guide the present. Dispute about that is considerable, but dispute extends to whether past rules *should* be taken to guide or should have somewhat less influence than the maximum possible. Theories of interpretation address such questions. A theory of constitutional adjudication that stresses the framers' intent places emphasis on past judgments. Acceptance of one theory or another is bound to affect somewhat how a judge interprets. The point is illustrated by the Contracts Clause cases during the Great Depression, in which the Supreme Court rendered a very unrestraining view of what the clause demanded of states dealing with mortgage debtors. The justices in the majority, as I indicated in Chapter 9, decided to depart from what the clause originally meant and had subsequently been interpreted to mean, essentially because they thought desperate social conditions strongly supported a permissive reading. Had they accepted a rigorous version of a framers' intent approach, they would almost certainly have decided differently.

A somewhat related inquiry concerns the boundaries of interpretation. Not everything that purports to be a legal interpretation really amounts to one. If someone focuses on the subjective state of mind of the person doing the interpreting, the possibility of disregard or subversion is clear. A corrupt court could issue an opinion in which it puts no credence, making its best attempt with the use of legal reasoning to conceal its financial motive for deciding as it does. But the law can be subverted for "noble" reasons as well as corrupt ones, as when a judge finds that the woman brought before him is not a fugitive slave despite overwhelming evidence that she is. Part I emphasized that there may be a difference between what the law requires and what it is best to do, taking everything into account. This reality can provide an incentive for judges to appear to comply with the law when they, in fact, do not comply. On some occasions, it may lead the judge to falsify his interpretive efforts. (Something similar can occur for other sorts of interpretations when a person is "playing a joke" or attempting to manipulate people by leading them to think something is true that the speaker believes is false.)

When can we say that the boundaries of interpretation have been transgressed? Imagine that an appellate judge thinks that a defendant was guilty under the law but that events after his criminal action suggest that the best disposition would be to acquit. The judge does not think, as a matter of interpretive practice, that events after a crime should determine liability, and she does not doubt that her initial interpretation would be correct for cases generally. The tension between preferred interpretation and desired result is not resolved by further reflection; that reflection does not lead her to think her initial interpretation is mistaken or that a conviction would be the best outcome. She decides to write an opinion holding that the criminal law does not cover the defendant's acts, a proposition which she does not believe. From a subjective perspective, the judge is now disregarding the law, but she may suppose that the opinion is within the range that others will find acceptable. Indeed, her opinion may be joined by fellow judges who are not self-consciously adopting anything less than a best interpretation.

The external observer can guess whether the writer of an opinion is subjectively giving the best interpretation she can and whether the writer subjectively thinks the interpretation is within a generally acceptable range. The external observer might recognize that one judge joining an opinion is a genuine interpreter and another is not.

What the observer who wants to judge an opinion on its face may say is more difficult. Of course, he can say whether an interpretation of law is one to which all reasonable lawyers would agree, is correct by a criterion of the balance of arguments, or is in a range to which there is no correct answer. But how does he decide if an interpretation he believes to be wrong is just a *bad interpretation* or a *subversion*? The observer must have a range of what he regards as within bounds and what is not. He may say something like, "No reasonable judge could write such an opinion, unless, rather than trying genuinely to interpret, she wished to subvert the law for this case or more generally." Like the opinion writer, the observer may think subversion is warranted. His judgment that the opinion bears no other reasonable explanation is not itself a judgment that, overall, anyone should have done anything differently.

So far, so good, but we reach some disturbing aspects of political judgment and rhetoric. Not only will political and moral views affect what one thinks about best interpretation, but also what one thinks or says about the line between interpretation and disregard or subversion. Consider how a conservative proponent of the status quo, a social reformer who favors an activist judiciary, and a genuine revolutionary might talk about what is a reasonable range of interpretation. The conservative may believe that the best interpretation takes past rules as highly constraining and views genuine interpretation narrowly, accusing activists of not doing real interpretation. The social reformer conceives interpretation as very much directed to modern and future needs. He stresses the openness of interpretation and perhaps even suggests that the conservative is either willfully manipulative or downright stupid, because the conservative's variety of interpretation is really impossible. The genuine revolutionary's approach is interesting. Believing reform from within the system is impossible and not wanting to credit the existing system with adequate flexibility, he may be inclined to say that the only interpretation is what the conservative suggests, and that this shows the need for overthrow of the present system.

It is troubling that rhetorical advantage can so influence what is said to count as interpretation of law and what crosses over into disregard of law. This may be a small part of the explanation why so much confusion has reigned over legal interpretation. I have no neat alternative if one wants to carry on the inquiry in a broader spirit than the pursuit of favored political objectives. I see no substitute for estimations of the subjective states of mind of those who write and join opinions—are they trying to comply with law or not?—and generous but measured judgments about the range of "in the ballpark" interpretive options.

Conclusion

In this third part of the book, we have come a long way from the relatively straightforward inquiry in Part I. Part I established that legal questions, that is, specific questions about legal consequences, often have determinate, or objectively correct, answers on which virtually all lawyers and others familiar with the law would agree. The foundations for such answers are shared understandings about language, social contexts, and values. To "play the game" of answering a legal question is to adhere to basic premises of a legal system, and that adherence will often yield clear answers to conceivable and real questions. Legal interpretation is a species of interpretation in general, but that does not mean that every legal question has more than one plausible answer.

Part III examined three other senses in which law might be thought objective. One is that law is tied to more general sources. Since law is interrelated with other aspects of social culture, there can be no doubt that law possesses this sort of objectivity, though argument is possible over how much of law is essentially independent.

The second sense of objectivity is that answers to legal questions are correct by standards that transcend particular cultures. A legal rule or outcome that conforms with sound political morality is objective in this sense. The legal issue is dealt with in a way that is *really right*, taking everything into account. In this sense, a legal rule prohibiting slavery is objectively correct. Because broader standards of correctness may take into account different social conditions, the right resolution for one society *may* be different from the right resolution for another, but the standard of judgment is either universal (happiness is preferable to unhappiness) or drawn from some basic type of political ordering (inequalities must be justified in a liberal democracy).

There is a tremendous range of disagreement among philosophers and lawyers over how far correct answers to questions of political morality are possible, and one's view about that will affect the degree to which one believes that law is, or can be, objective in this way. I take the position that significant standards of correctness exist. Many of these are generally accessible, but they leave unresolved some important questions. When religious sources of insight about correctness are included, I believe there are correct answers to all moral and political questions, but these sources are not, to oversimplify, generally accessible.

Much of Part II consisted of an effort to bring to bear general standards of judgment to determine what our law should look like. To take only the most obvious example, the discussion of fair classification in Chapter 7 was a treatment of whether possible legal standards are justifiable under sound principles of political morality (for all societies or liberal democracies).

A third sense of law's objectivity addressed in Part III is that the answer to a legal question often directly depends on the application of a broader standard of correctness. I considered the possibility that an apparently legal norm does not qualify as law if it violates a broader nonlegal standard. Simple invalidation because of incompatibility with a broader source is rare, but many legal standards, especially those in constitutions protecting rights, implicitly call for such judgments drawn from broader sources when judges review other legal rules. I treated at length the manner in which broader sources intertwine with narrower legal sources as standards for decision.

This discussion led to the renewed inquiry about answers to legal questions that are correct in the sense of being somehow required by the law as it then exists. Accepting notions of "best reasons" and an ideal judge, I agreed with Dworkin and others who urge that answers may be objectively correct in a significant sense even when reasonable lawyers disagree. I show that these answers often depend on there being correct answers to questions of political morality. For a liberal democracy, an answer to what existing law provides can be correct only if the crucial "best reasons" are generally accessible. When such reasons are inconclusive, that is, when the "right" answer to a legal question depends crucially on reasons accessible only to those with good religious insights or idiosyncratic values, I claimed that the law as it exists does not provide an answer to that question.

The discussion in Chapter 6 of Part II bears an interesting relation to the possibility of correct answers. The more the law makes external events and the perspectives of reasonable people determinative, the easier it will be to find relevant facts and reach normative conclusions that lawyers may agree upon. When a defendant's subjective perceptions are critical, the determination of fact will often be difficult, although the application of law to found facts may be fairly straightforward. Evaluations of individual blameworthiness are particularly hard and will often be controversial. It is impossible to say which standards of criminal liability will more often yield correct answers under a "best reasons" approach, but the nature of the inquiry alters significantly as the standards become more or less objective.

There are many important questions about law and objectivity. They bear complex relations to each other. Useful consideration demands that differences among the questions and the interrelations between them be seen with clear vision. That has been the overriding aim of this book.

NOTES

Chapter 1

1. This picture of the law managed to develop despite the fact that my father was a lawyer who knew better, and it was only mildly affected by an excellent seminar on constitutional law and legal theory under Roland Pennock at Swarthmore College and by a very rewarding term of studying philosophy of law under H. L. A. Hart at Oxford.

2. Since one aspect of legal positivism, perhaps a defining aspect, is that a law can count as law even if the law is immoral, it follows that not all law will be objectively grounded in morality. And if, as many people now believe, much of morality itself is not objective in some important sense, positivist legal reform cannot aspire to congruence with what is objectively correct morally in that sense.

3. Two related respects in which much writing in critical legal studies departs from traditional Marxism are in emphasizing the conflicting impulses within single cultures and claiming, as had Hegel long ago, that our conceptual apparatus determines the reality in which we live as much as external reality determines the way we think. If these insights are accepted, legal and other social concepts cannot flow straightforwardly from some more basic reality as Marx supposed.

Chapter 2

1. See, e.g., Anthony D'Amato, Pragmatic Indeterminacy, 85 Northwestern University Law Review 148 (1990); David Kairys, Law and Politics, 52 George Washington Law Review 243, 247–48 (1984); Joseph Singer, The Player and the Cards: Nihilism and Legal Theory, 94 Yale Law Journal 1, 8–9 (1984).

2. In discussions after my first lecture, Anthony D'Amato strongly challenged my position. In D'Amato, note 1 supra, and D'Amato, Can Any Legal Theory Constrain Any Judicial Decision?, 43 Miami Law Review 513, 514, 521, 530–32 (1989), he takes a position that seems to be contrary to mine.

3. No conceptualization can be wholly uncontroversial, and mine is not. Two clarifications are in order. I adopt an approach that is substantially "conventional" about the meaning of language and the significance of legal practices, words, and concepts. Some of what I say may not be compatible with what may be called a philosophical realist approach to legal judgment (not to be confused with a legal realist approach, which lies at the other end of the spectrum). Under that approach, judgment in law largely consists of ascertaining true moral and political positions to which the words of legal standards point. See, e.g., Michael

Moore, The Interpretive Turn in Modern Theory: A Turn for the Worse?, 41 Stanford Law Review 871 (1989); Heidi Hurd, Sovereignty in Silence, 99 Yale Law Journal 945 (1990). I do not in what follows make general arguments against a realist view of the matters I discuss. Perhaps it is enough to say here (1) that a realist view is fairly unusual today, (2) that it is not one on which skeptics can rely in challenging my position (except perhaps to show that no shared understanding about law, or our law, exists), and (3) that were one to accept a realist approach there would be clearly determinate answers to many cases, and the overlap of clearly determinate answers under that approach and my approach would be very great.

The relation between what I say and Ronald Dworkin's account of "conventionalism" and law as integrity, see Law's Empire (Cambridge, Mass., Harvard University Press 1986), is a bit more complicated. I definitely do not mean to endorse what Dworkin calls conventionalism, with its view that "law" is restricted to what is conventionally settled. Parts II and III of this book partly explain what more I believe is involved in legal judgment. Nor do I mean to reject Dworkin's fundamental idea that judges are involved in an effort to interpret legal materials that may properly lead them on some occasions to reject views about the content of law that are then widely accepted. I think that respect for what is widely accepted (because it is widely accepted) mixes with other elements as bases for decision, as I explain in Kent Greenawalt, The Rule of Recognition and the Constitution, 85 Michigan Law Review 621, 658–71 (1987), published in a compressed version as Hart's Rule of Recognition and the United States, in 1 Ratio Juris 40 (1988). Dworkin's own emphasis on coherence in the law, on "fairness" in deferring to widely held opinions, and on the place of paradigms in legal thought give a significant place to convention (or something very close to it) in judicial decision. I suspect that Dworkin's concentration on hard cases and the kind of imaginative reconstruction required for them tends to understate the place convention has as an overall source of judicial decision within his own thought; but it may well be that I think convention has a larger role than he does. In any event, I am confident that the practical conclusions I draw about determinate answers would not be affected by use of Dworkin's imaginatively constructed judge Hercules, given what Dworkin actually says about how Hercules would approach cases.

4. Allan Hutchinson says, for example, "The indeterminacy critique is fatal to the legitimacy of the current adjudicative enterprise, but it is not damaging to democracy." Democracy and Determinacy: An Essay on Legal Interpretation, 43 Miami Law Review 541 (1989).

5. Her tone of voice, for instance, might indicate a joke.

6. "Shutting the door" might mean cutting losses on a project Sam is supervising.

7. If a four-year-old child had just entered, Beth might feel a need to be more explicit about which door is to be shut.

8. He may not have heard Beth or understood her words. Only if further

words between Sam and Beth establish that he understood her request will it be clear to Beth and others that he has *consciously declined* to comply.

9. How a joke will be taken by Beth will depend on her relationship with Sam.

10. The lapse may be permanent or only temporary, depending on the circumstances.

11. Another conceptual possibility is that the directive exercises some force, but that the force is overridden by good reasons for noncompliance. This, however, is an inapt way of characterizing these situations, because Beth's request, made for normal circumstances, seems to have no relevance for these evidently abnormal circumstances.

12. I suggest below that one way of looking at the directive is: "Shut the door, unless [one among certain conditions arises]." One of the conditions then does arise. There is a sense in which doing nothing might be viewed as "complying with the directive including its unless clause." But this is a weak sense of "complying" that boils down to "not violating."

13. See generally John Searle, Expression and Meaning 117–36 (Cambridge, Cambridge University Press 1979).

14. Sometimes full meaning not only goes beyond literal meaning but contradicts it. This can occur when speaker and listener have a reason to conceal actual meaning from others; as when Nazi directives to kill Jews were phrased as instructions to "treat" them.

15. Suppose something *like* the circumstance has previously arisen: last time the president approached Beth's door, this time it is a vice-president. Whether an exception for the somewhat novel circumstance is best conceived as part of the directive's meaning will depend on how broadly the speaker and listener understood the original exception to be.

16. Frederick Schauer, Formalism, 97 Yale Law Journal 509, 534–38 (1988).

17. Such remarks might tip Sam off that something exceptional is going on, that Beth wants to hide her physical disability from the president, or that she fears the president is going to attack her physically.

18. I am here putting aside the possibility that the reasons for keeping the door open are so substantial that Sam thinks seriously about overriding Beth's directive. In the sense that such action always remains an option, Sam retains the final decision whether he should act. That problem is discussed below.

19. On the distinction between speaker's meaning and sentence meaning, see Hurd, note 3 supra, at 962–67, discussing various ways in which the kind of divergence indicated in the text might be dealt with under the highly influential approach of H. P. Grice, which emphasizes speaker's meaning, that is, what the speaker expects the hearer to understand the speaker as intending him to understand.

In some instances in which the speaker does not expect to be understood, speaker's meaning would appear to depend on how the speaker thinks it is more likely he will be understood than any other way *if* he is understood at all. If I try to give directions to someone who knows only a few words of English, I may think the greatest probability is that my words will not be understood at all, and I may think that the chance that the hearer will misconstrue them is greater than the chance that he will understand them correctly. Still, I usually choose words that I think will be more likely to be understood as I want than in any other single way.

20. See Terry Eagleton, Literary Theory 70–71 (Minneapolis, University of Minnesota Press 1983).

21. However, if she almost always says "door" instead of "window" and Sam is aware of this, the directive might be to shut the window. If Beth misspeaks some percentage of the time and Sam is aware of this, his appropriate response might be to ask her what she really wants. But, conceivably that might embarrass Beth, so Sam may be left with the option of moving to shut the door and hoping Beth has not misspoken on this occasion.

22. A purely "subjective" listener's approach seems obviously inapt. If Sam fails to shut the door because he has grossly misunderstood what Beth wants and expects, and the misunderstanding is the result of a personal failure of his, he has not complied with the directive.

23. It is possible that once the purpose of the inquiry is specified, there will be disagreement about the controlling perspective because of some evaluative difference. Someone *might* think that anyone who guesses wrong about a boss's actual intent should be punished. On that view, Beth's intent should govern Sam's possible punishment.

24. Conceivably, all people might be certain but disagree, or all people might be uncertain. But, for examples like these, uncertainty of some will usually mix with disagreement among others. Because of their temperaments, some people are usually sure one way or the other; other people are often uncertain.

25. Analysis would be more complicated if Sam correctly supposes Beth would wish him not to close the door, if keeping it open might help forestall company plans. One might say that this would then be an exceptional circumstance for which the directive's force would lapse. But as an employee, responsible to her own superiors, Beth might still have told Sam to shut the door and justified her doing so. Possibly she hopes as a whole human being that Sam will disobey a directive to promote company welfare that remains in force for that purpose.

26. I do not know whether running personal errands was *ever* understood to be an appropriate part of most secretaries' jobs. The practice might have been defended as freeing up the more valuable time of the boss for work.

27. Initial violations of conventional employee duties may not always be required to change conceptions of duties—one can imagine political activity or union-management agreements, or even a general reconceptualization of what is appropriate in light of novel notions of equality, doing so—but violations often make a contribution in that direction.

28. They also bear on whether his dismissal would be justified or fair.

29. As I have shown, a complex chain of argument can challenge the idea of

normative force when duties have less than ideal content and can even challenge the idea of conceptualization in terms of "duty" for such circumstances. Were the latter challenge to be seriously examined, many more complications about the conceptual boundaries of employee duties would need to be explored.

30. In strict form, "we would like" *may* state a fact about feelings rather than direct action, but such a statement, even without a "please," operates indirectly as an imperative in our culture. The "please" at the end of the sentence may turn the "would like" into explicitly imperative language. See Searle, note 13 supra, at 30–49.

31. Judges, unlike Sam vis-à-vis his superiors, may have a more complicated task, and a more creative role vis-à-vis legislatures. If the judicial role is properly highly creative, it is doubtful whether it makes good sense to say judges are ascertaining "collective intent." If it does, collective intent in law may depart from any ordinary sense of collective intent. If the term collective intent in law is to maintain close contact with collective intent in other spheres, delineating collective intent in law is not exclusively a matter of political philosophy. That is, one would need to think not only about optimal political arrangements between bodies issuing directives and those later interpreting them; one would also need to consider what collective intent signifies across a broad range of human activity.

32. This is Ronald Dworkin's recommendation of how judges should conceive legislation. See Dworkin, note 3 supra, at 313–54.

33. Of course, identification of violations would matter only if some possible consequences, such as criticism or disciplinary action, depended on committing a violation. The officials might have taken this attitude: "We're really concerned only about people who leave their doors open for long periods, but when we think we identify such people, we don't want to get into squabbles over whether they were only leaving doors open for short breaks." Sam's action here differs from his justified failures to close the door in my earlier hypothetical. His *closing* of the door when he takes coffee breaks would not defeat the purposes behind the closed-door rule or any likely countervailing purpose. His leaving the door open briefly *may* be appropriate; his closing the door certainly would be appropriate as well.

34. Roughly, for readers not familiar with baseball, a "strike" occurs when the ball is pitched into the "strike zone" above "home plate" and the batter fails to swing or swings and misses, or when the batter swings and hits the ball but does not hit it into "fair" territory (a "foul"). A batter is "out" after three strikes.

35. New York Times, Dec. 8, 1987, p. D25, col. 5.

36. Id. In December of 1987, the rules committee changed the upper limit to "the midpoint between the top of the shoulders and the top of the uniform pants," which was said to be "the middle of a player's chest." Id. The explanation for the *reduction* in the rule book strike zone was an attempt to *expand* the effective strike zone by providing a strike zone that umpires would enforce.

37. Packed into this conclusion is a judgment that consistency among umpires and fulfillment of player expectations matters more for a game like baseball than

strict adherence to original rule makers and a further judgment that virtually all those associated with the game of baseball would agree with the first judgment.

38. I am assuming here that betting is not intrinsically immoral, and that either it is legal or, if it is illegal in some sense, a loser still has a moral duty to pay off.

39. For most games, imagining an actual immoral rule is hard. But suppose that Kate is a voluntary gladiator and that at some stage of a contest the understood rules call on her to kill an opponent. Realizing the barbarity of this practice, she hits her opponent with a symbolic blow evidencing her ability to kill and then claims that the contest is over. If Kate can get Ralph to go along with her interpretation both will have acted in a praiseworthy way. Within the norms of the gladiatorial enterprise in which they are involved she and Ralph will have "failed to do their duties," but from a broader perspective, they will have performed morally preferable acts.

Chapter 3

1. Joseph Singer, The Player and the Cards: Nihilism and Legal Theory, 94 Yale Law Journal 1, 6 (1984).

2. David Kairys, Law and Politics, 52 George Washington Law Review 243, 244 (1984). Allan Hutchinson, in his Introduction to readings he has edited, Critical Legal Studies 7 (Totowa, N.J., Rowman and Littlefield 1989), has written that CLS has salvaged the powerful insights of realists "and insists that no objectively correct results exist, regardless of whether presented in terms of legal doctrine or policy analysis and no matter how skilled the judge or advocate." An article of his published the same year indicates that critics do not claim that all cases could be decided either way, that indeed most cases are easy, but this is because of extradoctrinal considerations of acceptability. Hutchinson, Democracy and Determinacy: An Essay on Legal Interpretation, 43 Miami Law Review 541, 557, 560, 567 (1989). Mark Kelman has said: "The Realists seem to me to be fixated on the indeterminacy of language, on the difficulties any rule maker would have in restraining the discretion of those who apply her rules simply by abstract verbal directive." A Guide to Critical Legal Studies 12 (Cambridge, Mass., Harvard University Press 1987). Noting that this position is "rehearsed by most CLS adherents," he believes that a stronger CLS claim is that the legal system is simultaneously philosophically committed to mirror-image contradictory norms. Id. at 13. See also id. at 45–46. Charles Yablon has urged that central to the CLS position on indeterminacy are statements about legal explanation that are neither descriptive nor normative about the law itself. The Indeterminacy of the Law: Critical Legal Studies and the Problem of Legal Explanation, 6 Cardozo Law Review 917, 937 (1985). For an extreme version of the indeterminist position, see Anthony D'Amato, Pragmatic Indeterminacy, 85 Northwestern University Law Review 148 (1990).

3. "No person under eighteen years old may vote" may amount to exactly the

same rule, with the same practical implications, as "only persons who are eighteen years old or over may vote." Even if, for some reason that I fail to see, these two formulations are not an exception to the idea that different formulations have different implications, other slighter differences may qualify: "Persons over eighteen years may vote" or "People over eighteen may vote." On the broader problem whether different linguistic forms can carry identical meaning, see E. D. Hirsch, Jr., The Aims of Interpretation 50–63 (Chicago, University of Chicago Press 1976). Even if different linguistic forms cannot carry precisely identical meanings, they could indicate the same practical consequences.

4. I use the term "standards" as a general term to cover both fairly precise rules and broader formulations that require contextual decisions by adjudicators. This usage differs from the division between rules and standards in Duncan Kennedy's important article, Form and Substance in Private Law Adjudication, 89 Harvard Law Review 1685 (1976).

5. Matters are somewhat more complicated with respect to civil law. The pushing in Warsaw is not immediately a tort in Vermont, but if the two Polish citizens then move to Vermont, one might be able to recover against the other given the conflicts of law rules in Vermont. (Conflicts of law rules indicate when one jurisdiction gives relief for events occurring in another jurisdiction and when it will enforce the substantive law of another jurisdiction.) How to characterize the situation in which Vermont courts use the tort doctrines of either Vermont or Poland to provide relief is not easy.

6. See Lawrence Solum, On the Indeterminacy Crisis: Critiquing Critical Dogma, 54 University of Chicago Law Review 462, 470–73 (1987).

Further, the law *might* make people liable for pure thoughts, and it might make animals or even plants liable for events. The question whether I am liable for a fleeting thought or a dog is liable for barking have determinate negative answers.

7. Many people have simple income tax questions answered by the instructions accompanying their forms.

8. For an extensive analysis of the elements that constitute a "case," see William Felstiner, Richard Abel, and Austin Sarat, The Emergence and Transformation of Disputes: Naming, Blaming, Claiming . . . , 15 Law & Society Review 631 (1980–81).

9. The reverse is also possible. It might be clear that certain grounds would assure a result in favor of one side; the answers to other questions the court addresses might be indeterminate.

10. As Lawrence Crocker pointed out to me, a defense lawyer would actually request an instruction that would tie the jury's evaluation of the alibi witnesses to the reasonable doubt standard that the prosecution must overcome in criminal cases. I have avoided this complication because there may be doubt in some jurisdictions about the appropriate phrasing of the reasonable doubt standard as it applies to alibi witnesses. I focus instead on the stark situation where the jury thinks the witnesses are probably telling the truth.

11. Benjamin Cardozo, The Growth of the Law 60 (New Haven, Conn., Yale University Press 1924). Walter Oberer has suggested that when a case belongs in court, legal doctrines do not decide it. On Law, Lawyering, and Law Professing: The Golden Sand, 39 Journal of Legal Education 203 (1989).

12. Jon Newman, Between Legal Realism and Neutral Principles: The Legitimacy of Institutional Values, 72 California Law Review 200, 204 (1984). Anthony D'Amato has suggested that the low rate of dissents may reflect judicial recognition that cases have no correct answers and that dissent is pointless. See Anthony D'Amato, Aspects of Deconstruction: Refuting Indeterminacy With One Bold Thought, 85 Northwestern University Law Review 113, 115 (1990). I do not claim to greater expertness in judicial psychology than Professor D'Amato, but as a general explanation for unanimity his proposal strikes me as highly implausible.

13. In How Courts Govern America 4 (New Haven, Conn., Yale University Press 1981), Richard Neely, Chief Justice of the West Virginia Supreme Court, wrote, "[m]y test for whether there is a clear legal principle is whether if ten lawyers were put in a room, given a legal principle and a set of facts as to which that principle could be applied to reach legal resolution of a dispute, nine out of ten would arrive at the same answer. I leave room for a tenth because in such a group one lawyer will inevitably be either stupid or eccentric."

14. This proposition would not be true for criminal cases in which taking an appeal is a routine obligation of representing a defendant. More generally, decisions about appeal based on economic calculation would lead to appeals when the cost of appeal is slight compared with the value of victory, even if the chances of victory are modest (assuming settlement after trial is not possible at a figure that would warrant relinquishing the chance to appeal).

15. See generally Ken Kress, Legal Indeterminacy, 77 California Law Review 283, 325–27 (1989), for a thoughtful discussion of the significance of predictability. See also Solum, note 6 supra, at 483.

16. See, for example, Kairys, note 2 supra, at 247–48; Singer, note 1 supra, at 22–24. See also Yablon, note 2 supra, who suggests that the common claim of indeterminacy is about neither imperative significance nor predictability.

17. Some answers are highly predictable even when the court is divided. On some questions, as to which a minority of one or two Supreme Court justices disagrees with the majority, one knows with great confidence that they will not carry the day in the near future.

18. See Michael Hancher, What Kind of Speech Act Is Interpretation, 10 Poetics 263, 269 (1981). Passages cited in notes 1 and 2 of this chapter might be read as concerning only cases in which some complicated reasoning is required.

19. I do not think the fit would be complete because there are some problems that are so complicated that interpretation may be required, but once the problems are understood, only one answer seems appropriate. When I was clerking for Justice Harlan, one case in which the Court actually reversed the decision below seemed to me to fall into this category. Massachusetts Trustees of Eastern Gas and Fuel Associates v. United States, 377 U.S. 235 (1964).

20. Similar to this claim of indeterminacy would be a claim that cases that the Supreme Court disposes of by full opinions are indeterminate. The Supreme Court does not often take cases and write full opinions when virtually all lawyers agree on answers; it spends most of its time only on relatively difficult cases.

21. See Allan Hutchinson, Democracy and Determinacy: An Essay on Legal Interpretation, 43 Miami Law Review 541, 543 (1989). According to Mark Tushnet, Following the Rules Laid Down: A Critique of Interpretivism and Neutral Principles, 96 Harvard Law Review 781, 819 (1983), the limits of craft are so broad that "in any *interesting* case any reasonably skilled lawyer can reach whatever result he or she wants" [emphasis added].

22. Neely, note 13 supra, at 110, remarks that the "real winners" are those who get justice without going to court.

23. I use the quotation marks around violated and violations because it could be argued that a cancelled violation is not a real violation, that each criminal provision somehow carries within it all valid claims of overriding justification.

24. I must confess that a change in circumstance and perspective has shaken me a bit on part of this point. When I initially drafted this example, I was a runner in a park frequented by unleashed dogs and a member of a household in which a firm decision had been reached that having a dog was impractical. As a consequence of my wife Sanja's death and my boys' pleas for a dog, I am now in a household with a big friendly dog that needs lots of exercise, and most of my running is now done with him. Most dogs in Riverside Park, including ours, are unleashed much of the time. For that large park with comparatively few people at most hours of the day, I believe a nonliteral interpretation might be practically effective. I still think it would not work for most New York parks, and I do not suppose judges sensibly can impose different rules for different parks.

25. In this sentence and elsewhere in the text, I assume that a judge would not properly reject present, central ideas of legislative supremacy in some radical way. To be more precise, if by the language it has chosen and by any other available indications of its purpose the legislature has disposed of a problem one way, and other relevant officials assume that way to be the law, a judge should not reject that disposition in favor of another he or she thinks is only somewhat better.

How does my assumption fit with Ronald Dworkin's interpretive approach of law as integrity? See Law's Empire (Cambridge, Mass., Harvard University Press 1986). This type of clear recent legislative mandate would certainly be part of the preinterpretive body of law according to Dworkin. On his view, the best interpretation of the law might lead to something previously regarded as the law not to be regarded as such. Even central paradigms might be overturned. But a minor issue such as this would certainly not be an occasion to overturn in one fell swoop basic notions of legislative supremacy. And as Dworkin says, id. at 255, "Any plausible working theory would disqualify an interpretation of our law that denied legislative competence or supremacy outright . . . ."

My discussion here and elsewhere also assumes that legislation should be regarded as a form of imperative. Challenging this position, Heidi Hurd, Sovereignty in Silence, 99 Yale Law Journal 945 (1990), has argued that legislation fails to meet the requisites of communication between a speaker and audience and should be conceived not as imperative but as "descriptive" comment (like a captain's entry in a ship's log) about "optimal legal arrangements." On this view, a legislature is a "theoretical" rather than "practical" authority. Professor Hurd's arguments are too complex for me to attempt to summarize and seriously respond to here; but (1) I believe that the communicative difficulties are still best handled by regarding legislation as a kind of imperfect imperative communication; (2) I do not perceive a feasible line between official directives that *are* communicative because they meet the requisites (a written order is sent to all those subject to it) and those that are not communicative; (3) in light of all the compromise and logrolling in legislatures, viewing legislation as a *description* of optimal legal arrangements seems severely strained; and (4) most importantly, the intricacies of communication theory in the philosophy of language seem a bad starting point for suggesting that courts treat legislation differently from how they have treated it previously. To be fair, Hurd's argument, as I understand it, is that by perceiving legislation to be noncommunicative, we are thereby *freed* to regard it in the most appropriate light. But whether legislation is genuinely communicative or not strikes me as not too important to whether legislation should be treated as directive or descriptive in Hurd's sense. In any event, the crucial practical significance in Hurd's approach for my purposes here would be how far judges could substitute their own views of "optimal legal arrangements" for those indicated by the legislature. As long as the legislature's view of "optimal legal arrangements" for matters of this sort would be taken as controlling (absent some serious immorality), Olive's case would remain an easy one. I do not think Professor Hurd suggests anything to the contrary.

26. I put aside the possibility that the judge thinks a literal leashing ordinance is grossly immoral or grossly misconceived. That might matter.

27. Within the law many terms that sound factual, such as "intentional" or "coerced," require a degree of judgment in their application. Two people who somehow understood every relevant event that transpired, including all relevant mental events, might disagree about whether a person acted "intentionally" or about whether the person had been "coerced." In such constructions, traditionally called mixed questions of law and fact, more is involved than ascertaining the bare facts. Although the issue is the application of a factual-sounding term, the real question, decided by judge or jury, may be how the law, including this term, applies to a given set of facts.

28. This conclusion is meaningful only if what is legally relevant is ordinarily determinate. In some circumstances it is arguable whether something is legally relevant. But there are not many sorts of facts relevant to whether scratching one's nose is murder.

29. The previous sentence mixes together challenges to what may be called metaphysical realism, epistemological realism, and realism of meaning. See Michael Moore, The Interpretive Turn in Modern Theory: A Turn For the Worse?,

41 Stanford Law Review 871, 874–81 (1989). I am self-consciously considering a skeptical view of each relevant issue. By my present understanding, I am a "realist" about metaphysics and about the meaning of factual statements, but I accept a coherentist test of knowledge.

30. A reference to an existing culture may be necessary since members of very different cultures might have radically different perceptions.

31. Probably much more complex reformulations would be required if one were to aim for a vocabulary that would be precise in rejecting the idea of facts as they actually occurred. Past presence at events and past perceptions are themselves facts. One who is skeptical about facts "as they occurred" must also be skeptical about "past presence" and "perceptions as they occurred"; so, to be precise, one might have to talk about what people without noticeable defects in memory who are reporting honestly would now recall as having been perceived by them (as most people now over forty recall having perceived from television or radio reportage in November of 1963 that John F. Kennedy was killed).

32. If the two are ultimately separable, a speaker might have to be a bit more precise about what he observed about a leaf or a dog in order to omit the kind of silent reliance on scientific generalizations suggested by words such as "fall" and "runs," which implicitly explain why the leaf and dog move as they do.

33. Thomas Kuhn, The Structure of Scientific Revolutions (Chicago, University of Chicago Press, 2d ed. 1970).

34. See Yablon, note 2 supra. If a full explanation of a legal conclusion must include an explanation why a judge actually chose to use the legal materials as he or she did, I do not see how existing materials could conceivably provide a full explanation.

35. *Some* discretion was, of course, left to Sam, such as which hand to use in closing the door.

36. See Dworkin, note 25 supra, at 15–23, 338–54, for cases in which the argument for a "nonliteral" application is very strong.

37. Gerald Graff, "Keep Off the Grass," "Drop Dead" and Other Indeterminacies: A Response to Sanford Levinson, 60 Texas Law Review 405, 407–8 (1982).

38. As I have noted, at least in the extreme case, where Beth says, "Shut the window," intending to say "door," the meaning of what she has said does seem to diverge from her intent.

39. On the difficulty in making sense of legislative intent, see Gerald MacCallum, *Legislative Intent*, in Robert Summers, ed., Essays in Legal Philosophy 237–73 (Berkeley, University of California Press).

40. A collective mental intent might exist about what a rule is meant *not* to do. Legislators voting on a bill entitled "A Leashing Ordinance" do not think they are adopting a death penalty for terrorists who hijack airplanes. One could perhaps speak of the legislators as intending that the rule not adopt such a penalty even though that possibility will not have occurred to them.

41. Something like the ignorance of legislators who do not think much about what they are adopting can occur with individual executive directives and private

contracts. With little awareness of content, individuals who have authority to act may sign documents prepared by others who lack authority.

42. Richard Posner has suggested that texts, including legal texts, can be clear by virtue of linguistic and cultural competence. Legal Formalism, Legal Realism, and the Interpretation of Statutes and the Constitution, 37 Case Western Law Review 179, 187, 191 (1986–87).

43. In Kent Greenawalt, Conflicts of Law and Morality 62–93 (New York, Oxford University Press 1987), I defend this assertion.

44. Matters may be different if the majority of the affected population rejects sets of rules altogether (e.g., the rules establishing apartheid in the Union of South Africa), and therefore would like to see the rules interpreted to be as ineffective as possible. Perhaps matters are also different if the particular accepted interpretation offends some higher normative principle drawn from the legal materials or directly from standards of political morality. Here I pass over such troubling examples.

45. I am assuming that no one thinks the Supreme Court *will* change its mind, despite the presence of good arguments for doing so. When lower courts think higher courts will overrule, it is arguable whether they should stick to the precedents they expect to be overruled.

46. Kelman, note 2 supra, at 46–51, emphasizes such uncertainties in application. See also Kenneth Davis, Police Discretion (St. Paul, West Publishing Company 1975).

47. I should say it does indicate that Joan should not pay less just because of a threat to drag Keith through the courts, but that is debatable.

48. Shortly after finishing law school, I was so angry that I got charged a $2.00 parking fee for a car I had left to be repaired (on the mistaken assurance by an employee that the garage would do that repair) that I sued for the fee in a court of small claims.

49. N.Y. Penal Law § 240.20 (McKinney 1989) (disorderly conduct).

50. People v. Pritchard, 27 N.Y.2d 246, 265 N.E.2d 532, 317 N.Y.S.2d 4 (1970).

51. The actual case was disposed of by an adjournment contemplating dismissal, so no decision on the merits was reached, but my acquaintance had the impression that the judge involved would have tried faithfully to apply the law of the statute and court of appeals.

52. I talk of "positive application" because proper exercises of discretion do not permit officials to *apply* legal standards that do not exist. Discretion, thus, does not threaten the conclusion that negative answers to legal questions—is Nick's scratching of his nose murder?—are often determinate.

53. See note 25 supra, for possible complexities regarding the judge's job description. See generally, Duncan Kennedy, Freedom and Constraint in Adjudication: A Critical Phenomenology, 36 Journal of Legal Education 518, 527 (1986).

Chapter 4

1. Model Penal Code, §3.02 (1985). The Commentary to the Code indicates the wide variations on this formulation that have been adopted and gives the content of other formulations. The main problem I discuss in the text is relevant for any of these formulations.

2. If all the defenses are sometimes determinate and sometimes not, instances will arise, of course, in which the general justification defense is determinate and some other defense, like insanity, is not. But in some instances when nonapplication of the general justification defense is determinate, nonapplication of the other defenses will also be determinate, and criminal liability will follow if a rule making certain behavior criminal applies.

3. A threshold difficulty with this argument is that the defense talks only about the harm to "himself" or "another," presumably human beings, but we can assume that the harm of a dog's not being healthy and happy is a harm to the owner. A second threshold difficulty Olive faces is that one harm to be avoided by leashing is serious injury to human beings from bites of dogs running free. It is hard to argue that that harm is not a more serious harm than the harm that results from leashing a dog. The answer to this threshold difficulty is that probabilities matter; avoidance of a near certain harm may be warranted even if this avoidance slightly increases the chance of a more serious harm. For example, breaking the speed limit may sometimes be warranted for reasons less than saving life even though the risk that someone will be killed is slightly increased.

4. Olive might respond that granting her the defense would not in fact undermine the ordinance because it carries such slight penalties most people would simply pay their fines without hiring a lawyer or contesting the matter in court. Olive's victory would be unknown to, or not worth invoking for, most dog owners. This response flies in the face of a premise of our legal system that courts should not consciously declare rights that they would be unwilling to declare if the rights were to be widely declared and acted upon by individuals and enforcement agencies. I do not say this "principle of legality" is never violated by courts, but it largely undercuts the force of Olive's argument. Further, if the legislature has decided most dogs should be leashed, and the court thinks that judgment should not be undermined, her making of a contrary argument is not a good reason to make an exception in Olive's case.

5. In a controversial 1917 case, a trial judge spoke of the necessity defense as one resting on "natural rights" that "cannot be taken away by statute." See Comment, The Law of Necessity as Applied in the Bisbee Deportation Case, 3 Arizona Law Review 264, 267 (1961). See note 25 in Chapter 3, supra, on the possibility of the judge rejecting standard ideas of legislative supremacy.

6. Olive might counter that few owners would contest summons for failing to leash dogs. This argument resembles the one considered and rejected in footnote 4, but its acceptance would be somewhat less offensive to principles of legality. Many dogs must be leashed; if owners of dogs who need not be leashed must

decide whether to establish that in court or pay a small fine, that is not *as troublesome* as having a system in which the great majority of those penalized are not appropriately subject to the penalty, the problem discussed in footnote 4.

7. The Fourteenth Amendment applies only to "persons," United States Constitution, Amendment XIV, § 1, and dogs do not qualify. That nonqualification could change over time (especially if it were learned that dogs have a high intelligence), but I assume that, barring some astonishing factual discoveries, a contemporary judge could not properly hold that dogs themselves are persons directly protected by the amendment.

8. Kenneth Karst, in Belonging to America: Equal Citizenship and the Constitution 141 (New Haven, Conn., Yale University Press 1989), suggests that the more a particular inequality tends to stigmatize, the more should be demanded in the way of justification. This wealth classification powerfully stigmatizes.

9. Probably this case does not yield a determinate answer for a Supreme Court justice, in the very narrow sense of "determinate" I am using in this part of the book. Since forms of analysis stated by judges and supported by others in the professional community would yield a contrary answer, a Supreme Court justice could reach the contrary answer without violating universally shared norms of the legal community and more general culture. Some people believe that the original language as historically intended is the only proper basis for an equal protection decision. More specifically, they believe that the Supreme Court has been mistaken to treat wealth discrimination as presumptively invalid under the equal protection clause (albeit the people that say this are usually thinking about the "indirect" wealth discrimination of charging set fees for vital services, not the explicit and direct wealth discrimination of my example). A Supreme Court justice might decide that, despite contrary precedent, the equal protection clause should henceforth be limited to racial discrimination and closely related forms of ethnic discrimination. That position has some limited support in the legal community. What can be said for Supreme Court justices as well as other judges is that if application of the equal protection clause to wealth classifications is granted, either because such "expansion" is intrinsically appropriate *or* because it is firmly established by precedent, then invalidation of this scheme follows objectively.

10. Some common law rules on technical subjects may have formulations that are repeated enough times so that a particular formulation is taken as distinctly authoritative.

11. Lest it be said that "some exception" may be infinitely malleable, we need to remember that there will be standard situations that do not arguably fall within any exception.

12. Indeed, the general justification defense itself remains a common law defense in many jurisdictions.

13. Melvin Eisenberg suggests a systematic approach to overruling in The Nature of the Common Law 104–45 (Cambridge, Mass., Harvard University Press 1988).

14. It may not be "off the wall," but I believe it very unsound.

Chapter 5

1. I leave open whether those understandings are actual understandings of real people or constructed understandings based on what they did. See Chapter 3.

2. By "broader standard" I mean approximately what Duncan Kennedy calls a "standard" in his Form and Substance in Private Law Adjudication, 89 Harvard Law Review 1685 (1976).

3. See Andrew Hayes, Chaos and Law (unpublished manuscript).

4. See generally, Heinz Pagels, The Cosmic Code (New York, Simon & Schuster 1982). It is conceivable that movements could be completely determinate in a way that an omnipotent observer could understand, but not be predictable for human beings. For people who believe that the only assertions about reality concern what human beings are capable of knowing, perhaps there is no meaningful distinction between actual indeterminacy and unavoidable human uncertainty.

5. One can imagine a physical regularity or many physical regularities simply ceasing, or being suspended on rare occasions by miracles or something like them.

6. This argument is developed by Andrew Hayes, in the manuscript cited in note 3 supra, which was submitted, in a much shorter version, as a paper in a seminar I was teaching.

7. What psychology and other "human sciences" may show is far more significant.

8. If someone is characterizing the status of an act at the time the act occurred, that judgment would not seem to be vulnerable to subsequent changes in social assumptions.

9. Saul Kripke, Wittgenstein On Rules and Private Language (Cambridge, Mass., Harvard University Press 1982).

10. Charles Yablon, Law and Metaphysics, 96 Yale Law Journal 613, 624 (1987). Professor Yablon's review is sensitive, however, to the limited relevance of Kripke's account for legal theory.

11. Dennis Patterson, Law's Pragmatism: Law as Practice and Narrative, 76 Virginia Law Review 937, 943 (1990). See generally Scott Landers, Wittgenstein, Realism, and CLS: Undermining Rule Scepticism, 9 Law & Philosophy 177 (1990), and the brief discussion in Anthony D'Amato, Pragmatic Indeterminacy, 85 Northwestern University Law Review 148, 173–74 (1990).

12. G. P. Baker and P. M. S. Hacker, Scepticism, Rules and Language (Oxford, Basil Blackwell Publisher, Ltd. 1984).

13. See Lawrence Solum, On the Indeterminacy Crisis: Critiquing Critical Dogma, 54 University of Chicago Law Review 462, 477–81 (1987).

14. Patterson, note 11 supra, does provide an illuminating account that focuses on law.

15. Margaret Jane Radin, Reconsidering the Rule of Law, 69 Boston University Law Review 781 (1989).

16. Id. at 807.

17. I am not sure whether Radin accepts the idea of obligation as I have used it in the sentence in the text. She does speak approvingly of the skeptical view that

one can neither tell if a rule is being applied nor show rule bindingness; she apparently endorses Wittgenstein's idea that a rule follower acts without reason or choice. Id. at 797, 799. Wittgenstein is focusing on rules of language and arithmetic that are followed without any thought that "disobedience" makes sense or is a wrong toward others. That is quite different from complying with *imperatives* when there are reasons not to comply. Part of many social practices is that people have a responsibility to act according to individual imperatives or general rules. When they participate in the social practice, that responsibility is a reason to act. This account of obligation to comply is not threatened by the notion that people follow "rules" of language and arithmetic without making a conscious choice.

18. I have not included the interpretation involved when a listener tries to ascertain what a speaker has said or when one language is translated into another. I also have not included ordinary scientific interpretation. Ronald Dworkin, in Law's Empire 49–53 (Cambridge, Mass., Harvard University Press 1986), comments illuminatingly about the relation between creative interpretation and conversational and scientific interpretation.

19. Hans-Georg Gadamer, Truth and Method 275 (New York, Cross Roads, 2d. rev ed. 1984).

20. Id.

21. Sanford Levinson, Law as Literature, 60 Texas Law Review 373, 374 (1982).

22. Id. at 375, fn. 7.

23. Id. at 379.

24. For similar reasons, I do not explore other possible categorizations in the process of applying norms. On a traditional distinction between interpretation and application, see E. D. Hirsch, Jr., The Aims of Interpretation 19 (Chicago, University of Chicago Press 1976).

25. I shall not consider the reproductive interpretation involved in the staging of plays and the playing of music because it seems to have the least relevance for our purposes, and for those purposes I am not sure it is significantly distinguishable from literary criticism.

26. Disagreements about the object of literary criticism make any simple generalizations about it difficult.

27. In an Epilogue to her account of early Christian understandings, Adam, Eve, and the Serpent 151–54 (New York, Random House 1989), Elaine Pagels indicates that she initially studied the origins of Christianity in the hope of finding the "real Christianity"; she discovered that historical inquiry "most often does not solve religious questions but can offer new perspectives upon those questions." Id. at 153.

28. See generally Robert Cover, The Supreme Court 1982 Term—Foreword: Nomos and Narrative, 97 Harvard Law Review 4 (1983). Ronald Dworkin has suggested that propositions of law "are interpretive of legal history, which com-

bines elements of both description and evaluation but is different from both."
Law as Interpretation, 60 Texas Law Review 527, 528 (1982).

29. Those who think they are not subject to the same criteria may believe normative judgments are not subject to truth or falsity at all, or are subject to different criteria of truth or falsity.

30. See Owen Fiss, Objectivity and Interpretation, 34 Stanford Law Review 739, 751 (1982): "What is being interpreted is a text, and the morality embodied in that text, not what individual people believe to be the good or right."

31. Even someone who thought evil laws did not count as laws could admit such a possibility since some good laws have unfortunate applications.

32. I am putting aside the view that *all* normative judgment involves interpretation. Even on that view, some kinds of normative interpretation, of the law or of social practices, would not be finally determinative of what one should do. A broader interpretation, say of moral duty or justice, would be required.

33. Levinson says, for example, that there are as many plausible readings of the Constitution as of *Hamlet*. Levinson, note 21 supra, at 391.

34. William Beaven Abernethy and Philip Joseph Mayher, Scripture and Imagination (New York, The Pilgrim Press 1988).

35. Michael Moore indicates various ways in which psychoanalytic interpretation of dreams may be understood. The Interpretive Turn in Modern Theory: A Turn for the Worse? 41 Stanford Law Review 871, 917–41 (1989). One way is that dream interpretation is not constrained by explanations of what caused the dream. A "successful" interpretation is one that helps the patient.

36. It is a little hard to put this question in a short form that yields the definite answer. If I asked whether Jesus was the most important human being, some might respond that he wasn't really a human being (although that answer is at odds with orthodox Christian theology). If I asked whether he was the most important person, some might respond that God is a person and God is the most important person. But my question is aimed at comparing Jesus to ordinary human beings who appear in the gospels.

37. It is *conceivable* that the privilege has actually been improperly invoked, if the witness is certain that nothing he truthfully says could *possibly* be used against him in any way, but as far as a judge is concerned, a witness has wide latitude to determine what might be incriminating and on these facts could certainly not require the testimony.

38. See Hirsch, note 24 supra, at 12, 125–39. I do not believe all valuable interpretations of a piece of literature could be said to be attempting "to show which way of reading the text . . . reveals it as the best work of art." Dworkin, note 28 supra, at 531. See also Dworkin, note 18 supra, at 50–62. One *might* think aesthetic value is what makes something art, but that interpretation should be in light of moral truth, even when such interpretation marginally reduces aesthetic value.

39. James Boyd White says, "It is indeed something of a critical truism that the meaning of a literary work is not in its message but in the experience it offers its

reader." Law as Language: Reading Law and Reading Literature, 60 Texas Law Review 415, 420 (1982). Even when a precise literary question is answered differently by two interpreters, the reader may profit. Suppose the question is: Looking at Alexey himself, does he represent a better moral exemplar if he is considered not to be motivated by malign feelings? Answering this question requires coming down on one side or the other, but the reader of competing interpretations may learn something significant about human nature and the qualities of a moral life from each interpretation.

40. Ronald Garet has pointed out that literal meanings are ordinarily a supplement or complement to nonliteral readings, and that early Christians did not read the Bible just literally. Ronald R. Garet, Comparative Normative Hermeneutics: Scripture, Literature, Constitution, 58 Southern California Law Review 35, 78–79 (1985).

41. See note 34 supra. Of course, *some* interpretations may be both highly implausible and without personal value.

Psychoanalytic interpretation of dreams is an interesting parallel. See note 35 supra.

42. Thomas Grey, The Constitution as Scripture, 37 Stanford Law Review 1, 13–14 (1984). Comparing a London Underground notice to a poem, Terry Eagleton, Literary Theory 88 (Minneapolis, University of Minnesota 1983), makes the point that interpretation of a poem is freer because for the notice "the language is part of a practical situation which tends to rule out certain readings of a text and legitimate others."

43. See, for example, Stanley Fish, Working on the Chain Gang: Interpretation in Law and Literature, 60 Texas Law Review 551, 562 (1982); Kenneth Abraham, Statutory Intepretation and Literary Theory: Some Common Concerns of an Unlikely Pair, 32 Rutgers Law Review 676 (1979).

44. I concentrate on legal interpretation by judges. Interpretation by lawyers is generally intended to predict what judges will do or to persuade them, and interpretation by scholars is often to recommend what judges should do.

45. Certain difficulties may arise in deciding what is to count as the text to be interpreted. Suppose an editor has insisted that a certain scene be cut because it will be offensive to readers. Does the critic take the manuscript as sent to the publisher or as edited? If it makes a large difference, each can be interpreted. There is another unimportant wrinkle of moderate interest. Any writer is familiar with printing and typing errors. Most of those get caught but a few do not. Even authors writing longhand occasionally "slip" and write the wrong word or leave out a word. What counts as the text? The interpreter must interpret the text he sees, which in turn may lead him to conclude that a slightly different text is what the author intended; he can then interpret that text.

46. Eagleton, note 42 supra, says that the relevant community includes publishers, editors, and reviewers, as well as academics.

47. See Hirsch, note 24 supra, at 40–41, 82–83, on the "fallacy" of the homogeneous present-day perspective.

48. I say "thoughtfully supposed" because people do have some tendency to *feel* that friends and associates whose views begin to diverge from their own have "let them down."

49. See A Quantity of Copies of Books v. Kansas, 378 U.S. 205, 215, n. 1 (1964) (dissenting opinion of Harlan, J.). I pick a book from this case because I actually read more than one of them as Justice Harlan's law clerk.

50. Graham Greene, The Heart of the Matter (London, The Reprint Society 1950). Of course, *The Brothers Karamazov*, which I have previously mentioned, has a strong religious perspective.

51. There may be intricate problems in deciding what counts as adultery, given the different practices of marriage and concept of adultery in ancient Israel.

52. Writings of Marx, Engels, and Lenin for many years had this status within the Soviet Union, and the Declaration of Independence has something close to this status in the United States.

53. Demonstrating the errors of one's contemporaries may be a very important part of one's task.

54. Further, if one knew the interpreter was likely to make such a statement one might not publicize one's contrary individual interpretation already reached.

55. As Chapter 4 argues, this does not mean that the norms are invariably indeterminate. Suppose when Sam joined the firm he was told by three different superiors that strong firm policy was that office doors should be kept shut except when people are entering and leaving the offices. One day a few weeks later when the air conditioner is operating full blast, he takes a two-hour lunch and neglects to shut his door on the way out. Though the rule has never been formulated in one authoritative version and though Sam cannot even recall the exact words each superior used, he can be as sure that he failed to comply as if a firm rule in canonical language had been circulated.

56. The distinction between a rule with exceptions and factors that must be weighed can be thin indeed.

57. The intermediate stage in reasoning might be that the clause forbids religious classifications for employment by the government even when a classification would favor members of a religious group that had previously suffered discrimination.

58. Levinson, note 21 supra, at 389, recalls Edward Randolph's words at the Philadelphia Convention proposing the new constitution: "There are great seasons when persons with limited powers are justified in exceeding them, and a person would be contemptible not to risk it."

59. Fiss, note 30 supra, at 755, talks of the judge as speaking with the authority of the pope. Of course, literary and historical interpreters judge the work of other interpreters, and these judgments may determine who is employed and who is not, but these are comparable to judgments of competence by an employer; they do not represent a determination of wrongdoing to be followed by a prescribed remedy against someone who would prefer to have nothing to do with the courts.

60. This includes discourse by judges off the bench.

61. These matters will, however, influence the amount of its force for subsequent cases.

62. See generally Fiss, note 30 supra; Owen Fiss, Conventionalism, 58 Southern California Law Review 177 (1985).

63. United States Constitution, Art. VI.

64. People would then be in the position of a couple who have been invited to a party each year but know that the hosts are free not to invite them this year.

Chapter 6

1. It might be responded that mental states of which the law takes cognizance should not be conceived as "real" but merely as constructions of the law. For most mental states important in law, however, such a position is mistaken. For example, theft is committed only if one intends to take the property of another; if I take a coat at a restaurant that belongs to someone else but that I think is mine, I have not committed theft. However much they are determined by my culture, I do experience mental states. I experience a difference between knowing that property is not mine and making a mistake about that. I assume others have the same basic experience, and I know they say they do. If my experience and reflection about this corresponds with that of almost everyone else, we can be sure that people connected with the law believe they are drawing distinctions in terms of real mental events of people when they distinguish knowledge that property belongs to someone else from a mistake about that. A similar demonstration could be made about most other basic distinctions in mental states drawn in the law.

2. Liberal governments do not entirely dissociate themselves from thoughts and attitudes apart from acts. In public schools, children are taught to believe certain things and to have certain attitudes, and official speeches and publications also promote beliefs and attitudes. Prisoners and mental patients are often encouraged and sometimes forced to undergo treatment that will affect basic attitudes. Some harmful behavior by these persons may be the trigger for the government's intervention, but part of the intervention is an attempt to deal directly with beliefs and attitudes. When I talk of the law not controlling beliefs and attitudes, I exclude education of children, broader educational efforts that are noncompulsory, and interventions triggered by harmful or bizarre behavior.

3. If I say to someone, "I now want you to drive eighty miles an hour," I am both expressing a feeling and encouraging forbidden behavior; the latter may make me guilty of criminal solicitation.

4. On some occasions the law deals with behavior that so far has not affected anyone because of the likelihood that dangerous action will follow; thus it is illegal for me to construct and possess a bomb or some other dangerous weapon.

5. See, Barbara Wootten, Social Science and Social Pathology (London, George Allen and Unwin 1959).

6. However, see note 13 infra, on the point that talking of someone's "action" already implies some mental element.

7. This terminology does not draw a sharp distinction between causes, in this sense, and conditions.

8. Almost certainly in such a system, it would be irrelevant whether James would probably have been hit by another car had Daisy not been driving, but I have simplified the example by removing that likelihood.

9. Let me defend this initial conclusion against possible objections. It might be said that because Daisy acted in an unexceptionable fashion she did not "cause" the harm in a legally significant sense. That would seem an appropriate way to deal with the problem, and it has support in present law, but doing so would depart from the pure harm-based approach to initial liability. It would make the reasonableness of Daisy's behavior, and perhaps her state of mind about possible harm, relevant to whether she is liable initially; that is exactly what the harm-based approach purports to avoid.

A narrower basis for letting Daisy off the hook might be that because James threw himself in front of the car, he caused his own injuries. That, again, would be a conceivable approach, but it also departs from a pure harm-based approach, as can be shown by four variations. Suppose that James had stumbled in front of the car, or that James was a two-year-old child who had just torn free from his mother's hand; in these cases, no intentional act of a responsible human agent would have "caused" the accident, and it would be more difficult to say that James caused it rather than Daisy. Indeed, the only basis for saying this would be that Daisy, and not James, had managed to behave in a careful and prudent way, one of the questions the harm-based approach means to put aside at the first stage. Another variation imagines Daisy as someone who lives down the road and hates James; she is chatting on the telephone with a guest at the party James is attending, who says "James got into another argument with his wife. Now he is sulking along the road." Knowing that James has recently tried to throw himself in front of a car, Daisy quickly gets into hers and drives by in the hope that James will try again. In a fourth variation, Daisy has independent reasons for driving by, but she recognizes James at a distance, knowing that he is deeply upset and has suicidal tendencies, she nonetheless proceeds at her normal speed. In these last two variations, we can see that even though James intentionally throws himself in front of Daisy's car, there are factual circumstances in which Daisy might very well be a proper subject of the criminal law. In summary, under a harm-based approach to criminal law, either Daisy's prudent driving and James's action do not let Daisy off the hook at the initial stage *or* matters of perceptions, intentions, and reasonable care will figure at that stage, something the harm-based approach claims to avoid. On the "purest" model Daisy is "liable" at stage one.

10. It might be claimed that dragging people who have shown no failing whatever through the criminal process would help to make people realize that criminal liability does not involve blameworthiness. This is a coherent strategy,

but one bought at the cost of forcing some people who are simply the victims of circumstance through a trying formal process. The strategy promises only marginal success, since people will probably suppose that actors whose behavior in an incident "requires" twenty years in prison are more to blame than those like Daisy for whom no treatment is indicated.

11. Whether her earlier statements of beliefs and feelings would be taken into account would be an important issue. If these could be taken into account, treatment would be based on more than dangerousness *manifested* by undesirable actions.

12. There is an approach to criminal liability and to much tort liability that is more simply harm based than the two-stage process. According to this approach, if a person causes a particular harm, he is strictly liable. A bar owner may be guilty of an offense if he serves a seventeen-year-old a drink, whatever his actual beliefs about the customer's age and whatever a reasonable person would have believed. (Indeed the bar owner can be guilty if an employee serves a drink to a minor, in which event his liability is both strict and vicarious.) If someone's pet rattlesnake escapes through no fault of the owner—say vandals let the snake loose—the owner will be civilly liable for damages if the snake injures someone with a bite. In the criminal law, strict liability is mainly used for "regulatory" offense for which proof of unreasonableness or mental states would be difficult and time-consuming. Since criminal sanctions represent in part a society's condemnation of the actor, it is widely agreed that serious criminal punishment should rarely be imposed on that basis, and many believe it should never be imposed, though strict liability may have a place for minor violations of such things as traffic laws and building codes.

The problem in torts is more difficult. The result in my snake example is based on the notion that someone who chooses to have a dangerous pet should pay for injuries rather than an innocent victim. There is a plausible case for saying more broadly that when action, even reasonable action, causes harm to an innocent victim, the actor should pay. Under such a system, deciding "who caused what" would be very important. On the original version of the accident involving Daisy and James, his throwing himself in front of the car, or even his standing in front of the car would relieve Daisy of liability; but if she suffered a wholly unexpected heart attack, and her car hit James because it jumped the curb, then she would be liable. The main ambit for expanding strict liability in tort would be to substitute for what would otherwise be liability for negligence, another "objective" standard.

13. To say that someone "acts" is to imply that he wills relevant movements of his body. (The notion of "willing" is itself highly complex, but I pass over that problem.) If my arm makes contact with someone else because it has been forcibly moved by a third person, I have not acted. A rigorous and completely "objective" approach would make "action" depend not on what the person involved had in his mind, but what a reasonable person would have had in his mind if his body had moved in that way.

14. I do not mean to be absolute. Perhaps it is sometimes necessary for the law to rely on certain myths about reality that are actually contrary to informed understanding of that reality.

15. One kind of possibly relevant "fact" is what the law prohibits. The traditional principle of common law jurisdictions is that "ignorance of the law is no excuse." This principle is less sweeping than it sounds because ignorance of some branch of law other than the criminal law may excuse. Suppose Rachel mistakenly thinks that the law of property confers ownership on her once she has repaired a car the "previous" owner has told her is totally worthless; when she takes the car away, she is not guilty of theft. But if Rachel just does not know there is a law prohibiting the acquisition of the property of others, if she is ignorant of the criminal law, she is guilty of theft. This requirement that one know the criminal law is a kind of strict liability feature of the criminal law. Its justifications are that people should be strongly encouraged to learn what the criminal law provides and that assessing many claims of ignorance is too difficult. Suggestions for reform in the United States have been primarily limited to situations in which an actor relies on an official (mistaken) statement of what the law provides. But there is an argument for even further reform to situations when actual ignorance of the law is joined with reasonable grounds for not knowing the law. If, for example, a newly arrived immigrant responds physically to a gross insult in a way that is permissible in his country of origin but not in the United States, whether he should be criminally liable is a troubling question. Except for misconstructions of relevant language, covered in a subsequent section, I shall not deal with ignorance of what the law provides.

16. I shall put aside the situation in which a person subjectively does, or objectively should, think the facts are such that his action might be criminal, but he is wrong; the action turns out to be perfectly all right. Heidi thinks the gun was a fake but it turns out to be real. Since the criminal law generally deals with harms that occur, for the most part one is not liable who makes mistakes in "this direction," but liability for attempting to commit a crime, and possibly reckless creation of risk, might be pinned on behavior in these circumstances. These are the reverse of the circumstances with which I deal, ones in which a genuine danger exists but there is a critical failure of the actor to perceive it.

17. See Model Penal Code §2.02 (c)(d)(1985).

18. This comment shows that even what counts as a "substantial risk" depends on what is involved; a one-in-a-thousand risk that one is shooting a human being is substantial, while a one-in-a-thousand risk that moving one's arm will make contact with a fellow pedestrian is not substantial.

19. For this purpose, the "reasonable person" would have at least *some* of Heidi's background. If, for example, the previous evening Joe had actually told Heidi that he was going to roam the nearby woods in a highly lifelike deer costume, the reasonable person would be someone to whom such a communication had been made.

20. A believer in the intermediate position might not necessarily opt to distin-

guish subjective risk taking in the substantive law of homicide. His decision would turn on factors like these: (1) Is the presence of *subjective* awareness of risk so important that it should be marked out by substantive categories? (2) Are the relevant facts better suited to being brought out in a criminal trial or sentencing proceedings? (3) Would judges consistently give adequate importance to actual awareness of risk in sentencing? These are not easy questions, but they show that one cannot move effortlessly from "intrinsic relevance" to "should be the basis for a separate category of crime."

21. If the crime is homicide, none of Heidi's three failures would qualify as consciously taking a substantial and unjustified risk of death occurring that amounts to a gross departure from how a reasonable person would act.

One form of careless behavior, drunkenness, has so often led to harms the criminal law seeks to prevent that for many instances drunkenness will not excuse. Sometimes it is not wholly clear how much is encompassed in this idea, but at a minimum one who fails to perceive a fact because of (voluntary) drunkenness will be treated as if he had perceived that fact for a crime of recklessness. This approach is widely accepted despite the element of unfairness in punishing a person who has never been drunk before, or who has been drunk before without any adverse effects, as if, when drunk, he possessed the capacities of a sober person.

22. However, if preceding acts of carelessness put an actor in a situation in which a reasonable person might find himself (failure to listen to a weather report leaves a party stranded on a mountain in a snowstorm), *necessary* choices made from that point on may be judged in terms of a reasonable person in the situation.

23. A 1962 New York case illustrates the latter approach. The state's highest court assumed that a man who intervened to save a youth from being beaten up by two men did so with complete reasonableness, but since it turned out the two men were plainclothes police officers making an arrest, the "good samaritan" intervenor was guilty of an assault under New York law. People v. Young, 11 N.Y. 2d 274, 183 N.E. 2d 319, 229 N.Y.S. 2d 1 (per curiam).

24. An example may be the rule in some states that one need not retreat rather than use deadly force in self-defense. Some who adopt such a rule may believe that retreat is definitely preferable but too much to insist upon for ordinary people.

25. In his illuminating book on the trial of Bernhard Goetz, George Fletcher points out that under the approach of the Model Code, one who shoots because of an unreasonable mistake in self-defense is guilty of no homicide crime if the victim does not die (he would be guilty of attempted murder if only reasonable mistakes provide any exoneration). Professor Fletcher says that the "code puts us in a comical position that its drafters would surely disown" because we would "have to watch the hospital charts" to see if the shooter is guilty of any crime of homicide. A Crime of Self-Defense 56 (New York, The Free Press 1988). It is not quite clear why this position is "comical." If the hunter unreasonably shoots someone thinking he is a deer, the hunter is guilty of no crime of homicide unless

the victim dies. We must "watch the hospital charts" to see if such a crime has occurred. The theory of the code is that the two situations should be treated similarly. In both situations, homicide liability depends on there being an actual death. If punishment is warranted for the person whose unreasonable belief in justification leads him to cause severe injury but not death, the better approach would be to have a general category of negligent assault, or a category of intentional or reckless assault with an unreasonable belief in justification.

26. New York Times, Jan. 22, 1982, at A 1, Col. 6.

27. See People v. Goetz, 131 Misc.2d 1, 502 N.Y.S.2d 577, aff'd, 116 A.D.2d 316, 501 N.Y.S.2d 326, rev'd, 68 N.Y.2d 96, 506 N.Y.S.2d 497 N.E.2d 41 (1986).

28. See generally Kent Greenawalt, The Perplexing Borders of Justification and Excuse, 84 Columbia Law Review 1897 (1984); Greenawalt, Distinguishing Justifications from Excuses, 49 Law & Contemporary Problems 89 (1986).

29. See Thomas Morawetz, Reconstructing the Criminal Defenses: The Significance of Justification, 77 Journal of Criminal Law and Criminology 277 (1986).

30. An independent reason for not drawing too fine a line in a code itself is that for many situations in which, on the actual and perceived facts, people widely agree that a defendant should be exonerated, they may disagree about whether what he does is genuinely warranted or only excused.

31. I am oversimplifying because the particular percentages may matter as well as the overall likelihood. For example, Heidi might have a better claim to be justified if the chance of the gun being real were 80 percent and the chance that shouting would not stop Jerry were 20 percent than if the chances were reversed.

32. I am not confident that misjudgments about likely consequences should always be treated like mistakes about immediately perceivable facts.

One possible exception concerns failures of judgment in which one is overwhelmed by present events and fails to consider consequences. Punishable fighting words may be defined as those likely to cause an addressee to fight. And the minimum level of culpability may be recklessness. Suppose the facts are as follows. The defendant has had two drinks at a bar and gets involved in an argument over a local firm's efforts to hire blacks. The argument gets so heated that the defendant utters a vicious racial epithet. If any remarks qualify as fighting, these do. But suppose the defendant says the following and is believed: "At the moment I spoke I was so angry I wasn't thinking clearly; it did not then pass my mind that my words might start a fight." It is true that in the heat of passion, people do not always consider consequences carefully, or at all, but if they reflect on matters in advance and inculcate a disposition of restraint, reminding themselves that some expressions should not be used, they will be much less likely to do what they know is dangerous on reflection. There is some element of conscious carelessness at an earlier stage, and there is a good argument that an actor in these circumstances should be punished even if the ordinary standard of recklessness requires conscious awareness of risk at the time of one's action.

33. See National Soc'y for the Prevention of Cruelty to Children v. Scottish National Soc'y for the Prevention of Cruelty to Children, 111 L.T.R. 869 (1915).

34. Even here one might distinguish a view that at least requires that a person subjectively intended to *act*, or acted with conscious awareness, from a view that attributes even action on the basis of what the movements of a reasonable person might represent. But I shall pass over this subtlety, which is also mentioned in note 13 supra.

35. Director of Public Prosecutions v. Smith (1961) A.C. 290 (H.L. 1960).

36. Another conceivable intermediate position would be to adopt a highly individualized objective concept of intent. That is, a person would be taken to have intended what a person with his prior characteristics would intend if he performed such an act. Perhaps this position is logically comprehensible; someone like me might almost always intend certain results when I perform a particular act, but because of some slip I do not intend them on one particular occasion. Thus, if I perform the movements of making coffee according to my regular pattern, on a rare day when I do not subjectively intend either to make or to drink coffee, I would still be taken to intend to make coffee. But this kind of "objective" standard makes no sense for practice. In most cases, subjective intent must be inferred from external facts, and a judge or jury actually determines subjective intent from a combination of what the actor has done and additional facts about the actor. For the judge or jury, a completely individualized objective standard would be virtually indistinguishable from a subjective standard, whose formulation better traces moral blame.

37. A variation involves innocent-looking acts that the actor mistakenly thinks will by themselves accomplish the criminal objective.

38. One can be guilty of murder or attempted murder if one performs an act that one knows has only a slight chance of causing death if one's aim is to cause death. An aspect of theft is one's intent to keep rather than to return property.

39. More precisely, he could not successfully rely on the defense if this attitude were revealed.

40. It is a much harder question whether I should be excused if my defect is a lesser degree of emotional control than the average person has. Perhaps that depends on the kind and causes of lack of emotional control.

41. Social science data could sometimes help, as in bolstering a Moslem's claim that a threat to shove pork down his throat was deeply upsetting.

42. Model Penal Code, § 210.3 (1)(b)(1985). The Code formulation does not quite meet the situation of someone whose disturbance has a reasonable explanation, but who acts in a way that is very unreasonable even given the disturbance.

Chapter 7

1. Private use of idiosyncratic uncommon criteria may present no serious moral issue. Suppose that in hiring an employee at a small grocery store I give positive weight to the fact that an applicant's family comes from my wife's region of Yugoslavia. This is a form of "discrimination" unrelated to the underlying purpose of my choice, but if there are many grocery jobs available and I am the only

employer with this particular ground of choice, my deviation from "merit" criteria may cause no serious unfairness. One might say I am "biased" in favor of Yugoslavs from the area around Opatija without necessarily implying condemnation.

2. I use the word "really" because I think people usually grossly overestimate their own capacities for concealment and grossly underestimate the perceptive capabilities of others.

3. Arguably, however, experiences like this might confirm in young males the sense that they are "meant to be" more aggressive than women and older men.

4. Webster's New Universal Unabridged Dictionary 1420 (deluxe 2d ed., New York, Simon & Schuster 1983).

5. Id. at 178.

6. Alternatively one might say that one is biased whenever a group characteristic is used negatively. But one would then be biased against youths and men if one regarded young men as more likely to be dangerous than older men and than women.

7. Often what is "reasonably feasible" will depend on a kind of balance, involving not only the cost and inconvenience of doing more but also the strength of social reasons against acting on a generalization without individualized evaluation.

8. Of course, in a real case a judgment of equal strength will almost certainly not involve equality in every important respect, but a balancing of positives and negatives for each side.

9. Someone who thinks the predicted welfare of the children before the court should dominate to the exclusion of all other factors could reject this argument. I am not setting out here to provide any systematic approach to how conflicting values should be assessed for this sort of choice.

10. This is obviously not true if they are searching for a particular suspected criminal who has been identified as being of a particular race. It is also not true if, say, a violent gang is composed of one race, and members of the gang all wear a similar unusual scarf. A young man of that race with the scarf properly engenders suspicion that a young man of another race with the scarf might not.

11. A form of this argument can also be used to continue existing discrimination. For example, a white man may be said to be better qualified to be an executive because he will have more rapport with the great majority of business customers, who are white men. It might be said that justice permits such arguments to count only when made on behalf of previously disadvantaged groups, but I shall not investigate that possibility.

12. The department certainly reflected President Reagan's own stated opinions on the subject. But some other parts of the executive branch did not act consistently with the positions taken by the Department of Justice before the courts. A facet of the issue has come to prominence in the Bush Administration with its struggles to develop a policy on scholarships restricted to minority students.

13. Kent Greenawalt, Discrimination and Reverse Discrimination (New York, Alfred A. Knopf 1983); The Unresolved Problems of Reverse Discrimination, 67

California Law Review 87 (1979); Judicial Scrutiny of "Benign" Racial Preference in Law School Admissions, 75 Columbia Law Review 559 (1975).

14. The strength of this last argument obviously depends greatly on the position involved. Highly qualified brain surgeons matter more than highly qualified tree surgeons. When the argument is made about students, much depends on whether, and how quickly, initial disadvantages can be overcome.

15. There is a question about what should happen to the white who got the job unfairly at Time 1, but it would be highly disruptive to take jobs away from beneficiaries of unjust discrimination in order to give them to better qualified applicants who lose out because rectification is given to the original victim at Time 2.

16. One among many problems is how to identify those who would have applied (say, for supervisors' jobs) but did not because they knew they would be denied the position regardless of qualifications.

17. I am by no means assuming either (1) that remarks and movements of the four youths had actually reached a stage that in any reasonable interpretation could have warranted deadly force against them by Goetz, or (2) that even were such deadly force warranted, Goetz's own shooting of the four youths, and particularly his shooting of one youth a second time, was warranted. I am using the case loosely to suggest an illustration in which the gender and race of potential attackers might be thought, or felt, to be relevant.

18. For a judge to acknowledge that is only to say that if potential attackers seem to *make* race relevant, potential victims can pay attention to it.

19. Reform can be by the legislature or by judicial interpretation of the common law, statutes, and constitutional law.

20. See Nancy Erickson, Sex Bias in Law School Courses: Some Common Issues, 38 Journal of Legal Education 101, 107 (1988). In her article, she focuses on the problem of immediacy and on misapplications of a reasonableness test, so it is not certain she would disagree with the analysis that follows. She cites Elizabeth Schneider, Equal Rights to Trial for Women: Sex Bias in the Law of Self Defense, 15 Harvard Civil Rights-Civil Liberties Law Review 623, 631–32 (1980). Because Schneider mainly considers battered women, she does not focus directly on the problem I address, although she suggests an individualized approach to the defense that would apparently eliminate any particular degree of feared harm as a threshold for using deadly force.

21. See generally Model Penal Code §3.04 (1985).

22. This separation could be challenged on the ground that "battered wife" situations are so important for female use of deadly force that their treatment should inform the general rules.

23. Griggs v. Duke Power Co., 401 U.S. 424 (1971).

24. For ordinary problems of admissibility there is another serious difficulty. Defense lawyers might manage to get highly prejudicial evidence heard by jurors before such evidence is "disallowed" as insufficiently relevant. I assume *that* diffi-

culty can be met by requiring an initial full showing on relevance *before* evidence is presented to jurors.

Chapter 8

1. This is not to say that an "act" adopted by a legislature that establishes a single corporation or deals with a named individual, say admitting him to citizenship, is not legally authoritative, only that it is not a typical "law".

2. I pass over here the obvious problem if judges are left free to decide which rule to apply, see Duncan Kennedy, Form and Substance in Private Law Adjudication, 89 Harvard Law Review 1685, 1700–1701 (1976).

3. The mundane and indisputable point I make here holds whatever the validity of a version of social contract theory that asserts that in some sense citizens accept the government. My skepticism about such theories is developed in Kent Greenawalt, Conflicts of Law and Morality 62–93 (New York, Oxford University Press 1987).

4. See Kennedy, note 2 supra, at 1685, 1688.

5. It has been suggested that the pro-rules position is privileged in liberal thought, Mark Kelman, A Guide to Critical Legal Studies 16–17, 26–27 (Cambridge, Mass., Harvard University Press 1987), and that our system is less rule bound then we suppose, Katharine Bartlett, Feminist Legal Methods, 103 Harvard Law Review 829, 853 (1990). See also Kennedy, note 2 supra.

6. The problem of pronouns is even more troublesome in complicated legislative drafting than in academic writing.

7. These sentences grossly oversimplify my own ideas on this topic, which are developed in Kent Greenawalt, Speech, Crime and the Uses of Language (New York, Oxford University Press 1989); and Greenawalt, Insults and Epithets: Are They Protected Speech?, 42 Rutgers Law Review 287 (1990).

8. See Ellison v. Brady, 924 F.2d 872 (9th Cir. 1991).

9. Catharine MacKinnon has written, in Feminism Unmodified 92 (Cambridge, Mass., Harvard University Press 1987), "when violence against women is eroticized as it is in this culture, it is very difficult to say that there is a major distinction in the level of sex involved between being assaulted by a penis and being assaulted by a fist, especially when the perpetrator is a man."

10. I am assuming here that reasonableness is not resolved by some economic analysis that gives little attention to actual behavior.

11. If the activity is an ordinary one like driving, and reasonableness is assessed by juries, and juries have a fair representation of women, the problem is minimized, since women will draw from their own experience to determine what is acceptable driving.

12. Nevertheless, for reasons given in the book and article cited in note 7 supra, the proper substantive standard should be something other than whether an average addressee is likely to fight.

13. Herbert Wechsler, Principles, Politics, and Fundamental Law 27 (Cambridge, Mass., Harvard University Press 1961).

14. My own analysis of the major challenges up to that time is in Kent Greenawalt, The Enduring Significance of Neutral Principles, 78 Columbia Law Review 982 (1978). I urge that Wechsler's sense of "neutral," probably an unfortunate term for his purposes, was much more modest than many critics supposed. That article develops at greater length many of the points made here.

15. See John Ladd, The Place of Practical Reason in Judicial Decision, Nomos VII: Rational Decision 126, 144, C. Friedrich ed. (New York, Atherton Press 1964), explaining the desirability of generality.

16. Robin West, Jurisprudence and Gender, 55 University of Chicago Law Review 1, 58 (1988). In that article and in West, The Difference in Women's Hedonic Lives: A Phenomenological Critique of Feminist Legal Theory, 3 Wisconsin Women's Law Journal 81 (1987), Professor West gives her understanding of fundamental differences in the experience of women and men.

17. Bartlett, note 5 supra, at 862. See also Deborah Rhode, Feminist Critical Theories, 42 Stanford Law Review 617, 629 (1990), who writes that the feminist critique joins critical legal studies in denying "that the rule of law in fact offers a principled, impartial, and determinate means of dispute resolution."

18. Ann Scales, The Emergence of Feminist Jurisprudence: An Essay, 95 Yale Law Journal 1373, 1376 (1986). About an objective standpoint more generally, Catharine MacKinnon, note 9 supra, at 55, claims that "the neutrality of objectivity and maleness are coextensive linguistically." See also id. at 50.

19. See generally Kennedy, note 2 supra; Kelman, note 5 supra.

20. Not all feminist scholars object to *this* aspect of existing law.

21. Carol Gilligan, In A Different Voice (Cambridge, Mass., Harvard University Press 1982).

22. Id. at 19. She continues, "This conception of morality as concerned with the activity of care centers moral development around the understanding of responsibility and relationships, just as the conception of morality as fairness ties moral development to the understanding of rights and rules." See also the two articles by West, cited in note 16 supra.

23. Gilligan, note 2 supra, at 22.

24. Catharine MacKinnon argues that the emphasis on care and relations in women's morality is a product of male domination. MacKinnon, supra note 9, at 38–39.

25. See Scales, note 18 supra, at 583–87; Rhode, note 17 supra, at 631. See generally Bartlett, note 5 supra, at 873.

26. The major problem is that the second approach involves both more care for the people involved and more attention to particular context than the first. One can imagine uncaring decisions closely attentive to contextual nuances and decisions based on principle by those who care deeply. Any single word label, such as "caring," "affective," "contextual," or "individualized," tends to emphasize one element at the expense of the others.

27. Simone de Beauvoir, The Second Sex (New York, Knopf 1953).

28. See generally Deborah Rhode, Justice and Gender (Cambridge, Mass., Harvard University Press 1989); Carrie Menkel-Meadow, Portia in a Different Voice: Speculations on a Women's Lawyering Process, 1 Berkeley Women's Law Journal 39 (1985).

29. See Bartlett, note 5 supra, at 853–56.

30. I have not, of course, demonstrated, or even seriously argued, that *any* competitive sports would survive in a better, more fully relational, society, or that any that did survive would retain the feature of being relatively rule governed. Any illustrations of the sort I have sketched are open to the objection that the practices should not survive in anything like their present form.

31. This is not to say that I actually manage to be this way, but I wish I did.

32. Similarly to what I indicate in note 30 supra, the illustration I have used does not demonstrate what student evaluation should be like and is open to the objection that nothing like grading is defensible or to the objection that grade giving and changing should be much more sensitive to personal factors. I have not tried to meet such objections in a sustained way.

33. However, the insistence of younger children that they get the privileges of their predecessors is a powerful force for principled treatment.

34. In some areas, but not others, the either–or character of legal decisions can reasonably be reduced.

Chapter 9

1. I very definitely do not mean to suggest that one could describe a cultural morality without explicit or implicit reference to law. The example I use concerns unmarried couples; whether two people are married or not is determined by the law.

2. For a powerful modern defense, see John Finnis, Natural Law and Natural Rights (Oxford, Clarendon Press 1980). Some of my own reservations are indicated in a review of the book, 10 Political Theory 133 (1982).

3. See Friedrich von Savigny, Of the Vocation of Our Age for Legislation and Jurisprudence (A. Hayward trans. London, Littlewood & Co. 1831). For brief accounts of Savigny's theory, see Wolfgang Friedmann, Legal Theory (London, Stevens & Sons Ltd., 4th ed. 1960); Edwin Patterson, Jurisprudence: Men and Ideas of the Law 410–14 (Brooklyn, Foundation Press 1953).

4. In The Nature of the Common Law 14–42 (Cambridge, Mass., Harvard University Press 1988), Melvin Eisenberg usefully divides "social propositions" that are relevant to legal decisions into moral norms, policies, and experiential propositions. It is perhaps a stretch of the term, but I am taking "cultural morality" to include community opinion on all of these, when that opinion bears on what individuals or the government should do.

5. I put the point this way because it is always possible to argue that other legal changes help set the conditions under which more liberal attitudes toward sexual involvement could flourish.

6. One might instead admit that critics can evaluate cultural moralities, and features of them, as good or bad, but claim that no external standards exist for judging the evaluations. On this view, cultural moralities would not have to be accepted as "proper," but none would be "objectively" better than any other.

7. Those standards must include something more than the undesirability of radical disruptive change. It would be an extremely weak claim to say that a society should not abandon abruptly the cultural morality it now has. A cultural morality does not become "proper" simply because overthrowing it very quickly would be bad.

8. This way of putting it is less than ideal, because in ordinary usage cultural morality is a constitutive element of a society. One needs to think of people living together in some respect who might have (or have had) different standards of cultural morality.

9. I am not sure whether any critical legal scholar adopts this stark position, though occasional passages intimate something like it. Roberto Unger's praise of human self-transcendence and his recommendation of destabilization rights in The Critical Legal Studies Movement, 96 Harvard Law Review 561 (1983), may seem to point in this direction, but a seminar paper by Derek Spitz that reviews much of Unger's work has persuaded me that Unger should not be so understood.

10. There is a difference between saying that efficiency is a means of achieving cultural values and saying that efficiency is actually a culturally shared value. That is why I distinguish its being an "aspect" from being a "means" in the text. It could, of course, be an aspect because it is widely recognized as a means.

11. More precisely, the Kaldor-Hicks approach leaves open how the utility of people involved is to be measured. See John Hicks, The Foundations of Welfare Economics, 49 Economics Journal 696 (1939); Nicholas Kaldor, Welfare Propositions of Economies and Interpersonal Comparisons of Utility, 40 Economics Journal 549 (1939). Using monetary wealth as the crucial measure is only one application of a Kaldor-Hicks approach, but it is the application that characterizes modern American "law and economics," especially that of Richard Posner and the "Chicago school." See, for example, Richard Posner, Economic Analysis of Law (Boston, Little Brown, 3d ed. 1986); Posner, Utilitarianism, Economics, and Legal Theory, 8 Journal of Legal Studies 103 (1979).

12. See Paul Rubin, Business Firms and the Common Law: The Evolution of Efficient Rules pp. 13–14 (New York, Praeger 1983); Rubin, Why is the Common Law Efficient? 6 Journal of Legal Studies 51 (1977); George Priest, The Common Law Process and the Selection of Efficient Rules, 6 Journal of Legal Studies 65 (1977), William Landes and Richard Posner, Salvors, Finders, Good Samaritans, and Other Rescuers: An Economic Study of Law and Altruism, 7 Journal of Legal Studies 83 (1978); Posner, note 11 supra, at 239.

13. See Margaret Jane Radin, Market-Inalienability, 100 Harvard Law Review 1849, 1921-25 (1987).

14. On another variation, the wealth standard, without further specification, does not yield an answer. Suppose the residents care very much about staying

put, but have almost no money for anything but bare necessities. They could *pay* only $500,000 to have the noise stopped, but they would rather have the noise stopped than receive $1,500,000. Such discontinuities are not uncommon; when they exist the guideline to maximize wealth does not provide an answer.

15. I have some serious doubts about how the composite wealth of a society is to be measured. In any sensible account, exchanges of value (paying for a tennis lesson) cannot be valued higher in general than voluntary joint activities (two friends playing a game of tennis); voluntary joint activities cannot be valued higher than solitary activities (two friends each reading a book); solitary *activities* cannot be valued higher than passivity (sleeping). A measure of wealth must somehow assign a monetary value to all these possibilities, presumably in terms of opportunities foregone. But what opportunities count? Suppose one can earn $1000 an hour for extremely dangerous work. Further, the monetary value of opportunities will depend on how other people want to spend their time. As permissible activities and preferences change, I do not understand what sense it makes to say that a society has, overall, increased in wealth.

16. See, for example, Ronald Dworkin, Is Wealth A Value?, 9 Journal of Legal Studies 191 (1980); Lewis Kornhauser, A Guide to the Perplexed Claims of Efficiency in Law, 8 Hofstra Law Review 591 (1980).

17. H. L. A. Hart, The Concept of Law 181–98 (Oxford, Clarendon Press 1961).

18. See Finnis, note 2 supra. Many interpreters of Aquinas have emphasized a purposive view of the world; we understand what is good for human beings by understanding their true purposes. Finnis, instead, also drawing from Aquinas, claims that certain human goods are self-evident.

19. I talk about adults, but there are closely related questions about how children are to be educated. Although some people may believe it is feasible, I assume that children cannot be educated in a way that avoids proposing orderings of values, and I think it would be a grave mistake to attempt that ("children, whether you should care about other people is an open question you should resolve for yourselves"). Nevertheless, there remain critical questions about *how much* the orderings of values should be part of education.

20. Another view is that the *language* of morality implies equality. That view is also mistaken, but even if it were correct, it would not indicate why someone should really *do* what the language of morality requires rather than act according to some other principles.

21. Conceivably an argument could be made that for vastly different social conditions, say those of the ancient world, one could not confidently reach this conclusion.

22. A hard issue of equal consideration concerns the severely retarded: if some members of the human species will never develop the capacities of higher non-human animals, are they entitled to consideration that far exceeds that accorded other animals?

23. See John Rawls, "Justice as Fairness: Political not Metaphysical," 14 Philosophy and Public Affairs 223, 229 (1983).

24. See Thomas Scanlon, "Contractualism and Utilitarianism," in Utilitarianism and Beyond, eds. Amartya Sen and Bernard Williams, at pp. 108–28 (London, Cambridge University Press 1982).

25. See John Rawls, A Theory of Justice (Cambridge, Mass., Harvard University Press 1971).

26. See Bruce Ackerman, Social Justice in the Liberal State (New Haven, Conn., Yale University Press 1980).

27. My views on this difficult topic are developed in Religious Convictions and Political Choice (New York, Oxford University Press 1988).

28. See id.; and Greenawalt, Religious Convictions and Political Choice: Some Further Thoughts, 39 De Paul Law Review 1019 (1990).

29. See Eisenberg, note 4 supra, at 14–26.

30. That is what the book and article cited in note 28 supra are about.

31. See Eisenberg, note 4 supra, at 14–49, 104–45.

32. Conceivably a general justification claim might be based on an assertion that complying with more specific criminal law provisions would have been incredibly wasteful; conceivably a claim might be made that legislation is so counterproductive from the standpoint of efficiency that it violates due process.

33. Palko v. Connecticut, 302 U.S. 319 (1937).

34. See Duncan v. Louisiana, 391 U.S. 145 (1968).

35. Sanford Kadish's account of due process methodology places great importance on how the law of various jurisdictions treats problems. Methodology and Criteria in Due Process Adjudication–A Survey and Criticism, 66 Yale Law Journal 319 (1957).

36. I treat general issues of nonenforcement at some length in Kent Greenawalt, Conflicts of Law and Morality 348–76 (New York, Oxford University Press 1987).

37. Id.

38. These might be understood in terms of historical or contemporary standards on the particular subject, such as the death penalty, or as some kind of distillation and construction based on the community's most basic values.

39. Restatement (Second) of Torts § 826.

40. Trop v. Dulles, 356 U.S. 86 (1958).

41. Repouille v. United States, 165 F. 2d 152 (2d Cir. 1947).

42. 290 U.S. 398 (1934).

43. United States Constitution, Art. I, § 10(1).

Chapter 10

1. Compare Charles Fried, The Artificial Reason of the Law or: What Lawyers Know, 60 Texas Law Review 35 (1982), with Richard Posner, The Decline of Law as an Autonomous Discipline: 1962–1987, 100 Harvard Law Review 761 (1987).

2. It, however, does not distinguish "legal reasoning" from reasoning that

takes a discovered norm of social morality as authoritative and seeks to discern its implications.

3. See, for example, Edward Levi, An Introduction to Legal Reasoning (Chicago, University of Chicago Press 1949).

4. Melvin Eisenberg, The Nature of the Common Law 50–96 (Cambridge, Mass., Harvard University Press 1988).

5. See generally id., and Ronald Dworkin, Law's Empire (Cambridge, Mass., Harvard University Press 1986).

6. Fried, note 1 supra, at 57. Fried speaks of ideals and values as constraining, limiting, informing, and inspiring the foundation, and thus may agree with the following two sentences in the text.

7. Roscoe Pound, A Survey of Social Interests, 57 Harvard Law Review 1 (1943).

Chapter 11

1. Some people believe that what it is really right for them to do is to act in accord with the will of God; they also believe that as to some subjects what God wills is beyond human understanding. Of course, most religious believers think human beings are incapable of fully understanding God's will, but I am referring here to a more extreme position that denies even partial understanding for some subjects. Perhaps one could defend the idea that what it is right to do *morally* is to act in accord with God's will, even if that is wholly beyond human understanding, but the law involves human norms and practical reason. The criteria for a right answer in the law cannot be inaccessible to human beings. Just *how* these criteria must be accessible is a much harder question to which I shall return.

2. See Benjamin Nathan Cardozo, The Nature of the Judicial Process (New Haven, Conn., Yale University Press 1921).

3. See H. L. A. Hart, The Concept of Law (Oxford, Clarendon Press 1961).

4. There is an interesting asymmetry about judicial psychology and a conceptual descriptive account of how cases are decided. If judges believe they are discovering the law, that is not proof that they are doing so; if analysis suggests there is no correct answer to be discovered, one may conclude that judges are mistaken in their understanding. Suppose, however, judges believe they are legislating, and they say in response to more detailed questions that for some decisions at some points, they really do not regard the law as constraining but approach issues like a legislator might. If judges sometimes do not even try to discover the law, it is hard to conclude that they are really doing that. One might, of course, still contend that correct answers are there to be discovered and that judges should discover them, but a descriptive account would need to acknowledge that they are not now doing so. See Kent Greenawalt, The Perceived Authority of Law In Judging Constitutional Cases, 61 University of Colorado Law Review 783 (1990).

5. See Paul Brest, Interpretation and Interest, 34 Stanford Law Review 765 (1982).

6. See Owen Fiss, Objectivity and Interpretation, 34 Stanford Law Review 739 (1982).

7. See Rolf Sartorius, Individual Conduct and Social Norms (Encino, Calif., Dickenson Publishing Co. 1975).

8. See, for example, Duncan Kennedy, Form and Substance in Private Law Adjudication, 89 Harvard Law Review 1685 (1976).

9. In id. at 1724, Kennedy acknowledges that, despite the absence of meta-principles to choose between altruist and individualist approaches, "we find that we are able to distinguish particular fact situations in which one side is much more plausible than the other."

10. It is logically conceivable that whenever the broader source yields no determinate answer, one would be returned to values as reflected within the law. That would be an extremely implausible way to construe our legal system, for reasons that the chapters in this part of the book suggest, but I do not attempt a full refutation of that possibility here.

11. Restatement (Second) of Torts § 826.

12. See generally, for example, Richard Posner, The Federal Courts: Crisis and Reform 286 ff (Cambridge, Mass., Harvard University Press 1985); Frank Easterbrook, Statutes' Domains, 50 University of Chicago Law Review 533 (1983).

13. Ronald Dworkin, Taking Rights Seriously (rev. ed.) 335–45 (Cambridge, Mass., Harvard University Press 1978).

14. A formulation like this raises an interesting dilemma about the precise relation between fit and independent views. Is the idea that the independent views only come into play when the "fits" are, or are perceived to be, absolutely equal in some sense? It is doubtful that any actual judge would ever have such a perception, but an ideal judge might. It is troubling to think what exactly equal "fits" would entail, and it is not surprising that Dworkin chose the more cautious phrase of "adequate." Are there inequalities of "fit" among adequate "fits," or is the notion of equal and unequal somehow inapposite if one talks about adequate fits? I am not sure. In any event, this whole idea of using independent views to decide among adequate fits raises the question whether, for example, as an interpreter of South African law, one can prefer a theory that "fits" a little less well but is far superior on independent moral grounds. We can imagine an approach that concedes that fit cannot resolve everything, but argues that independent views can never be employed to choose a less well fitting theory over a better fitting theory, however slightly the better fitting theory fits. I am doubtful that this theory could be coherently defended, and in any event no one has tried, since the increasing emphasis on law as related to other interpretive endeavors has led to wide acceptance of the idea that one's own independent perspectives will inevitably and appropriately affect how one interprets materials.

15. Ronald Dworkin, Law's Empire (Cambridge, Mass., Harvard University Press 1986).

16. Melvin Eisenberg, The Nature of the Common Law (Cambridge, Mass., Harvard University Press 1988).

17. I use the term "cultural morality" broadly here. See Chapter 9 for an explanation.

18. Repouille v. United States, 165 F.2d. 152, 154 (2d cir. 1947) dissent of Frank, J.

19. Eisenberg, note 16 supra, at 22–24.

20. Id. at 140–42.

21. Id. at 9–10.

22. Id. at 18.

23. Id. at 14–15 says courts should rely on standards that have substantial support, can be derived from norms that have such support, or appear as if they would have such support. It is doubtful if judges can manage either the process of derivation or the decision to give effect to norms that do not yet have community support without some independent judgments of political morality. One problem is the determination whether to give effect to a standard that seems to enjoy community support but is in conflict with what can be derived from another broader norm supported by the community.

24. Id. at 19.

25. One might argue that if disputes are to be regulated by existing community standards, a judge's correct estimate of the social future of a norm should be irrelevant.

26. Id. at 42–49.

27. I am considering interpersonal calculations of welfare as a subcategory of sound judgments of political morality. One might, instead, emphasize the relation between them and cultural morality, claiming that cultural morality authorizes such judgments by courts and guides their determination. The mere authorization of a judgment by cultural morality, or by law, does not assure that the question for judgment has a correct answer. For cultural morality to *provide that*, it would need to yield a weighing of interpersonal interests. Without doubt, cultural morality, and law, do say something about how competing interests are to be weighed, but it is unrealistic to suppose that if only the ideal judge could dig deep enough, cultural morality would yield a definitive outcome for every conflict of interests.

28. See also the possibility discussed in note 10 supra.

29. If it is argued that on a highly sophisticated understanding such judgments are not resolvable, that alone would not be a sufficient reason for saying that the law never requires such judgments.

30. Perhaps a bare minimum of private property would be necessary; once someone's food or shelter were provided, others could not freely take it over.

31. As I indicate at pp. 239–41 of Religious Conviction and Political Choice (New York, Oxford University Press 1988), I think it is appropriate for judges in rare cases to rely on religious reasons. At first glance, that conclusion may seem

at odds with what I say here, but it is not. My point here is that we should not say "the law requires" an answer that can be reached only on the basis of a religious reason. Cases in which reliance on a religious reason is appropriate are ones in which the law, including nontheological reasons of moral and political philosophy, does not yield a correct answer either way, but the judge must resolve the issue.

32. I am concentrating here on theological, or religious, reasons, but the same exclusion would extend to all reasons that lack interpersonal validity.

33. See, for example, Kennedy, note 8 supra; Kennedy, The Structure of Blackstone's Commentaries, 28 Buffalo Law Review 205 (1979). The word "contradiction" has a powerful rhetorical force, and I think its use is somewhat misleading when the conditions for having a "contradiction" are very weak. Kennedy, note 8 supra, at 1775, suggests that if no abstract unit of measurement exists to resolve conflicts, then contradiction is present. On this understanding, life is certainly full of contradictions. If I believe no abstract unit of measurement resolves conflicts between happiness and increased knowledge, then each time I face a choice between these I face a contradiction. We deal with many such "contradictions" comfortably.

34. Civil Rights Act of 1964, §601, 42 U.S.C.§2000d.

35. United States Constitution, Amendment XIV, §1.

36. I have oversimplified. There are, at least, four factual variations: private money at private universities, public money given to private universities, private money given to public universities, and public money at public universities. Some experts, but not all, think it matters for legality which variation is involved. I have also oversimplified in not considering the possibility that, correctly interpreted, Title VI may forbid more or less than the Constitution does.

37. See Greenawalt, note 31 supra.

38. See Stanley Fish, Dennis Martinez and the Uses of Theory, 96 Yale Law Journal 1773, 1779 (1987).

BIBLIOGRAPHY

Books

Abernethy, William Beaven, and Mayher, Philip Joseph. *Scripture and Imagination*. New York: The Pilgrim Press, 1988.

Ackerman, Bruce A. *Social Justice in the Liberal State*. New Haven, Connecticut: Yale University Press, 1980.

Baker, G. P., and Hacker, P. M. S. *Skepticism, Rules and Language*. Oxford: Basil Blackwell Publisher Ltd., 1984.

Cardozo, Benjamin Nathan. *The Growth of the Law*. New Haven, Connecticut: Yale University Press, 1924.

——. *The Nature of the Judicial Process*. New Haven, Connecticut: Yale University Press, 1921.

Davis, Kenneth C. *Police Discretion*. St. Paul: West Publishing Co., 1975.

de Beauvoir, Simone. *The Second Sex*. H. M. Parshley, trans. and ed. New York: Alfred A. Knopf, 1953.

Dworkin, Ronald M. *Law's Empire*. Cambridge, Massachusetts: Harvard University Press, 1986.

——. *Taking Rights Seriously*. Cambridge, Massachusetts: Harvard University Press, rev. ed., 1978.

Eagleton, Terry. *Literary Theory*. Minneapolis: University of Minnesota Press, 1983.

Eisenberg, Melvin Aron. *The Nature of the Common Law*. Cambridge, Massachusetts: Harvard University Press, 1988.

Finnis, John. *Natural Law and Natural Rights*. Oxford: Clarendon Press, 1980.

Fletcher, George. *A Crime of Self-Defense*. New York: The Free Press, 1988.

Friedmann, Wolfgang. *Legal Theory*. London: Stevens & Sons Ltd., 4th ed., 1960.

Friedrich, Carl J., ed. *Nomos VII: Rational Decision*. New York: Atherton Press, 1964.

Gadamer, Hans Georg. *Truth and Method*. J. Weinsheimer and D. Marshall, trans. New York: Cross Road, 2d rev. ed., 1984.

Gilligan, Carol. *In a Different Voice*. Cambridge, Massachusetts: Harvard University Press, 1982.

Greenawalt, Kent. *Conflicts of Law and Morality*. New York: Oxford University Press, 1987.

——. *Discrimination and Reverse Discrimination*. New York: Alfred A. Knopf, 1983.

——. *Religious Convictions and Political Choice*. New York: Oxford University Press, 1988.

——. *Speech, Crime and the Uses of Language*. New York: Oxford University Press, 1989.

Hart, H. L. A. *The Concept of Law*. Oxford: Clarendon Press, 1961.

Hirsch, E. D., Jr. *The Aims of Interpretation*. Chicago: University of Chicago Press, 1976.

Hutchinson, Allan C., ed. *Critical Legal Studies*. Totowa, New Jersey: Rowman and Littlefield, 1989.

Karst, Kenneth L. *Belonging to America: Equal Citizenship and the Constitution*. New Haven, Connecticut: Yale University Press, 1989.

Kelman, Mark. *A Guide to Critical Legal Studies*. Cambridge, Massachusetts: Harvard University Press, 1987.

Kripke, Saul A. *Wittgenstein On Rules and Private Language*. Cambridge, Massachusetts: Harvard University Press, 1982.

Kuhn, Thomas. *The Structure of Scientific Revolutions*. Chicago: University of Chicago Press, 2d ed., 1970.

Levi, Edward. *An Introduction to Legal Reasoning*. Chicago: University of Chicago Press, 1949.

MacKinnon, Catherine A. *Feminism Unmodified*. Cambridge, Massachusetts: Harvard University Press, 1987.

Neely, Richard. *How Courts Govern America*. New Haven, Connecticut: Yale University Press, 1981.

Pagels, Elaine. *Adam, Eve and the Serpent*. New York: Random House, 1989.

Pagels, Heinz. *The Cosmic Code*. New York: Simon & Schuster, 1982.

Patterson, Edwin. *Jurisprudence: Men and Ideas of the Law*. Brooklyn: Foundation Press, 1953.

Posner, Richard A. *Economic Analysis of Law*. Boston: Little Brown, 3d ed., 1986.

——. *The Federal Courts: Crisis and Reform*. Cambridge, Massachusetts: Harvard University Press, 1985.

Rawls, John. *A Theory of Justice*. Cambridge, Massachusetts: Harvard University Press, 1971.

Rhode, Deborah L. *Justice and Gender*. Cambridge, Massachusetts: Harvard University Press, 1989.

Rubin, Paul. *Business Firms and the Common Law: The Evolution of Efficient Rules*. New York: Praeger, 1983.

Sartorius, Rolf E. *Individual Conduct and Social Norms*. Encino, California: Dickenson Publishing Co., 1975.

Savigny, Friedrich von. *Of the Vocation of Our Age for Legislation and Jurisprudence*. A. Hayward, trans. London: Littlewood & Co., 1831.

Searle, John. *Expression and Meaning*. Cambridge: Cambridge University Press, 1979.

Sen, Amartya, and Williams, Bernard, eds. *Utilitarianism and Beyond*. London: Cambridge University Press, 1982.

Summers, Robert, ed. *Essays in Legal Philosophy*. Berkeley: University of California Press, 1968.

Wechsler, Herbert. *Principles, Politics, and Fundamental Law*. Cambridge, Massachusetts: Harvard University Press, 1961.

Wootten, Barbara. *Social Science and Social Pathology*. London: George, Allen and Unwin, 1959.

Articles

Abraham, Kenneth S. "Statutory Interpretation and Literary Theory: Some Common Concerns of an Unlikely Pair." 32 *Rutgers Law Review* (1979), 676–694.

Bartlett, Katherine T. "Feminist Legal Methods." 103 *Harvard Law Review* (1990), 829–888.

Brest, Paul. "Interpretation and Interest." 34 *Stanford Law Review* (1982), 765–773.

Cover, Robert M. "The Supreme Court 1982 Term—Foreword: Nomos and Narrative." 97 *Harvard Law Review* (1983), 4–68.

D'Amato, Anthony. "Aspects of Deconstruction: Refuting Indeterminacy With One Bold Thought." 85 *Northwestern University Law Review* (1990), 113–118.

———. "Can Any Legal Theory Constrain Any Judicial Decision?" 43 *University of Miami Law Review* (1989), 513–539.

———. "Pragmatic Indeterminacy." 85 *Northwestern University Law Review* (1990), 148–189.

Dworkin, Ronald M. "Is Wealth A Value?" 9 *Journal of Legal Studies* (1980), 191–226.

———. "Law As Interpretation." 60 *Texas Law Review* (1982), 527–550.

Easterbrook, Frank H. "Statutes' Domains." 50 *University of Chicago Law Review* (1983), 533–552.

Erickson, Nancy S. "Sex Bias in Law School Courses: Some Common Issues." 38 *Journal of Legal Education* (1988), 101–116.

Felstiner, William L. F., Abel, Richard L., and Sarat, Austin. "The Emergence and Transformation of Disputes: Naming, Blaming, Claiming. . . ." 15 *Law & Society Review* (1980–81), 631–654.

Fish, Stanley. "Dennis Martinez and the Uses of Theory." 96 *Yale Law Journal* (1987), 1773–1800.

———. "Working on the Chain Gang: Interpretation in Law and Literature." 60 *Texas Law Review* (1982), 551–567.

Fiss, Owen M. "Conventionalism." 58 *Southern California Law Review* (1985), 177–197.

———. "Objectivity and Interpretation." 34 *Stanford Law Review* (1982), 739–763.

Fried, Charles. "The Artificial Reason of the Law or: What Lawyers Know." 60 *Texas Law Review* (1982), 35–58.

Garet, Ronald R. "Comparative Normative Hermeneutics: Scripture, Literature, Constitution." 58 *Southern California Law Review* (1985), 35–134.

Graff, Gerald. "'Keep Off the Grass,' 'Drop Dead,' and Other Indeterminacies: A Response to Sanford Levinson." 60 *Texas Law Review* (1982), 405–413.

Greenawalt, Kent. "Distinguishing Justifications From Excuses." 49 *Law & Contemporary Problems* (Summer 1986), 89–108.

———. "The Enduring Significance of Neutral Principles." 78 *Columbia Law Review* (1978), 982–1021.

———. "Hart's Rule of Recognition and the United States." 1 *Ratio Juris* (1988), 40–57.

———. "Insults and Epithets: Are They Protected Speech?" 42 *Rutgers Law Review* (1990), 287–307.

———. "Judicial Scrutiny of 'Benign' Racial Preference in Law School Admissions." 75 *Columbia Law Review* (1975), 559–602.

———. "The Perceived Authority of Law In Judging Constitutional Cases." 61 *University of Colorado Law Review* (1990), 783–793.

———. "The Perplexing Borders of Justification and Excuse." 84 *Columbia Law Review* (1984), 1897–1927.

———. "Religious Convictions and Political Choice: Some Further Thoughts." 39 *De Paul Law Review* (1990), 1019–1046.

———. "The Rule of Recognition and the Constitution." 85 *Michigan Law Review* (1987), 621–671.

———. "The Unresolved Problems of Reverse Discrimination." 67 *California Law Review* (1979), 87–130.

Grey, Thomas C. "The Constitution as Scripture." 37 *Stanford Law Review* (1984), 1–25.

Hancher, Michael. "What Kind of Speech Act is Interpretation?" 10 *Poetics: International Review for the Theory of Literature* (1981), 263–281.

Hicks, John R. "The Foundations of Welfare Economics." 49 *Economics Journal* (December 1939), 696–712.

Hurd, Heidi M. "Sovereignty in Silence." 99 *Yale Law Journal* (1990), 945–1008.

Hutchinson, Allan C. "Democracy and Determinacy: An Essay on Legal Interpretation." 43 *University of Miami Law Review* (1989), 541–576.

Kadish, Sanford. "Methodology and Criteria in Due Process Adjudication—A Survey and Criticism." 66 *Yale Law Journal* (1957), 319–363.

Kairys, David. "Law and Politics." 52 *George Washington Law Review* (1984), 243–262.

Kaldor, Nicholas. "Welfare Propositions of Economies and Interpersonal Comparisons of Utility." 40 *Economics Journal* (September 1939), 549–552.

Kennedy, Duncan. "Form and Substance in Private Law Adjudication." 89 *Harvard Law Review* (1976), 1685–1778.

———. "Freedom and Constraint in Adjudication: A Critical Phenomenology." 36 *Journal of Legal Education* (1986), 518–562.

———. "The Structure of Blackstone's Commentaries." 28 *Buffalo Law Review* (1979), 205–382.

Kornhauser, Lewis A. " A Guide to the Perplexed Claims of Efficiency in Law." 8 *Hofstra Law Review* (1980), 591–639.

Kress, Ken. "Legal Indeterminacy." 77 *California Law Review* (1989), 283–337.

Landers, Scott. "Wittgenstein, Realism, and CLS: Undermining Rule Skepticism." 9 *Law & Philosophy: An International Journal for Jurisprudence and Legal Philosophy* (1990), 177–203.

Landes, William, and Posner, Richard A. "Salvors, Finders, Good Samaritans and Other Rescuers: An Economic Study of Law and Altruism." 7 *Journal of Legal Studies* (1978), 83–128.

Levinson, Sanford. "Law as Literature." 60 *Texas Law Review* (1982), 373–403.

Menkel-Meadow, Carrie. "Portia in a Different Voice: Speculations on a Woman's Lawyering Process." 1 *Berkeley Women's Law Journal* (1985), 39–63.

Moore, Michael S. "The Interpretive Turn in Modern Theory: A Turn for the Worse?" 41 *Stanford Law Review* (1989), 871–957.

Morawetz, Thomas. "Reconstructing the Criminal Defenses: The Significance of Justification." 77 *Journal of Criminal Law and Criminology* (1986), 277–307.

Newman, Jon O. "Between Legal Realism and Neutral Principles: The Legitimacy of Institutional Values." 72 *California Law Review* (1984), 200–216.

Oberer, Walter E. "On Law, Lawyering and Law Professing: The Golden Sand." 39 *Journal of Legal Education* (1989), 203–211.

Patterson, Dennis. "Law's Pragmatism: Law as Practice and Narrative." 76 *Virginia Law Review* (1990), 937–996.

Posner, Richard A. "The Decline of Law as an Autonomous Discipline: 1962–1987." 100 *Harvard Law Review* (1987), 761–780.

———. "Legal Formalism, Legal Realism, and the Interpretation of Statutes and the Constitution." 37 *Case Western Law Review* (1986–87), 179–217.

———. "Utilitarianism, Economics, and Legal Theory." 8 *Journal of Legal Studies* (1979), 103–140.

Pound, Roscoe. "A Survey of Social Interests." 57 *Harvard Law Review* (1943), 1–39.

Priest, George L. "The Common Law Process and the Selection of Efficient Rules." 6 *Journal of Legal Studies* (1977), 65–82.

Radin, Margaret Jane. "Market-Inalienability." 100 *Harvard Law Review* (1987), 1849–1937.

———. "Reconsidering the Rule of Law." 69 *Boston University Law Review* (1989), 781–819.

Rawls, John. "Justice as Fairness: Political Not Metaphysical." 14 *Philosophy and Public Affairs* (Summer 1983), 223–251.

Rhode, Deborah L. "Feminist Critical Theories." 42 *Stanford Law Review* (1990), 617–638.

Rubin, Paul. "Why is the Common Law Efficient?" 6 *Journal of Legal Studies* (1977), 51–63.

Scales, Ann C. "The Emergence of Feminist Jurisprudence: An Essay." 95 *Yale Law Journal* (1986), 1373–1403.

Schauer, Frederick. "Formalism." 97 *Yale Law Journal* (1988), 509–548.

Schneider, Elizabeth. "Equal Rights to Trial for Women: Sex Bias in the Law of Self Defense." 15 *Harvard Civil Rights–Civil Liberties Law Review* (1980), 623–647.

Singer, Joseph William. "The Player and the Cards: Nihilism and Legal Theory." 94 *Yale Law Journal* (1984), 1–70.

Solum, Lawrence B. "On the Indeterminacy Crisis: Critiquing Critical Dogma." 54 *University of Chicago Law Review* (1987), 462–503.

Tushnet, Mark V. "Following the Rules Laid Down: A Critique of Interpretivism and Neutral Principles." 96 *Harvard Law Review* (1983), 781–827.

Unger, Roberto Mangabeira. "The Critical Legal Studies Movement." 96 *Harvard Law Review* (1983), 561–675.

West, Robin L. "The Difference in Women's Hedonic Lives: A Phenomenological Critique of Feminist Legal Theory." 3 *Wisconsin Women's Law Journal* (1987), 81–145.

———. "Jurisprudence and Gender." 55 *University of Chicago Law Review* (1988), 1–72.

White, James Boyd. "Law as Language: Reading Law and Reading Literature." 60 *Texas Law Review* (1982), 415–445.

Yablon, Charles M. "The Indeterminacy of the Law: Critical Legal Studies and the Problem of Legal Explanation." 6 *Cardozo Law Review* (1985), 917–945.

———. "Law and Metaphysics." 96 *Yale Law Journal* (1987), 613–636.

INDEX